Feminist Theory,
Women's Writing

Reading
WOMEN
Writing

a series edited by
Shari Benstock and Celeste Schenck

Reading Women Writing is dedicated to furthering international feminist debate. The series publishes books on all aspects of feminist theory and textual practice. *Reading Women Writing* especially welcomes books that address cultures, histories, and experiences beyond first-world academic boundaries.

FEMINIST THEORY, WOMEN'S WRITING

Laurie A. Finke

Cornell University Press

ITHACA AND LONDON

First published 1992 by Cornell University Press.

International Standard Book Number 0-8014-2547-6 (cloth)
International Standard Book Number 0-8014-9784-1 (paper)
Library of Congress Catalog Card Number 91-55566
Printed in the United States of America
Librarians: Library of Congress cataloging information appears on the last page of the book.

To Stephen and Hannah and
in memory of my mother

Contents

Preface

The first draft of the introductory chapter of this book began by recounting exhaustively—and rather dryly—the history of feminist criticism between 1975 and 1985. I tore it up. Instead, by way of preface to the chapters that follow, it seems appropriate, because I am writing about women writers, to offer some account of myself as a woman writer and, because I am writing about feminist theory, to offer a brief history of my own encounters with a developing and dynamic feminist theory during those years. But like the medieval saints' lives that are the subject of my third chapter, this brief autobiographical excursion is meant to function emblematically: my political situation is, I think, characteristic of a generation of female scholars who entered graduate school before there was such a thing as feminist theory and who, having been trained in the patriarchal traditions of careful scholarship, found by 1980 or so that the tradition to which we had pledged our fealty had been exposed, to varying degrees, as a procession of false idols. In this respect, my experiences in the profession disclose a political (and generational) history that I hope will focus attention on the institutional consequences of my analyses of feminist theory.

I spent the years between 1974 and 1978 in Philadelphia as a graduate student training in medieval studies. I sweated, willingly, over at least nine dead languages, from Old Irish to Middle High German. Except for learning those languages, I was not really doing anything I had not already done as an undergraduate. The restlessness and boredom I experienced during those years was symptomatic of the ennui of a profession that was growing disenchanted with New Criticism but had nothing else to "do" to justify its existence except to spawn "newer" and "newer" readings of the same canonical texts or ever more arcane and esoteric dissertations and monographs on inaccessible ones. In the 1970s feminist criticism was neither required nor recommended reading for field exams in Old or Middle English. Upon completing a dissertation on *Piers Plowman* which I had little desire to revise for publication, I tried to get a job. I spent the years between 1979 and 1984 during the worst period of the job crunch in English in a series of temporary and underpaid positions (in Virginia and Oklahoma) and unemployed (in Lubbock, Texas); I taught freshman English and wrote dozens of applications each year for tenure-track positions.

During those years I made two discoveries that changed (or perhaps I should say confounded) my sense of professional purpose. I read Gayatri Spivak's translation of Jacques Derrida's *Of Grammatology* and, shortly thereafter, Sandra Gilbert and Susan Gubar's *Madwoman in the Attic*. My discovery of feminist literary criticism thus became inextricably intertwined in my own mind with my discovery of literary theory. My understanding of each has been, from the start, informed by the other; I do not think even now I could easily separate the two. I began reading in both feminist criticism and literary theory, spending five years literally retraining myself in new fields that in graduate school I had not even known existed—and indeed, at least in the institution where I studied, did not exist. Although always a politically committed feminist, I had assumed that, except for such workplace issues as discrimination and harassment, my feminism was separate from my scholarly work. My specialized areas of expertise had always seemed remote from women's issues, irrelevant to contemporary debates about abortion or comparable worth. Soon, however, my reading began to politicize my teaching and research. Like many of my contemporaries, I began to recognize that the political circumstances that created what we glumly referred to as "the job market" might be related to the restlessness that seemed evident in so much American theory during this time. If the New Criticism, as some have argued, was a response to the need to find pedagogical methods adaptable to the influx of new students into the universities after World War II, it was equally plausible that the "new theorizing," including feminist theorizing, might be a response to the dilemma facing literary faculties in the 1970s—a vicious circle that created a surplus of new Ph.D.s trained for a very few tenure-track jobs, coupled with a lack of turnover in mostly tenured-in departments that required more and more graduate students to fill classes. My reading in feminist criticism satisfied my desire to recontextualize and to subvert the orthodoxies I had been taught as an undergraduate and graduate student. I began to forge connections, to think about the intersections and conflicts among my personal, political, and professional lives and among the several disciplines I encountered as a teacher of writing. Like many of my generation—victims of the same peculiar forms of late capitalist logic—I had discovered that feminism, along with literary theory, offered a means to bring the political idealism of the 1960s into academic institutions by transgressing the boundaries between politics and the separate "disciplines" that divided knowledge in the university.

In the midst of this excitement of discovery, however, I found myself once again marginalized, an outsider, this time because of the field I had chosen. I had known all along that most medievalists did not really have much use for feminism. I soon learned that feminism had as little use for medieval studies, or for any literature before 1800, unless it was to catalog images of women as portrayed by the canonical male writers. The more feminist criticism I read, the more it seemed clear that, as a practice, feminist literary criticism had been created from a canon of works by women written during the nineteenth and twentieth centuries in England and America. Rarely did feminists venture on the other side of a great divide erected around 1800, when, as Virginia Woolf comments in *A Room of One's Own*, women supposedly first became writers. If, as many critics complained, Western feminism had excluded and silenced women of other races and other cultures, it had also excluded its own history before the nineteenth century.

Even more disheartening, literary theorists—who also did not seem much interested in literature written before the eighteenth century—often seemed only marginally concerned with what was happening in feminist criticism, while many feminists seemed downright hostile to literary theory, which they characterized as obscurantist and elitist. This hostility between literary and feminist theory, which began to be addressed only in the late 1980s, struck me as so shocking that around 1985 I began to explore it as a starting point for a series of investigations into feminist literary theory. To dismiss the theoretical insights of the previous decade— or to claim that theory is tangential, even hostile, to the processes of resurrecting or celebrating women writers—seemed to me to force feminist criticism into a single-voiced, authoritarian mode of discourse, which domesticated the subversive, demystifying potential of the feminist theory I found so exciting. As I suggest in Chapter 1, the challenges posed by contemporary theory have begun to spur feminists, including myself, to articulate a dialogic concept of what feminist theory might accomplish by encouraging a decentralized, polyvocal alternative to the dominant discourses of Anglo-American literary criticism and theory.

This book, which examines feminism's ambivalent and often conflicted relationships with the institutions of literary study, was begun during my own somewhat rocky initiation into the profession. In 1984, months after giving birth to my first child, I landed my first tenure-track job at Lewis & Clark College, moved from Texas to Oregon, began a commuter marriage, and settled into both mothering and teaching. Hired to teach primarily Chaucer and medieval literature, I found myself teaching linguistics, literary theory, and feminist theory as well. I became involved in designing and administering an interdisciplinary gender studies minor, one of the first programs in the country to take seriously the insight that gender is a relational system and that "women" cannot be studied in isolation from the forces that shape gender relationships in any social formation. As I worked on this book, I found myself juggling several commitments—teaching schedules, cross-country commutes, baby sitters, a second child, day care, and committee meetings. I discovered that I no longer had the luxury—if I had wanted it—of separating my personal, political, and professional lives. Circumstances brought them into sharp and often painful juxtapositions. But these juxtapositions also revealed any number of intersections among feminist political activism, the structures of everyday life, the specialized periodization that organizes the teaching of English literature, and the linguistic and cultural theory that is challenging those structures. These issues have inevitably found their way into the chapters that follow.

I originally conceived of this book as a means to bring together three fields that have been designated as "specialties" and compartmentalized by literary studies: feminist literary criticism, literary theory, and literature before 1800. I would not pretend that I am the first to look at the effect of literary theory or early English literature on feminist literary criticism. I could not have written this book without engaging the important feminist scholarship on both subjects. I hope to contribute to this scholarship not simply by demonstrating how the concerns of these three areas are compatible but by exploring their conflicts as well. This project grew out of my dissatisfaction with the antipathy of many (though certainly not all) feminists to the theoretical criticism—including poststructuralism, semiotics, psychoanalysis, and cultural hermeneutics—that, along with feminist criticism, prompted a rethinking of traditional literary scholarship in the 1970s and 1980s. For this reason, and because it is intended to initiate new debates rather than to command assent, the book articulates no single overriding theory or pat thesis; instead it stages a series of encounters between theoretical issues that have figured prominently in critical discussions since 1980 and several texts that illuminate those issues in new and, I hope, disruptive ways. Rather than focus exclusively on the earlier texts in which I specialize, I have chosen to include both modern and premodern texts to dismantle the ideologies of specialized "periods" which dominate professional writing by investigating the historical multiplicity of texts by and about women, their difference for feminist theorizing, and the dialogues they generate.

I want to criticize those assumptions—both explicit and implicit—that have guided feminist criticism, for they have walled feminism off from important historical and theoretical concerns. Feminist literary critics, in an attempt to counter the marginal status of women writers and women critics in the study of literature, have championed several concepts as the bases for new approaches to literary and cultural evaluation. These include "female oppression," "women's experience," "women's language," and even "the woman writer." The assumptions, however, about gender, the self, language, and the text which underwrite these notions—and the methodologies that have been adapted to explicate them—have been generated by scholars specializing primarily in nineteenth- and twentieth-century fiction and poetry. These concepts depend heavily on the New Criticism, a theoretical model that paradoxically emphasizes the independence of literary texts from the very social and political concerns feminists are trying to raise. These are the assumptions that I challenge in this book. Through specific readings of disparate historical texts—those of contemporary feminist theory, linguistic theory, and medieval mysticism, as well as Mary Wollstonecraft's *Vindication of the Rights of Woman* and Kate Chopin's *Awakening*—I offer a critique of conventional feminist notions of women's language, women's experience, and women's writing. My purpose is to analyze some intellectual currents of the 1970s and 1980s and to offer both a means of working through the theoretical problems of feminism and a reevaluation of the achievements and limitations of feminist literary criticism since 1975. The key concepts that have structured feminist literary criticism need to be reexamined both within the historical context in which they were raised and within the larger framework of contemporary theoretical formulations about language, representation, subjectivity, and value.

This book is a record of my dialogues with many people whose words are inextricably intertwined with mine. Some are published words and are recognized in the footnotes and bibliography. Others are less tangible and must be acknowledged, as is customary, in the preface. First and foremost are my students at Lewis & Clark College, past and present, who have been a constant source of inspiration and stimulation. There is hardly a sentence in this book which has not been informed by their often trenchant questions and their unwillingness to be fobbed off with conventional answers. Several seminars in literary theory and feminist theory, as well as several linguistics classes, helped me to think through the theoretical problems of language, subjectivity, and literary value this book addresses. Students in "Women Writers before 1800" showed me why the medieval mystics and the trobairitz are important for feminism and made me think for the first time about the histories of such apparently ahistorical phenomena as love and pain. My Feminist Literary Theory seminar in 1986—Bonnie Anderson, Lisa Hoesel, and Jill Marts in particular—helped me to think through the initial organizational principles of this book, and though the book has been reorganized several times since then, I could not have begun it without their input.

Several colleagues read parts of the book in manuscript and offered their reactions and advice. I thank Robert Con Davis, Robert Ginsberg, Valerie Lagorio, Ronald Schleifer, Martin Shichtman, Ulrike Wiethaus, and my Feminist Research Group in Portland: Dorothy Berkson, Kathleen Clay, Kathleen Erndl, Virginia Darney, Deborah Heath, Barbara Seidman, Jean Ward, and Kristi Williams. I am indebted to Carol Patrick, Cinda Smaasgaard, and Karin Gates for assistance in preparing the manuscript. I thank both the editors of the Reading Women Writing series, Shari Benstock and Celeste Schenck, and the anonymous readers for Cornell University Press who read several versions of the manuscript and offered both encouragement and criticisms. Their friendly but rigorous responses compelled me to articulate my arguments ever more precisely. My dialogues with them have proved a model of scholarly exchange. Bernhard Kendler, as always, has been a supportive and facilitative editor. I thank him for his help.

I was fortunate to hold summer stipends from Lewis & Clark College in 1985 and 1990 and from the Oregon Committee for the Humanities in 1986 and 1990. These grants helped me begin this project and carry it to its completion. A sabbatical from Lewis & Clark in 1987 enabled me to write a substantial part of the manuscript. Portions of Chapter 3 appeared in *Philological Quarterly* 67 (1988) and in *Maps of Flesh and Light: Aspects of the Religious Experience of Medieval Women*, ed. Ulrike Wiethaus (Syracuse: Syracuse University Press, forthcoming), and an earlier version of Chapter 4 appeared in *The Philospher as Writer: The Eighteenth Century*, ed. Robert Ginsberg (Selinsgrove, Pa.: Susquehanna University Press, 1987). I thank these publishers for granting me permission to reprint.

To my husband, Robert Markley, I owe more than I can say. I could not have written this book without his constant help and companionship, his love and patience. His perceptive editorial advice, computer assistance, and moral support, as well as babysitting and the occasional meal, were all equally invaluable. Finally, I dedicate the book to the memory of my mother, Patricia Halpin Finke, to whom I owe my emotional commitment to feminism, and to my children, Stephen and Hannah Markley, who I hope will one day share that commitment.

LAURIE FINKE

Portland, Oregon

Feminist Theory,
Women's Writing

A Powerful Infidel Heteroglossia: Toward a Feminist Theory of Complexity

> As a concept "woman" is too fragile to bear the weight of all the contents and meanings now ascribed to it.
>
> —Rosalind Delmar

> The real political task in a society such as ours is to criticize the working of institutions which appear to be both neutral and independent; to criticize them in such a manner that the political violence which has always exercised itself obscurely through them will be unmasked, so that one can fight them.
>
> —Michel Foucault

During the 1980s, feminist literary criticism was marked by an often contentious split between those pragmatically committed to the recovery of the woman writer and, with her, something usually called women's experience,[1] and those concerned to explore the implications for feminism of postmodern theories that question the legitimacy of such constructs as the author and experience. This book explores feminist contributions to poststructuralist debates about language, texts, the status of the real, and the nature of political oppression and resistance; it locates both the "woman writer" and "feminist theory" within a series of cultural and historical matrices to reveal the complexities of these critical formulations. Finally, it offers a dialogical materialism through which to understand the ways in which traditionally marginalized women writers challenge notions of what constitutes the institutions of literature and criticism.

The increasing prominence of theory within feminism is evident from the sheer proliferation of hybrid labels during the 1980s: Marxist feminism, feminist reader-response criticism, feminist new historicism, and feminist psychoanalysis, to name just a few. This

---

[1]Elaine Showalter called this activity "gynocritics" (1981).

dissemination of theoretical allegiances has not gone unremarked. To some feminists it represents a dangerous sectarianism that threatens the ability of women to engage in meaningful political action; to others, it offers a productive diversity that may lead to a more effective, because more inclusive, activism. "Theory"—by which we almost always mean poststructuralist theory—has been an almost obsessive subject of polemics, defenses, dialogues, and debates among feminist literary critics. Elaine Showalter's 1981 essay "Feminist Criticism in the Wilderness" and her 1983 "Critical Cross-Dressing" both warn against too close an alliance with "misogynist" theories. In 1982 Peggy Kamuf and Nancy K. Miller debated in *Diacritics* how French theories of language and subjectivity affect the feminist project of recovering "lost" women writers. As late as 1987, Barbara Christian was decrying theory for its "linguistic jargon, its emphasis on quoting its prophets, its tendency toward 'Biblical' exegesis, . . . its preoccupations with mechanical analyses of language, graphs, algebraic equations, [and] its gross generalizations about culture" (1987, 53), while Mary Jacobus, in contrast, was criticizing the "untheorized, experiential, and literary herstorical tendency" of much American feminist criticism (1986, xii).[2] This obsession with the place of theory in feminism is not merely an academic question: what is at stake for feminists in these debates, in Foucauldian terms, is how best to expose the political violence that inheres in the institution of literary studies under the guise of neutral and objective scholarship, and how most effectively to implement strategies of political resistance to sexual oppression.

Debates about theory within feminism are, significantly, also struggles to define the status of the "real." At least since Simone de Beauvoir's celebrated manifesto in 1952—"One is not born, but rather becomes a woman" (1974, 301)—most feminists have committed themselves to a social constructivist view of gender, to a belief that "male" and "female" are functions of historically specific forms of mediation, cultural narratives through which we structure

---

[2]There is no indication that this argument will be decided any time soon. For other voices in the debate, see Treichler 1986; Finke 1986; the 1988 issue of *Feminist Studies* with essays by Leslie Rabine, Joan Scott, and Mary Poovey; Straub in Davis and Finke 1989, 855–76; Malson et al. 1989; and Kauffman 1989.

the world, and not fixed ontological essences. At the same time, they have voiced strong ambivalence about that position. Feminists (myself included) have insisted upon the social construction of gender because we have perceived that our oppression has always been fobbed off on us as "natural," the result of universal and immutable "differences" between the sexes. To change these gender relations we have to conceive of such concepts as human nature, masculinity, and femininity not as unitary and unchanging but as heterogeneous cultural fields, always sensitive to historical contingencies. In short, a progressive feminist politics depends upon perceiving gender and, indeed, reality as social constructs that can be dismantled and reconstructed in new and perhaps more egalitarian ways.[3]

But the constructivist insistence on the linguistic and rhetorical nature of reality can rebound in ways that have been troubling for many feminists. If reality is nothing more than narratives we tell ourselves, if the world is a "contestable text," then these "stories" can have no greater claim to inherent authority than the old ones feminists have rejected. The dilemma becomes how to proclaim new, politically progressive "truths." As Donna Haraway puts it, "We would like to think our appeals to real worlds are more than a desperate lurch away from cynicism and an act of faith like any other cult's" (1988, 577). For feminist literary critics the problems posed by a social constructivist perspective are immediate and political. Women have been denied access to the means of producing culture, and the ultimate aim of feminist criticism for many of its practitioners is to create the opportunity to help construct the conditions of their existence. In the 1970s and 1980s this meant recovering the woman writer and validating women's experiences. But social constructivism suggests that there is no author (Foucault 1979) and that experience is a simulacrum, a set of *discursive* practices (de Lauretis 1987, 18). Furthermore, women's "experience" is saturated with and not separate from the practices by which masculinist cultures reproduce their domination. The problem for feminist theorists, then, as Haraway succinctly puts it, is "how to have

---

[3]Thomas Laqueur has even suggested that biological notions of sex, which seem so fundamental to twentieth-century consciousness, may not be as stable and unchanging as we tend to think they are (1990).

simultaneously an account of radical historical contingency for all knowledge claims and knowing subjects, a critical practice for recognizing our own 'semiotic technologies' for making meanings, *and* a no-nonsense commitment to faithful accounts of a 'real' world, one that can be partially shared and that is friendly to earthwide projects of finite freedom, adequate material abundance, modest meaning in suffering, and limited happiness" (1988, 579). The recognition that knowledge and truth claims are radically contingent and historically specific does not, however, strand us in some never-never land of relativistic paralysis—far from it—although this is precisely what the forces of conservative reaction want us to think. Nor does this recognition of the social and semiotic construction of gender deny the real, material oppression of many women by reducing it to "simply language." A brick wall is a social construct, produced by the socioeconomic relations of production and labor, but if I run into it, my head still hurts. The task for feminist criticism in the 1990s is to develop more sophisticated theoretical models that offer a way out of the impasse described by Haraway, models that enable women to recognize the "historical contingency" of the social relations of gender, while allowing them to claim their own "truths," however partial or contingent.

In this regard, my concern is with feminism's need for what I shall call a politics of complexity. I use *complexity* in a technical as well as an evaluative sense, drawing specifically on the works of cultural critics such as Donna Haraway, N. Katherine Hayles, Bruno Latour, and Michel Serres, who work in hybrid fields at the intersections of science and culture. *Complexity* describes a cultural poetics of indeterminacy, informed by contemporary theoretical debates in a variety of fields but without the political paralysis often attributed to poststructuralism. By collecting the difficult questions posed by contemporary theory about language, representation, history, culture, and difference under the rubric of "complexity," I hope to move away from the still-prevalent tendencies to construct theory in terms of totalizing systems and the "maze of dualisms" that require us to view reality in binary terms (Haraway 1985, 100). The discussion that follows, then, serves two purposes. The first is frankly polemical. I contend that feminist criticism can neither ignore theory nor simply celebrate an untheorized "difference"; it must engage—and challenge—many aspects of the competing languages that constitute contemporary theoretical discourse. The second purpose is to introduce the theoretical issues that figure prominently in later chapters, whose primary aim is to articulate a dynamic description of cultural and literary activity sensitive to the complexities of gender and the semiotic practices of culture which constitute it.

I turn to the cultural critiques of science to suggest a critical rhetoric for my argument precisely because I am concerned to de-center notions of objectivity and totalizing theory which underwrite a host of disciplinary and critical practices that inform feminist theory. Understanding these critiques provides an opportunity to expose the violence masked by the claim of science to objectivity. The warrant for such a project has been suggested by the conclusion of Haraway's 1985 essay "A Manifesto for Cyborgs."

> Taking responsibility for the social relations of science and technology means refusing an anti-science metaphysics, a demonology of technology, and so means embracing the skillful task of reconstructing the boundaries of daily life, in partial connection with others, in communication with all of our parts. It is not just that science and technology are possible means of great human satisfaction, as well as a matrix of complex dominations. Cyborg imagery can suggest a way out of the maze of dualisms in which we have explained our bodies and our tools to ourselves. (100)

Haraway's cyborg is, in effect, a figure for a theory of complexity. Like Haraway, I believe it is important for feminists to go beyond simply showing the myriad ways in which the sciences and other institutions have oppressed women; the more difficult task is to rethink the boundaries separating different cultural practices, to examine how structures of knowledge function as strategies of oppression, and to explore how feminism might help to restructure larger cultural institutions. This project must ask not only how science or literature might be changed by feminism but also how we might appropriate aspects of dominant discourses to offer feminist theory a way out of the "maze of dualisms"—nature/culture, mind/body, fact/fiction, real/artificial, theory/praxis, objectivity/

subjectivity, order/disorder—by which we have traditionally defined ourselves and our politics.

As Haraway suggests, some of the problems being posed in contemporary scientific thinking—in nonlinear dynamics, information theory, and fluid mechanics—may help feminists think about how to move away from the production of universal, totalizing theory and toward a "feminist theory of complexity" which is at the same time nontotalizing and theoretically aware of what complexity implies. These fields pose problems that cannot be solved by resorting to any simple principles of order or linear determinism. In Luce Irigaray's terms, they resist "adequate symbolization" and signify "the powerlessness of logic to incorporate in its writing all the characteristic features of nature" (1985b, 106–7). I will forgo all the usual disclaimers about the dangers of analogies between such disparate fields of inquiry as, say, fluid mechanics and literary criticism because what I am proposing is precisely the need to explore the possibilities of circulation and exchange between artificially erected cultural boundaries, as well as to examine the institutional structures that hold them in place. I am interested in the emergence at this particular historical moment of disorder as a productive theoretical principle in the sciences—in chaos and information theory—as well as in such critical theories as deconstruction. My perception that feminist theory needs to articulate noncoercive theories of complexity and disorder seems consistent with developments in several fields. In her book, *Chaos Bound*, Katherine Hayles speculates "that disorder has become a focal point for contemporary theories because it offers the possibility of escaping from what are increasingly perceived as coercive structures of order" (1990, 265). Disrupting cultural boundaries and tracing the possibilities for exchanges among disparate fields exposes the political interests masked by our ideas about order. As Irigaray suggests, disorder and chaos constitute a threat to Western economies of representation. Order is coercive because it is achieved through the exclusion, neutralization, or marginalization (sometimes through violence) of whatever lies outside of artificially constructed "norms," whether the norm is constructed as an electron, a human genome, or a ruling class. To move from scientific conceptions of complexity to their implications for women's writing in different cultural and historical contexts, though, requires that we define *complexity* as precisely as possible.

A theory of complexity is exactly the opposite of what physicists call a theory of everything (or TOE), a single succinct (if quixotic) mathematical description that is supposed to unify the four fundamental forces of nature: the strong force, weak force, electromagnetic force, and gravity. "A good TOE should consist of much more than a mere catalogue of underlying laws and objects; it should have explanatory power and it should establish *linkages* between the various facets of nature" (Davies and Brown 1988, 6). A TOE would be marked by elegance and simplicity. It would be a totalizing, universalizing theory; as E. David Peat remarks in his popular account, "A perfect theory would be forced on physicists by nature itself; there would be no room for arbitrary assumptions or for making adjustments. The theory would stand or fall on its own" (1988, 104). What is significant for my purposes is that most literary critics—including feminist literary critics—consciously or unconsciously, have derived their beliefs about what a theory is from precisely this kind scientific idealism, itself a remnant of totalizing misinterpretations of eighteenth-century Newtonianism (Markley 1991). Stanley Fish, for example, describes theory as "formal, abstract, general, and invariant," as "a recipe with premeasured ingredients which when ordered and combined according to absolutely explicit instructions . . . will produce the desired results" regardless of the political commitments of the investigator (1985, 110–11). In other words, literary and feminist theory—according to both its detractors and its proponents—is implicitly or explicitly modeled on the "rigor" and denotative clarity idealistically attributed to deterministic science and mathematics.

Scientists in many fields, however, are routinely challenging totalizing beliefs about theory. Stephen Hawking, for example, has remarked that "quantum mechanics is essentially a theory of what we do not know and cannot predict" (1989, 138). As Hayles notes, in both the postmodern sciences and in literary theory, the 1970s and 1980s brought "a break away from universalizing, totalizing perspectives and a move toward local, fractured systems and modes of analysis (1990, 2), in other words, toward theories of complexity. In contrast to a TOE, a theory of complexity reveals the messiness behind the illusion of unified narratives about the world by restoring information—what I shall call noise—previously marginalized and excluded by those narratives. It attempts to expose the "ficticity"—or the constructed nature—of facts.

Consider disorder. Ordinarily we think of disorder as the absence of order and assign a negative value to it. Theory, in this mindset, exists to make the disorderly orderly, to discover order in it—or impose order on it. One of the insights of chaos theory, however, is that disorder is perhaps more productively conceived of as the presence of information. In the sciences, chaotic or complex systems turn out to be far more prevalent than we might at first suspect—from dripping faucets and the smoke swirls produced by a cup of hot coffee to epidemics, the weather, and even the complicated rhythms of the human heart. Although the sciences of chaos are primarily quantitative, their implications for theory are far more suggestive than the "application" of a few odd principles to feminist theories or even (though I recognize that this assumption is implicit in scientific descriptions of chaos) for promoting a deep structural explanation for disorder. My concern is to enable feminism to account for more information from those sources that have most often been marginalized by dominant systems of "order" and to create new ways of discussing and using this new information to challenge the political repression of complexity.

In this respect, I prefer to think of complexity as a trope occupying a site somewhere between an evaluative standard and a self-justifying and self-sustaining theory. To suggest briefly something of the explanatory power of this trope let me return to the dilemma of social constructivism I raised at the beginning of this chapter. The concept of complexity enables us more completely to articulate what we mean when we say that culture is the collective means by which societies represent themselves to themselves. In political theory, it is customary to think of society as a collection of preexistent individuals who relate to one another either randomly and voluntarily (the perspective of the social contract) or in ways that are overdetermined and coercive (the perspective of dialectical Marxism). But we might more productively envision society and culture as complex and interrelated systems that link individuals, institutions, discourses, texts, and material objects in relations of interdependence—of alliance and solidarity as well as struggle and conflict—which confer meaning on them but which are neither predetermined by some fixed laws of history nor existentially "free." None of these constituents of society exists before it or independently of it; they have meaning only in relation to it and to one another. A society, then, is not a fixed and stable entity but an always shifting, always changing process. In fact, a considerable amount of cultural work is required to maintain the illusion of stasis and permanence, to deny the workings of complexity in and through society. In a more complex, "disorderly" model, societies both maintain themselves and change through elaborate feedback mechanisms by which their cultural productions— individuals, genders, class identities, and written texts —feed back into them, reorganizing and reproducing social structures and the strategies that maintain and refashion them.

Complexity, as Hayles notes, insists on local applications rather than global laws or principles. An individual assumes a gendered identity, in this regard, only within a set of social practices specific to a historical time, place, and culture. There are no universal roles or meanings attached to male or female, no "eternal feminine" or masculine principle, only networks of differential relations that construct men and women, masculine and feminine, in culturally and historically specific ways. Uncovering the full range of social meanings attached to gender within any particular cultural forma-tion, then, requires a method sensitive to the historical particu-larities of time and place, as well as to the heterogeneity of so-cioeconomic formations, the intersecting and competing interests of different groups, and the hegemonic practices that work to smooth over or to suppress these conflicts.

The intersections, collisions, and perturbations created by the many different agents, institutions, and discourses at work within a society create patterns that cannot be resolved into coherent nar-ratives. The unidirectional laws of cause and effect—of history— which have traditionally been used to explain social relations are inadequate to represent the complexities of the production we call society, but so too are the very images I have employed— networks, for example. Attempts to produce totalizing representations of society, culture, and history risk mistaking local contingencies for global patterns. Any understanding we may have of the formation of gender identity within a particular society, consequently, will always be incomplete and fragmentary, limited to partial representations of local networks. This recognition of our contingency, however, does not need to be disabling; it can create the impetus to challenge hegemonic, totalizing constructions of self and society.

Those cultural practices, meanings, and values that attempt to bring together power and knowledge to create order and hierarchy may be examined by drawing on something like Foucault's notion of the *disposatif*, or "grid of intelligibility." The *disposatif* locates a set of specific practices that organize some aspect of social life. It establishes links among such disparate practices as "discourses, institutions, architectural arrangements, regulations, laws, administrative measures, scientific statements, philosophic propositions, morality, philanthropy, etc." (1980, 194) as a means of demonstrating how societies construct, organize, and control their constituent subjects.[4] But those practices that serve to create "docile" subjects have to be continually "renewed, recreated, and defended" and therefore can be challenged, resisted, and modified (Williams 1977, 112). Michel de Certeau uses the term "poaching" to describe those strategies that parasitically undermine hegemonic cultural practices and enable the disempowered to manipulate the conditions of their existence. "Everyday life," he writes, "invents itself by poaching in countless ways on the property of others" (1984, xii).[5] These appropriations of the dominant social order deflect its power without challenging it overtly. Poaching is neither staightforward conformity nor rebellion but a dialogic and destabilizing encounter between conflicting cultural codes. If we accept this complex model of social relations, the dilemma for feminists becomes not how to overturn the oppressive social relations of gender but, how to poach most effectively, how to influence the direction and velocity of change in a social formation that is constantly in flux.

[4]For a discussion of Foucault's use of *disposatif*, see Dreyfus and Rabinow 1982, 120–25.

[5]Foucault uses the term "technologies of the self" to describe the same process of resistance (Blonsky 1985, 367); Williams refers to these practices, meanings, and values as "counterhegemonic" (1977).

Subsequent chapters of this book attempt to suggest rather than demonstrate authoritatively an analytic of complexity by examining the conflicts and struggles that have gone into the production of the "woman writer" as a critical concept for feminism, looking at specific historical instances of that production: in the Middle Ages, the Enlightenment, at the turn of the twentieth century. Each chapter builds on the recognition that both gender identity and the cultural authority conveyed by authorship are socially produced within a specific grid of intelligibility and that the subjects they produce—the woman writer and her texts—in turn contribute to the reproduction of the system of gender relations. But before turning to those specific instances, I would like to outline three "propositions," or key assumptions, that will guide this study and then elaborate on each of them in subsequent sections of this chapter.

(1) A feminist theory of complexity must be dialogic, double voiced, in that its explorations of social and cultural phenomena will be "half-ours, half-someone else's" (Bakhtin 1981, 345).

(2) Dialogic complexity restores the history of conflict and struggle that went into the making of the "fact" but was suppressed to create the appearance of unquestioned "fact."

(3) History, conceived of as an unresolvable tension between "what really happened" and the multiple and dialogic narratives about it, provides a means by which feminists might destabilize oppressive representations of gender and locate on the margins of discourse—in the "noise" of history—possibilities for more egalitarian cultural formations not yet even recognizable as representations.

Dialogic Feminism

"There is no utterance without relation to other utterances, and that is essential," writes Tzvetan Todorov in his introduction to the work of Mikhail Bakhtin (1984, 60). Elsewhere, I have suggested that Bakhtin's conception of the "dialogic" word provides feminist theory with a critical rhetoric that enables feminists to examine the complex social relations of gender and to engage in contemporary theoretical debates without falling into either essentialist arguments about a "women's language" uncontaminated by "male thought" or a too uncritical assimilation of literary theory (Finke 1986). Because the field of utterance is the space in which feminist theories must be contested, a feminist theory of complexity might usefully begin with a dialogic notion of the utterance to counter the totalizing structuralist concept of the sign which has dominated contemporary literary theory almost as thoroughly as it has dominated contemporary linguistics.

To provide a model for the historical transformation of social values and ideologies we must understand the utterance as an ideological construct produced through conflict and struggle within a specific social and historical context. The dialogics described by Bakhtin and members of his circle, most notably V. N. Vološinov and P. N. Medvedev, provides the impetus for a more complex understanding of how discourse functions. Bakhtin argues that all discourse is inherently dialogic and double-voiced, that it involves "intense interaction and struggle between one's own and another's word, . . . in which [these words] oppose or . . . interanimate one another" (1981, 354).[6] In using the term *double-voiced* I am not im-

---

[6] I have drawn primarily upon the essay "Discourse in the Novel" for my discussion of dialogism because it seems to me Bakhtin's most accessible discussion of that term. The concept informs all his work, however, and that of the Bakhtin circle, including those works signed by V. N. Vološinov and P. N. Medvedev, which some scholars attribute to Bakhtin. Many of the same points are made in *Problems of Dostoevsky's Poetics* and *Marxism and the Philosophy of Language*, which is usually attributed to Vološinov. To call attention to the dialogic nature of Bakhtin's own work, I adopt Todorov's practice of citing the texts associated with Bakhtin which were published under someone else's name by keeping the name under which they were published and following it with a slash and Bakhtin's name: e.g. Vološinov/Bakhtin. For the sake of clarity, I have followed the same practice in the bibliography. I have chosen this typographical convention for the ambiguity it conveys about the relationship between the "authors." I do not have the space here for a long digression on the politics of the Bakhtin authorship controversy, although in themselves they provide a fascinating study of the dialogic nature of discourse as well as of Foucault's notion of the author function (1979). For discussions of the problems of authorship, see Todorov 1984, 6–13; Clark and Holquist 1984, 146–70; Godzich, Foreword to Medvedev 1985, vii–xiv; and Morson and Emerson 1989, 31–48. I tend to agree with Clark, Holquist, and Godzich that if he did not write it entirely himself, then Bakhtin had a large hand in the writing of *Marxism and the Philosophy of Language*. I disagree with Clark and Holquist that the Marxism in the book is superficial and only added to get the book by the censors. The book's Marxist philosophy seems to me an integral part of its linguistics.

plying that this dialogue is structured around such binary oppositions as male speech/female speech; rather, language that is
double-voiced calls into question the fiction of authoritative or
monologic discourse. Every utterance is always inhabited by the
voice of the "other," or of many others, because the interests of
race, class, gender, ethnicity, age, and any number of other related
"accents" intersect in any utterance. These perturbations in the
theoretically linear flow of speech are not simply additive; we cannot just append them to conventional structural descriptions of
grammar and syntax. Instead, they create labyrinthine complexities that are masked by traditional linguistic concepts. For this
reason, the dynamics of this complex system might be better represented by the term *heteroglossia*, a rough translation of Bakhtin's
raznojazychie for the ideologically contested field of utterances.

Bakhtin rejects the Saussurean distinction between *langue* and
parole central to contemporary linguistics, arguing that language
exists not as an abstract, holistic entity but only as a series of
utterances in a "dialogically agitated environment." He liberates
language from the constraints of structuralist abstractions and returns it to the realm of cultural activity, where it participates in the
historical, social, and political life of its speakers—the powerless
no less than the powerful—as both a production and a producer of
social relations. In "Discourse in the Novel" he writes, "Any concrete discourse (utterance) finds the object at which it was directed
already as it were overlain with qualification, open to dispute,
charged with value, already enveloped in an obscuring mist—or,
on the contrary, by the 'light' of alien words that have already been
spoken about it" (1981, 276). This formulation of language as a
struggle among competing codes, interpretations, and reconstruc-
tions of meaning, offers feminists a radical critique of language
which calls attention to the ideological and discursive bases of
identity (the woman writer) and experience (women's experience),
as well as the values we assign to these constructs. The dialogic
utterance is never simply citation, never an uncritical or passive
acceptance of the other's words, because what both speaker and
listener must grasp in any utterance is not, as Saussure suggests,
what is invariant in all its uses but what is different, novel in its use
in particular situations. It is the context, a particular social and

cultural situation, that creates the sign's provisional, local meaning. Repetition can never be repetitiousness.

The other's speech in our own is open, unfinished; it may become assimilated to our voices, but it is always the occasion for the struggle with another's words which Bakhtin sees as crucial to ideological consciousness. We learn from the other's speech, but we also "take it into new contexts, attach it to new material, put it in new situations in order to wrest new answers from it, new insights into its meaning, and even wrest from it new words of our *own* (since another's discourse, if productive, gives birth to a new word from us in response)" (1981, 346–47). Bakhtin's notion of the dialogized word is useful to feminist critics precisely because it refuses to see the oppressed or marginalized as passive victims of their oppression; it returns to them a culturally specific agency and the power to participate in defining their struggles, in turning the oppressor's words against him. In this respect, feminist theorists might see their encounters with poststructuralist thought, including Bakhtin's, not as the imposition of another "master" discourse but as the opportunity to engage in a productive, complex exchange with the other's words.

Because all language is dialogic, it can never be the sole property of any individual group, any more than it can of any man or woman. In Vološinov/Bakhtin's words, "Class does not coincide with the sign community, i.e., with the community which is the totality of users of the same set of signs for ideological communication. Thus various different classes will use one and the same language. As a result, differently oriented accents intersect in every ideological sign. Sign becomes an arena of the class struggle" (1986, 23). The sign is also an arena of the sexual struggle. Both sexes use the "same" language, or more radically, both sexes contest the "same" language. For Bakhtin, the struggle for and within language is ongoing. If patriarchy has created the illusion of monologic utterances monopolized by men, then feminists can dispel that illusion by appropriating the notion of heteroglossia, highlighting the dialogic nature of all discourse, insisting that those contested voices be heard. In doing so, feminists substitute for the dream of a "common women's language," or *écriture féminine*, what Haraway has called "a powerful infidel heteroglossia" (1985, 101).[7] Hetero-glossia, according to Bakhtin, is "another's speech in another's language, serving to express [the speaker's] intentions, but in a refracted way" (1981, 324). Feminist discourse is by its very nature the model of a complex heteroglossia because it always contains and struggles against another's—in this case masculinist—speech. To invoke "the female" in any sign is automatically to invoke "the male." The female contains the male not monologically, as the universal masculine is said to contain the female, but dialogically, as the possibility of politically refracting the utterance of the other.

Bakhtin's notion of the dialogic word has not been without its recent critics, and I am far from urging an uncritical acceptance of his work. Two objections in particular have been raised. The first, and perhaps more obvious, is that Bakhtin ignores the workings of gender in articulating his notion of dialogism.[8] This criticism can hardly be overlooked in any feminist appropriation of the dialogic, but it is worth pointing out, as I have done elsewhere (1986), that *all* the theories feminists have drawn upon—both explicitly and implicitly—ignore the workings of gender. Indeed, that is the whole point of feminism: to call attention to the marginalization of gender relations, and of the feminine, in Western cultural narratives about order. The feminine, as Dale Bauer suggests, becomes a "disruptive excess," the voice of gender, which cannot be accounted for in Bakhtin's dialogic model but which provides the basis for a feminist dialogics (1988, 6). We can apply the notion of dialogism to Bakhtin's own thought, using it as a means to stage an encounter between Bakhtinian heteroglossia and feminist theory. Feminism can encounter Bakhtin's words not as authoritative but as "internally persuasive discourse," discourse from which we can wrest our own—feminist—meanings. Forms of poaching, I would add, are always complex.

The second important critique of the dialogic is that Bakhtin

---

[7] For a Bakhtinian reading of the notion of women's language see Yaeger 1984, 955.
[8] See Booth 1982; Yaeger 1984, 959, 971 n.6; Mary Russo, "Female Grotesques: Carnival and Theory," in de Lauretis 1986, 218–21; Bauer 1988, 6; and Bernard Duyfhuizen, "Deconstruction and Feminist Literary Theory II," in Kauffman 1989, 179.

somehow promises dialogic exchanges that are "free, natural, spontaneous, informal, or lively" as a natural, "human" condition, when, in fact, one could point out many instances in which speech is coercive and highly unequal or in which individuals have been completely silenced.[9] This criticism, which domesticates Bakhtin, making him into a weak-kneed pluralist, is based on a liberal humanist misreading of the dialogic. It is all too easy for Western commentators to lose sight of Bakhtin's "otherness." He writes in what for all but a small elite of Western literary critics is a strange and exotic language. His work, for most of us, must be mediated through translations that are not without their own political agendas. Because he is a Soviet writer, translations of his work into Western languages have been mediated by the academic politics of the cold war, by the attempts of Western Marxists and liberals to appropriate the concept of the dialogic for their own purposes. However dead the cold war may be in international politics, in academia the question of the success or failure of Marxist analytics is far from settled.

Rather than suggest that the dialogic is a natural and essential element of the "human condition," conceived of as some static and universal entity, Bakhtin argues that the dialogic is a function of language conceived of as a thoroughly social and intersubjective phenomenon. For this reason, any analysis of the dialogic must account for the elements of coercion and constraint, of power as well as solidarity, which are obviously at play in any social encounter. Bakhtin does not say that dialogue is always spontaneous or informal; his illuminating essay on speech genres suggests that virtually all speech is governed by social conventions and institutions that dictate the style of any utterance, from the tritest social conventions of salutation to highly complex literary genres (1986). Therefore, no dialogue is ever free and equal. Rather, the notion of the dialogic requires precisely an investigation of the power relations that inform and shape any discourse. It calls for an investiga-

[9]See the essays by Fogel (173–96) and Bernstein (197–223) in Morson and Emerson 1989; the quotation is from Fogel, 174. Bauer to some extent shares this belief, although she at least credits Bakhtin for some analysis of the institutional forces that limit the dialogic (see 1988, 5–15). For a critique of liberal readings of Bakhtin see Hirschkopf 1985.

tion of the social institutions that control who speaks, in what situation, and with what force.[10] That Bakhtin did most of his writing during the years of Stalinist totalitarianism, that much of his writing was censored and went unpublished during his life-time, that during the years he was interned in a labor camp, Bakhtin used his writings to roll cigarettes—all suggest that he is sensitive to the ways in which the operations of power shape the dialogic and limit its "free play." Yet despite the inequalities in-volved in discourse, Bakhtin insists that within the dialogic the powerless are not simply passive and silenced victims of their op-pressors. However totalitarian the oppression, the powerless con-struct more or less subversive forms of agency; they are capable of defining their own struggles and of acting in—as well as against— their own interests. That is why Bakhtin says that the sign is the arena of the class *struggle*. However powerful the oppressor and however constrained the dialogue, Bakhtin argues, all classes with-in a sign community use and contest the same language, and their interests and "accents" contend within it. In this regard, he is talking not about opposition or oppression but about the materialist complexity of discourse.

It is theoretically and politically crucial, then, to hold onto the term *dialogic* (and its complement *heteroglossia*) despite these crit-icisms because its emphasis on the power relations that govern discourse offers a means to recast feminist debates in terms of complexity. Dialogics facilitates the movement toward a nonlinear and nondeterministic model of cultural analysis which enables feminists to move beyond ritualistic invocations of global concepts such as "difference" and "diversity" to an investigation of the spe-cific local and historical conditions that govern discourse and cul-ture. Unlike the New Critical paradox or the Hegelian dialectic, the dialogic refuses to synthesize and thus erase opposition. Unlike

[10] A related problem is Todorov's concern that Bakhtin is inconsistent, claiming all language is dialogic and yet making use of the term *monologic* to distinguish certain kinds of speech situations (1984). All language *is* dialogic, but the powerful are able to create the illusion that their discourse is monologic. They are able, at least intermittently, to enforce the social consequences of their power of utterance. It is the task of a dialogic criticism to expose this authoritative pose as one of the fictions held in place by the particular deployment of power within a social formation.

the binary oppositions of some forms of American deconstruction, the dialogic insists on the local and particularistic nature of the utterance. Finally, unlike the pluralism that has figured so prominently in feminist literary criticism, Bakhtin's dialogics insists upon exposing the power relations that govern discourse, including the mystifications of power implicit in pluralism's philosophical commitment to diversity. The feminist analysis of dialogic speech genres begins to examine the complex dynamics of social relations by unpacking this largely invisible, yet powerful network of social relations and institutions that both promote and limit heteroglossia. In such an analysis, every utterance partakes of both the centripetal forces that impel societies toward order, centralization, and control—toward the monologic—and the centrifugal forces that impel it toward chaos, heteroglossia, and change.

The Ficticity of Fact

The superimposition of the dialogic and complexity raises the question of my own "authority." If I have argued persuasively in the previous section, I have now created a "fact": all languages are dialogic. The form of this statement—its simplicity and the absence of any markers of ownership or fabrication—conveys a high level of confidence in its truth-value. My fact would seem to be self-contradictory, however, in that I am now in the position of declaring monologically that language is dialogic. I want to embrace this contradiction and exploit it as an example of the second aim of this book, which is to investigate the constructedness of what we call facts and to call attention to the processes involved in their construction.

Common sense tells us that fictions are made, but facts are discovered. Traces of this distinction are sedimented in the words themselves and their etymological relation to each other. *Fiction* comes from the active present of the Latin root, which emphasizes the process of making, whereas *fact* comes from the past participle, which masks the generative processes that go into making fact (Haraway 1989, 3). If fiction is open to possibilities, facts are finished. Facts appear to be monologic; they show no traces of fabrication, construction, or ownership. "The facts speak for themselves." "You can't dispute the facts." These truisms, like all clichés, have some element of truth in them. All academic disciplines deal in facts; without them discourse of most kinds would be impossible. But like most of what we call common sense, these clichés also mask their own hegemony, their own complicity in perpetuating certain preferred interpretations of the world, in particular the be-lief that there is a preexistent "reality" that the objective observer encounters, discovers, and then records as facts.

Following the extremely suggestive work of Bruno Latour and feminist adaptations of it by Haraway (1989), I offer a provisional or heuristic account of the processes by which facts take on qualities that appear to place them beyond dispute, that erase the history of their making. Latour and Woolgar's description of the creation of scientific facts is significant because it challenges a scientific prac-tice that, more than any other area of our culture, defines itself by its allegiance to the monologic, authoritative discourse of fact in opposition to, say, the consciously "political" orientation of femi-nism. According to Latour and Woolgar, however, in science an utterance becomes a fact only when it has been cut off from the circumstances of its production, "when it loses its temporal qualifi-cations and becomes incorporated into a large body of knowledge drawn upon by others" (1986, 106), that is, when the utterance presents itself as finished rather than in the process of becoming. Despite such attempts at forging universals—an ongoing project of both science and culture facts are always embedded in history and in the particular, local practices of a dialogic culture.

What Latour's work suggests is that we do not encounter a ready-made world through objective observation. "We" "make" "it." This we is radically heterogeneous, the making is contentious, dialogic, and its products are complex. To control the destabilizing implications of this process, science traditionally presents for con-sumption tidy narratives of discovery. Latour's analysis of the sem-iotic processes by which we sort through the complexity and chaos of our competing fabrications suggests a radical theory of complex-ity, which insists that facts have histories and that these histories include alliances, associations, conflicts, struggles, and negotia-tions among competing interpretations of the real.

What we call a fact is really a kind of "black box," an utterance that has effaced, at least for the moment, the history of its construction. In cybernetics, a black box designates a piece of machinery or a set of commands too complex to be repeated when the only information needed for a particular operation is the input and output. The complexities of its working, the networks that hold it in place, and the histories and controversies that went into its construction can and often must be temporarily ignored (Latour 1987, 2–3). One purpose of this book is to examine facts while they are in the making, to open up the black boxes and explore the networks of associations and alliances that hold them in place, as well as the controversies that threaten to dislodge them. Exposing the fact as a thing made and not discovered, the chapters that follow explore the "ficticity" of facts about women's writing. At the same time, it would be naïve to assert that I could undertake to expose the constructedness of facts without asserting any facts myself, without falling prey to the same practices of erasure I am unmasking. Like everyone else, I must write from within my particular social, historical, and institutional situation, using those discourses that are available to me and the speech genres that govern their deployment. My provisional, heuristic assertions must be subject to the same scrutiny in a process that is, at least in theory, endlessly complex and endlessly recursive.

The linguistic practices of modality offer one means to examine how facts are rhetorically constructed. *Modality* is the term used for those linguistic markers that designate the status, authority, and reliability of an utterance, markers that confer upon or deny an utterance value as truth or fact.[11] Consider the following three sentences:

(1) All language is dialogic.

(2) Because [all language is dialogic], it follows that statements of fact are utterances that have temporarily suppressed the dialogues, the histories of conflict and struggle that went into their making.

(3) In one of his later essays, "Discourse in the Novel," Bakhtin claims that the utterances that make up [language are dialogic], but

---

[11]My argument about modality is indebted to the insightful analyses of Hodge and Kress 1988, 121–61; and Latour 1987, 22–26.

others (notably Aaron Fogel and Michael André Bernstein) contend that this formulation ignores the institutional inequalities among speakers which silence the powerless.

The first sentence states a fact. All traces of fabrication or owner-ship have been suppressed; the utterance is cut off from its produc-tion and its producers. This sentence has a high or positive modality because it leads us away from the conditions of its pro-duction and presents itself as already made. Like a prefabricated brick, it can now be used in the construction of other larger and more complex structures. Because the conditions of its production have been removed, it is free to form alliances with other utter-ances, as in the second sentence. In this sentence, through the process of embedding, the fact allies itself with another, less potent utterance and lends the force of its high modality to strengthen the weaker statement. A statement with a high modality can ally itself with statements that are either stronger or weaker than itself to create ever stronger and more complex structures.

But other stresses might work in the opposite direction, to un-dercut the modality of any fact by highlighting the struggles that went into its production. Consider sentence 3. This utterance has a low or negative modality because it calls attention to the processes of its construction. The statement is produced by a particular per-son in a particular place at a particular time. It no longer carries universal force. Furthermore, the reader or listener is invited to question the authority of the speaker by the "but"—a marker of low modality—that begins the second clause. Other authorities who could contest, modify, or utterly deny the validity of the state-ment are ranged against the speaker. Those authorities form al-liances that undercut the force of the original utterance, isolating its speaker and rendering it considerably weaker than it is in either of the first two sentences. In this sentence, the fact with which I began has been obscured by conflict, controversy, and the strug-gles among competing interpretations of the real.

Theoretically the processes that create high and low modalities can proliferate endlessly, creating more complex structures of argu-ment, counterargument, documentation, and citation. As these structures accumulate, they are organized into a paradigm; as they grow more elaborate, a field, specialization, or discipline begins to emerge from the chaos, defining what questions can be asked and what counts as evidence in answering those questions. The complex structures of argumentation which circulate around these questions can then, once again, be "black-boxed."

Feminism, I would claim, has been created as a black box in this way. Its name gives it, if not a sense of solidity, at least a sense of solidarity, even though most recognize that feminism is hardly a single, unified movement or ideology. It is a term without a single referent, a complex network of conflicts and struggles, alliances and negotiations which many parties contend to appropriate. The complexities contained within the black box of feminism are designated by such terms as "female oppression," "women's experience," the "woman writer," and more recently, "the lesbian," the "third-world woman," and the "woman of color." If we think of these concepts as homogeneous or total—as finished "facts"—we are in danger of mythologizing them, of shoving them into their own black boxes to create an illusion of "sisterhood." This book attempts to restore to only one of these terms its historical complexity. Arguing that feminism has "black-boxed" the woman writer as a critical "fact," the chapters that follow trace the complex networks of institutions, power relations, resistance, and co-optation which have been effaced in the creation of the woman writer as an object of study for feminist literary criticism.

History as Noise

Implicit in my first two points about the dialogic nature of both utterances and facts is a shift in what we mean by history. At the same time that it insists upon the contingent and historical nature of the semiotic practices of gender, a feminist theory of complexity requires that the historical fact, no less than any other, be conceived as a site of political and social struggle. History of the kind I am envisioning depends on two completely interdependent and opposing formulations: the textuality of history and the historicity of textuality.

Claude Lévi-Strauss notes that the past is never experienced in any unmediated way simply as "what really happened." "What really happened," the raw unprocessed data of the past, is unattainable, and even if we could somehow obtain it, we would not be able to process it. Instead, history is always created by particular individuals for particular purposes. As Lévi-Strauss puts it, "The historian and the agent of history choose, sever and carve [historical events] up, for a truly total history would confront them with chaos. . . . Insofar as history aspires to meaning, it is doomed to select regions, periods, groups of men [sic] and individuals in these groups and to make them stand out as discontinuous figures, against a continuity barely good enough to be used as a backdrop. A truly total history would cancel itself out—its products would be nought. . . . History is therefore never history, but history-for" (1966, 257). Historical events come into being already fully textualized, their cultural "meanings" already the subject of disputation and competition. This intertextual field of conflicting and competing meanings hardens into historical "fact" when the dialogical interplay of competing versions of reality is suppressed in favor of a synthetic narrative that masks competing versions through the deployment of the markers of modality I discussed in the last section. When the utterance has enough positive modality to erase the process of its own production it becomes a historical fact.

It has become almost routine among contemporary historiographers to admit that history cannot give us any privileged access to "what really happened."[12] They recognize that the historian's task is to divide the present from the past and make order and meaning out of the chaos presented by the "past" and its discourses. History is a set of narratives that, as Hayden White has observed, create a past from which we would like to be descended (1987). It resides in the essential tension between "what really happened" and the multiple and shifting narratives about it. In the words of Roland Barthes, "Historical discourse does not follow the real; rather, it only signifies it, endlessly reiterating that *it happened*, but without having this assertion be anything other than the obvious underside of all historical narrative" (1967, 65). Reference to the real, however, has not been entirely obliterated; it has been displaced into

[12]See, for instance, Barthes 1967; White 1987; de Certeau 1988. For a feminist perspective, see Scott 1988b.

narrative and inserted within a particular, historical economy of social production. That is, an acceptance of the textuality of history does not imply a flattening out of its particularities in favor of a universalized theory of the text. We cannot now posit a univocal genre of "the historical" over the ages. Instead, the text is radically historicized, its production and reception governed by specific relations among individuals, other texts, and events.

History, then, for Lévi-Strauss, as for many other contemporary historiographers, is what gets constructed as meaningful narratives. History comes to us through documents, through texts of various kinds; we have no immediate access to the events themselves. Even if we did, those events are already bound up in textuality and intertextuality, in the competition among discourses to define what they mean. Even as they are occurring, historical events—battles, coronations, inventions, marriages, social revolutions, conquests, and palace coups—are filled with contested meanings and with a variety of dialogically agitated semiotic practices and utterances: rituals, ceremonies, rationalizations, speeches, pamphlets, sermons, tax rolls, charters. It is the historian's task to make order out of the "chaos" produced by these discourses, to "choose, sever, and carve up" the raw data of the past to produce a meaningful narrative. The selection of one interpretation always implies the suppression—the exclusion—of other interpretations, of other sources of information. However unfortunate such exclusions may be, historians claim, they are the price we pay to keep chaos at bay.

But a crucial insight of chaos theory is that chaos is not disorder and meaninglessness but a form of complex information. The apparent randomness of that information results from the inadequacy of our linear representations of historical narrative to comprehend, to represent, complexity. The conception of history as competing discourses, as contested meanings, produces patterns of interference, patterns we might refer to as "noise," following Michel Serres's use of the term (1982). Drawing on mathematical theories of information, Serres defines noise as "anything that survives as part of the message, but which was not part of the message when sent" (Paulson 1988). Noise is information that is not in itself meaningful, that resists being coerced into meaning, but against which meaning must emerge. A message—say, a narrative about the past—can emerge only by distinguishing itself from background noise, from details that are deemed irrelevant or unnecessary. But Serres argues that this noise is not parasitic on or secondary to the message: it is always an integral part of it. A message, a discourse, or a text can have no positive value, no meaning in and of itself, but must define itself differentially as that which is not noise. The transmission of noise along with information leads to more complex forms of organization so that noise becomes a positive factor in the organization of more complex representations of systems: society and history, for example.

In one respect, the chapters in this book examine what has traditionally been defined as the noise of history. Translating these notions about information to the site of discourses about history, I argue that noise is central to any dialogic conception of history. My purpose, in this regard, is not to create oppositional counternarratives out of either feminist theory or women's writing, but to foreground that which has been defined as noise and then marginalized or excluded as nonmeaningful, to make complex that which has traditionally been considered "true" or "factual." As Alice Jardine has suggested, noise in Western history—that against which the meaning of Western history has fashioned itself—has often been troped as the feminine. "The space 'outside of' the conscious subject has always connoted the feminine in the history of Western thought—and every movement into alterity is a movement into that female space; any attempt to give a place to that alterity within discourse involves a putting into discourse of 'woman'" (1985, 114-15). What Jardine calls alterity I am calling noise. Because, as I demonstrate in Chapter 4, the conscious subject of Western history has been constructed as male, the examination of historical noise most often requires the "putting into discourse of 'woman.'" The chapters that follow examine the ways in which subjects gendered as women in different cultures at different times have practiced poaching, using whatever means were at hand to struggle against their oppression and to wrest their own meaning from patriarchal cultural practices designed to keep them in their places. This book, then, can be neither a straightforward narrative of linear "progress" nor a reiteration of an abstract, ahistorical women's solidarity; instead, it must be an exploration of the cultural and historical specificity of oppression, resistance, co-optation, and subversion which marks writing by and about women. It is an essay in the politics of complexity, which seeks to resist narrative—and critical—tropings of coherence, linear causation, and "definitive" interpretations.

The texts I examine in the following chapters have all been characterized, in one or more ways, as noise, as that which violates the integrity of dominant patriarchal narratives. The texts produced by the female troubadours of the twelfth and thirteenth centuries, the medieval mystics, Mary Wollstonecraft, and Kate Chopin represent styles, ideologies, speech genres, perspectives, and sentiments that have been, until recently, marginalized within or excluded from literary history. There is no historical "continuity" among these texts, no linear progress to chart. Any "tradition" that might emerge from their conjunction is constructed by the historical and cultural contexts of feminist scholarship at the end of the twentieth century. My interest in them is to foreground the noise, the dissonances among the texts. Rather than offer pat syntheses of these works, I explore their dialogic relations of intersection, resistance, and conflict, looking at where they form alliances, part company, and modify each other. The argument of this chapter, then, extends itself both synchronically and diachronically in later chapters as a series of encounters between theoretical issues raised by complexity and texts that illuminate these issues in new and potentially disruptive ways. To focus on the dialogues these texts create calls into question in some respects the ideologies of specialized "periods" which dominate professional literary studies. I seek, then, not a continuous history that links literary developments between the twelfth and the nineteenth centuries but a series of disruptive moments—discontinuities—that call into question those standard narratives of literary history and its arbitrary division into periods.[13]

Chapter 2 examines the emergence of the trobairitz—the women troubadours of twelfth- and thirteenth-century Provence—from

[13]In "Women's Time, Women's Space," Elaine Showalter warns against uncritical acceptance of traditional historical periodization, which she sees as an imposition of a masculine and patriarchal perspective upon history (1984).

the system of gender and class relations we have come to call "courtly love." Usually considered only as a literary phenomenon, courtly love provides a grid of intelligibility through which to examine the complex interrelations among historical discourses about economics, politics, genealogy, kinship, patronage, and love which ordered both gender and class relations in feudal society. My examination of the trobairitz's poetry illustrates the ways in which women's self-representations both encode and resist hegemonic narratives about female desire and sexuality.

Chapter 3 moves from erotic love to spiritual love. The discourses of medieval mysticism provide an opportunity to revise the narratives of disempowerment that mark many feminist accounts of female authorship. This chapter examines the religious technologies of the Middle Ages, which were designed to produce docile female bodies, as well as the various ways in which certain oppressed subjects, primarily women, were able to poach, to use their visionary experiences to reconstruct their oppression as a form of power. Traditionally, the mystics' excesses of religious fervor are constructed as noise against the scholastic rationalism that is the historical legacy of the medieval Church, but the interactions among repression, power/knowledge, and the resistances of the repressed suggest that mysticism produced forms of empowerment for women which both challenged and accommodated a masculinist theology.

Chapter 4 examines the creation of an explicitly feminist discourse in Mary Wollstonecraft's *Vindication of the Rights of Woman*, which is nonetheless marked by traces of the masculinist ideologies it rebuts. As Wollstonecraft herself admits, style in a political treatise must be constructed as noise; it conveys significations apart from the "content" which in eighteenth-century political philosophy are supposed to be effaced in favor of a universal ideal of rationality. But style is also, for Wollstonecraft, a polemical instrument that challenges the hegemony of "meaning." The style of *A Vindication of the Rights of Woman*, then, both strains against and fails to recognize this ideal.

In the final chapter I return to the dialogic conception of history to consider what it does to the literary canon and to our beliefs about aesthetic value. Much of gynocriticism, the recovery of lost women writers, has been concerned with the recovery of texts we might consider cultural noise, ephemeral texts that supposedly lack the universality and permanence of canonical texts. The question is whether those texts will simply be valued as meaningful and appended to the canon—without fundamentally challenging its hegemonic power—or whether our interest in these texts will force us to rethink the ideology of aesthetic value. Will the canon finally simply exclude that noise which cannot be co-opted into its linear structure, or will texts of the kind represented in this book require more complex structures through which to articulate cultural and aesthetic values?

My method in this study is to work by parataxis, juxtaposing different representations of women not to show that they are ultimately similar but to study the myriad forms gender relations have assumed in Western culture and the kinds of social functions it has performed at different times and in different places. My aim is to suggest a dialogical and nonauthoritarian theoretical orientation and method for feminist literary criticism. My purpose, in this sense, is not to provide authoritative readings or methodological imperatives but to suggest something of the complex ways in which the symbolic representations of gender that figure in art and literature interact with, shape, and are shaped by the social institutions that organize gender roles. The chapters that follow, then, attempt to articulate a series of heteroglossic narratives, to describe a polyphonic practice of history and literary criticism which exposes the complexity behind the "unified truth" of the facts.

2

The Rhetoric of Desire
in the Courtly Lyric

A feminine text cannot fail to be more than subversive. It
is volcanic; as it is written it brings about an upheaval of
the old property crust, carrier of masculine investment;
there's no other way.

—Hélène Cixous

Woman is never anything more than the scene of more
or less rival exchange between two men.

—Luce Irigaray

This book attempts to rethink the concept of the woman writer
as it was theorized by feminism during the 1980s by looking at the
so-called feminine text as the noise of culture, uncovering the dialogically agitated contexts of its utterance. The texts I have chosen
for this task are those that expose discontinuities—ruptures and
gaps—within a literary history that has, since the eighteenth century, been characterized as linear and progressive. Thus, if the
Middle Ages seems an unpromising place to begin a study of the
"feminine" text, a forbiddingly masculine territory, with its glorifi-
cation of warfare, jousting, and hunting, its homosocial feudal ties
that bound man to man, vassal to lord; and its institutionalized
clerical misogyny, it also provides an opportunity to challenge traditional literary histories that filter out the anomalies in their narratives as irrelevant noise, thereby reproducing the cultural biases
they purport to document. The term "Middle Ages"—itself an
invention of the eighteenth century—marks the period as an interruption of progressive history, a gap between classical Rome and
the enlightenment of the Renaissance. Because feminist literary
histories have, for the most part, reproduced conventional historical periodization and, with it, conventional platitudes about progress and enlightenment, the rupture signified by the term "Middle Ages" provides a starting point for a revisionary investigation
of feminist theories of writing.

To challenge the view of medieval Europe as a benightedly masculine culture we need to locate and tease out the cultural spaces
for the "feminine." In doing so, it is critical to distinguish the
cultural representations of "woman" available at any given time—
discourse about women—from those individuals who might represent themselves as women both in conformity and in opposition to
those cultural representations. Any theory of women's writing
must position itself somewhere in the gap between cultural representations of Woman and the self-representations of individual,
historical women (de Lauretis 1987). One such space for the feminine is marked out by the development in the twelfth century in
the area of southern France known as Occitania or Provençe of a set
of attitudes toward love and women known as *fin' amor* or, more
popularly, courtly love.[1] "Farai chansoneta nueva," "I shall make a
new song," writes the first troubadour, Guillaume, ninth duke of
Aquitaine, at the beginning of the twelfth century. In the poetry of
the troubadours who followed Guillaume, and later in that of the
trouvères of France, the poets of the *dolce stil novo* of Italy, and the
minnesingers of Germany, woman becomes the object of the poet's
adoration; the noblewoman, or "lady," becomes the recipient of the
poet's homage and obedience. But whereas some have claimed that
the ideals articulated in these erotic lyrics suggest a "feminization"
of medieval culture, which expressed, as Meg Bogin says, a "deep
psychological need left unmet by the unrelenting masculinity of
feudal culture" (1980, 44–45), others, such as Jacques Lacan, suggest that it is "truly the most staggering thing that has ever been
tried," a "fraud," and the "only way of coming off elegantly from
the absence of sexual relations" in medieval society (1982, 141).
Lacan argues that *fin' amor* has nothing whatever to do with
women—at least not with women as subjects—and everything to
do with women's subjugation. The poetry that articulated *fin' amor*
remained primarily a vehicle for the expression of masculine desire, a means of articulating the relationships between men at a
time when the old feudal ties were being undermined by new
economic, social, and political developments.

[1]Gaston Paris in 1883 gave this name to the system of manners articulated by the
troubadour lyric; see *Romania* 12 (1883): 519.

While *fin' amor*, with its veneration of women, spread widely throughout Europe in the late twelfth and early thirteenth centuries, reaching northern France, Spain, Portugal, Italy, England, and even Germany, only in Provençe were the lyrical forms of troubadour poetry adapted to allow women to express their own desire. The poems of some twenty Occitan noblewomen who wrote between 1150 and 1250 survive. Until recently, the existence of these women troubadours, called the trobairitz, was known only to a handful of specialized scholars who wrote on relatively technical and largely linguistic features of their poetry. The appearance in 1976 of Meg Bogin's edition of the trobairitz, with facing-page translations, made their lyrics accessible for the first time to a much wider audience and sparked new interest in these medieval women poets.[2]

The tone of much recent writing on the trobairitz has been set by the introduction to Bogin's book. She writes: "Unlike the men, who created a complex poetic vision, the women wrote about their own intimate feelings. . . . This gives the women's poems a sense of urgency that makes them more like journals than like carefully constructed works of art" (67–68). Recent criticism of the individual poets characteristically focuses on the emotional, subjective aspects of their work—their joy and suffering in love—at the expense of their "art." They are denied a complex "poetic vision." Their works, too often, have been treated as ideologically overdetermined by the gender of their creators and as therapeutic outbursts rather than "carefully constructed works of art." For Peter Dronke, the countess of Dia, the only regularly anthologized trobairitz, is "Cleopatra-like in her variety of attitudes toward love" (in Wilson 1984, 131–32). Another, Castelloza, is no virtuoso: "Her language is narrowly concentrated; she does not create dazzling forms in the way, for instance, of her somewhat older contemporary Raimbaut de Vaqueiras" (in Wilson 1984, 144). William Paden

[2]Before 1970, the only complete study of all twenty trobairitz was Schultz-Gora's monograph from 1888, *Die Provenzalischen Dichterinnen*. Since the appearance of Bogin's book, the complete poems of Castelloza have been edited by William Paden (1981) and translated by Peter Dronke in Wilson 1984. Dronke also devotes a chapter to the trobairitz in *Women Writers in the Middle Ages* (1984), Marianne Shapiro has written about them for *Signs* (1978), and Paden has edited an anthology of essays on the trobairitz (1989).

writes that "the songs of Castelloza concentrate on feelings of melancholy and affliction with a single-mindedness that borders on masochism—not masochism in a narrow sense as sexual perversion, but the derivative form in which satisfaction comes from suffering or humiliation apart from any sexual pleasure" (Paden et al. 1981, 165). This emphasis on the emotional, subjective, and therapeutic aspects of these women's poetry miniaturizes it, perpetuating even in feminist criticism a literary double standard by which male poets' works are judged and canonized by so-called objective artistic criteria, while women's poetry is deemed emotional and personal, more like a diary than poetry.

To challenge this double standard it will be necessary to explore more fully the operations of gender in the courtly lyric. My interest in the trobairitz, about whom virtually nothing is known beyond their names and poems, lies less in what they might say about the "experience" of being a woman in twelfth-century France than in the complex ways in which the symbolic representations of gender which figure in the rhetoric of courtly love interact with, shape, and are shaped by the social institutions that organized gender roles among the aristocracy of twelfth-century Europe. In short, I want to know how sexuality, what Georges Duby has called "those fundamentally important mechanisms that ensure the reproduction of any society and the perpetuation of its structures," is discursively encoded in the courtly lyric as a genre (1983, xvii). The "subjects" created and displayed in the lyrics produced by the troubadours and trobairitz are constructed by the dialogical languages of feudalism and a newly emerging economics, as well as by the languages of sexual passion. They provide a grid of intelligibility through which to examine the exchanges between discourses about desire and those about politics, economics, and genealogy. The "intimate feelings" given form in the courtly lyric present desire not simply as a "natural" psychological state but as a form of ideology, one that both sustains and subverts hegemonic social relations.

All courtly poets—whether male or female—shared and contested the same cultural representations, the same language, the same forms. It is this interplay among representation, language, and form that creates genres, understood not merely as formal, aesthetic systems of classification but as agents of social and cultural behaviors—producers as well as products of social meanings. The forms within which poets can express themselves are as ideologically determined, and as ideologically significant, as their subject matter. The courtly lyric's forms were determined by culturally articulated relations between the sexes, conceived not as biological givens but as historically specific constructions. Women's self-representations in twelfth-century France, no less than men's, had to emerge from within a genre that promoted a very narrow range of social relations between the sexes. In claiming the power to speak—to represent themselves—the trobairitz created noise; they put into discourse what had remained outside the discourse of courtliness, which required the silence of the beloved. This rupture of feminine noise into the homosocial relations of the courtly lyric constituted a potential threat to the ideological project of *fin'amor*.

The rhetoric of desire in the tradition of the courtly lyric worked to legitimate the interests of a ruling aristocracy, which, during a period of rapid and disturbing change, was concerned to consolidate its power and limit its membership. The poetry of the trobairitz represents a potential challenge to this hegemony by giving voice to the unspoken understandings that structured social relations under feudalism, especially those of kinship and patronage. The trobairitz's poetry, then, illustrates how women's writing both encodes and resists cultural representations of femininity. But before turning to women's self-representations, it is necessary first to unpack the intricate web of social relationships that constituted *fin' amor* as a discourse about desire in twelfth-century France, the different ideological positions occupied by aristocratic men and women within that network, and the different rhetorical strategies occasioned by those positions.

Patronage and the Biopolitics of Lineage

The conventions of *fin' amor* were articulated in the first years of the twelfth century in the erotic lyrics of Guillaume IX. Whether or not the themes of courtly love were a "revolution in sentiment" or as old as the relations between men and women, they were the inspiration for a "new poetry" and for the creation of a poetic diction in the vernacular (Bogin 1980, 44). As even he seemed to recognize, Guillaume's songs were startlingly new, both formally and ideologically.

> Farai chansoneta nueva
> ans que vent ni gel ni plueva;
> ma dona m'assai' e.m prueva,
> quossi de qual guiza l'am;
> e ja per plag que m'en mueva
> no.m solvera de son liam.
>
> Q'ans mi rent a lieys e.m liure,
> qu'en sa carta.m pot escriure. . . .
>
> Que plus etz blanca qu'evori,
> per qu'ieu autra non azori.
> Si.m breu non ai ajutori,
> cum ma bona dompna m'am,
> morrai, pel cap sanh Gregori,
> si no.m bayz' en cambr' o sotz ram.
>
> [I shall make a new song
> before the wind blows and it freezes and rains.
> My lady is trying me, putting me to the test
> to find out how I love her.
> Well now, no matter what quarrel she moves for that reason,
> She shall not loose me from her bond.
>
> Instead, I become her man, deliver myself up to her,
> And she can write my name down in her charter . . . .
>
> For you are whiter than ivory,
> I worship no other woman.
> If I do not get help soon
> and my good lady does not give me love,
> by Saint Gregory's holy head I'll die
> if she doesn't kiss me in a chamber or under a tree.][3]

[3]Goldin 1973, 40–43; unless noted otherwise, all troubadour poems and translations cited here are from this edition. Page numbers will be noted parenthetically in the text.

Fin' amor celebrates and objectifies women extravagantly. The songs through which these ideals spread have as their principal subject the *dompna* (the term of address directed to the married noblewoman). She is the most virtuous ("bona") and beautiful woman in the world: "plus etz blanca qu'evori." The lover serves and worships his beloved, while she tests him ("prueva"). His joy and pain equally proceed from her. When she is kind, he is joyful: "Tant ai mo cor ple de joya, / tot me desnatura," writes Bernart de Ventadorn ["My heart is so full of joy / it changes every nature"] (128–29). When she is cold, he suffers, even to the point of death, as Guillaume's song suggests. But his love for her is ennobling; it makes him a better man. Arnaut Daniel writes, "Tot iorn meillur et esmeri / car la gensor serv e coli [Each day I am a better man and purer, / for I serve and celebrate the noblest lady]" (216–17).

This sudden appearance of poetry celebrating women and granting them absolute power in love coincides with a period of material changes in the social and economic life of twelfth-century Occitania. The sparse historical records from this period suggest an economic revolution that produced what Marc Bloch has called the second feudal age. He points to a combination of factors between 1050 and 1250, including a possible change in weather patterns, technological improvements in agriculture, and a steady extension of agricultural lands, which resulted in an increase in population throughout Europe, accompanied by increased urbanization, the expansion of trade, and the discovery of new sources of wealth. Although these developments were unevenly distributed throughout Europe, in the north and south of France the higher aristocracy—the kings, great nobles, and manorial lords—began to amass great fortunes (M. Bloch 1961, 69). The Church also continued to grow more wealthy and influential as it extended its hegemony over more and more of Europe.[4] Accompanying this new wealth was a desire for increased political stability.

Prior to the twelfth century, feudalism in the south of France was characterized by decentralized social and political relationships. The political structure was marked by multiple centers of power dominated by local strongmen. Politics was local and alliances

[4]Duby argues that the Church's wealth grew in proportion to its ability to persuade those it converted not to bury their wealth with their dead but to keep it in circulation by donating it to the Church (1974, 54–55).

could shift quickly. Because power was disseminated among several powerful magnates rather than concentrated in a single monarch, no one ruler or family could hope to maintain control indefinitely. Order in this region was perceived as an "ever-shifting configuration of competing forces," and stability as a "temporary balance of conflicting forces" (Kendrick 1988, 7–8). Such a political structure favors instability, a reasonable response to an unstable and hostile environment. The exercise of power under these conditions required the physical presence of the ruler. A lord could control and effectively administer only those holdings he could personally inhabit. Distant holdings that could not be visited frequently were easily lost to those who administered them on a day-to-day basis. Guillaume IX's attempts to occupy the Toulousain after his marriage in 1094 to Philippa, widow of the king of Aragon and heir to the Toulousain, suggests how difficult it was for even a very powerful duke to extend his power beyond the territories he could physically occupy. Leaving his wife to govern both her lands and Aquitaine, Guillaume went off to fight in Normandy and then Jerusalem. By 1113 he had forfeited his wife's rights in the Toulousain, and he spent the rest of his life fighting his own vassals in Aquitaine (Topsfield 1975, 13).

Instability and decentralization also marked kinship structures. The most powerful families in the region might best be described, in Howard Bloch's terms, as "a loosely defined grouping of relatives and retainers, 'friends' and neighbors [who] gravitated around the residence of a lord who was, above all, a patron, a distributor of gifts and lands, the spoils of war or exchange" (1983, 65). Kinship was calculated horizontally, and little distinction was made between the lineage of the husband and that of the wife. Marital alliances were often temporary. When property was passed on, inheritance might be shared among brothers and even sisters.[5] Noblewomen in southern France, then, occupied a more complex and ambiguous position within the feudal hierarchy than their counterparts in the north. If they were not exactly powerful, they were, at least, less absolutely disempowered. Women appear as

[5]Women could inherit land in the absence of male heirs. Eleanor of Aquitaine, Ermengarde of Narbonne, and Marie of Montpellier were among the prominent Occitan women who inherited and managed large estates (Paden 1989, 9).

landowners and land managers more frequently in southern France than anywhere else in medieval Europe. They frequently function as the heads of families, at least in name, as evidenced by the increasing use of the matronymic in place of the patronymic in charters between the tenth and twelfth centuries. The matronymic her son bore would be a sign of the woman's duties and privileges which would give her prominence within the community (Herlihy 1976, 18–21). Inheritance laws did not restrict a woman's freedom to administer family property (as they did, for instance, in northern France and Italy) either jointly with her husband or by herself as a widow.

By the twelfth century, the political and social structures that organized the aristocracy in the south of France were coming into conflict with attempts by both the Church and the monarchies of France and England to extend their sphere of influence into that region and impose upon it a new vision of feudalism dominated by order, hierarchy, and centralization. The concentration of wealth and power in fewer and fewer hands created the need for new technologies of control. To limit both the growth of the aristocracy and the dilution of feudal holdings through partition among multiple heirs, the aristocratic family came increasingly to calculate lineage vertically, based on descent from a single male founder; to practice strict primogeniture; and to privilege blood ties over marital ties. The family estate was to be passed on intact from eldest son to eldest son.[6]

As primogeniture and the resulting control of marriage and female sexuality enabled the aristocracy to concentrate larger and larger estates among fewer and fewer aristocratic families, effective governance required the development of administrative bureaucracies that could exercise executive and judicial power in the absence of the ruler. One of the most basic technologies of this new political order was writing—an order of representation without which neither primogeniture nor monarchial rule could long survive. Writing enabled the ruler to delegate power in his absence and so to rule from a distance. But it required the stabilization and

---

[6]For discussions of this transformation, see H. Bloch 1983, 64–75; Duby 1983, 16–19, 250; and Herlihy 1985, 79–111.

regulation of the vernacular, so that such elementary administrative tasks as executing contracts, recording debts and payments, and preserving judicial testimony would be possible. This new deployment of writing as a technology for political control in the service of the centralization and hierarchization of church and state, required a new class of administrators. The "new men" who filled these administrative positions often came from outside the aristocracy (Green 1986, 139–57). They needed to bring to their new positions skill in language and writing which they could then use to advance in the administrative service of their patron.

Troubadour poetry, some scholars have maintained, became a contested ground between the centripetal forces of feudal society—those that sought to hierarchize, order, and centralize political and economic life through the skillful deployment of representation—and the centrifugal forces of resistance that impelled it toward heterogeneity, complexity, and change. In resisting the push toward centralization, the decentralized and dispersed aristocracy of Occitania, whose power derived from their physical presence, rejected the most basic principle of representation: that there can be authority in absence and that representations are signs of that authority. It is perhaps not surprising, then, that the first troubadour, Guillaume IX, was one of the most powerful of the lords of Occitania. For the male poet of the aristocracy, this new poetry of sexual desire became a means of challenging the power of representation and, with it, the "centered, hierarchizing moral and social order" of lineage and primogeniture (Kendrick 1988, 15). It became a means of creating a poetry out of the linguistic noise of Occitan culture, out of the "foolishness" that resists being coerced into meaning. "Farai un vers de dreyt nien," writes Guillaume ["I will make a verse out of strictly nothing"] (24–25).

Guillaume IX, however, was a notable exception; most of the troubadours were of modest origins and depended for their livelihood on the patronage of the lords of Occitan.[7] The creation of a new, less rigidly defined administrative class, which negotiated its relationship to the aristocracy through patronage and which

[7]My own informal survey of the *vidas* of the troubadours turned up some thirteen troubadours of modest origins and only three—Guillaume, Raimbaut d'Aurenga, and Jaufre Rudel—of aristocratic origins.

served the new order of representation, may be reflected in this poem by Arnaut Daniel:

> En cest sonet coind'e leri
> fauc motz e capuig e doli,
> que serant verai e cert
> qan n'aurai passat la lima;
> q'Amors marves plan'e daura
> mon chantar, que de liei mou
> qui pretz manten e governa.

> [To this sweet and pretty air
> I set words that I plane and finish;
> and every word will fit well,
> once I have passed the file there,
> for at once Love polishes and aureates
> my song, which proceeds from her,
> ruler and guardian of merit.]

(216–17)

The new poetry of sexual desire emerged from within the same cultural matrix that demanded the regularization of the vernacular for administrative purposes; both the rhetoric of desire and that of government service are aspects of the same technology of hegemonic abstraction.[8] The distant love for the idealized lady stands in a metonymic relation to service to the absent ruler. The metaphor structuring this *cobla* (strophe) is that of the poet as artisan. Daniel compares his craft to the planing and polishing ("capuig e doli") the artisan requires to finish his work of art. Like the artisan with his file ("la lima"), the poet too has his tools—the tools of representation, words. The metaphor suggests an awareness that art is a commodity, which might structure relations of patronage between individuals through the mediation of representations. The poet and artisan seem to have more in common than the poet and his beloved, the patron who "rules and maintains

---

[8]Kendrick makes the stronger argument that the troubadours were in fact informal language teachers for the lay public. They traveled from court to court teaching the most basic skills of vernacular grammar: reading, writing, composition, and interpretation (1988, 72).

worth" ("qui pretz manten e governa"). Daniel's language suggests the extent to which money by the twelfth century has also become a representational medium of exchange, functioning to establish relative value among commodities, including art and poetry, and, by extension, relations between individuals (M. Bloch 1961, 71). The value of the poet's love is measured by a gold standard; it is gilded ("daura"). Its worth is monetary. The lover hopes to receive from his beloved not only value or merit but, perhaps implicitly, rewards or even wages.

What troubadour poetry contests, then, is nothing less than the power of representations—of language, of economics, of kinship, of lineage, of desire—to replace the "real" and to construct a new order of feudalism. This reading of the courtly lyric has been persuasively argued by Howard Bloch (1983) and Laura Kendrick (1988). But their readings fail to explain why, far from being explicitly political, courtly poetry is in fact explicitly erotic and why the object of that eroticism is most often the lord's wife, the dompna. They fail to suggest why representations of women and sexuality figure so prominently in this new poetry. To understand the place of desire in the courtly lyric, we must examine how social relations of gender were represented within this new feudal order. If writing and representation were necessary for the success of political centralization, so was the control of women. Fin' amor functioned as an ideology that smoothed over the contradictions brought about by homosocial competition to control women as resources. It provided the means to negotiate between the contradictory demands of marriage, which required the control of women's sexuality, and patronage, which demanded its exploitation. It represented aristocratic women as simultaneously on display and inaccessible.

The transformation of the medieval aristocracy into a "closed and patroclinous caste," to use Bloch's words, required a marital strategy based on monogamy, exogamy, and the repression of pleasure (1983, 68). It required that families marry off all daughters but only the eldest son in order to protect the family estate. Paden and other commentators have tried to locate the freedom of aristocratic women in southern France to participate in the extramarital liaisons described by fin' amor within the institution of marriage (1989, 4–

13), but the politics of marriage did not work to women's advantage. Within marriage a woman's sexuality would have to be strictly controlled to assure the legitimacy of any heirs produced. She must be a virgin upon marriage and after marriage must have no other sexual partner besides her husband. If women in twelfth-century Occitania enjoyed a somewhat more privileged position than women elsewhere in Europe, they were still pawns in a patrilinear culture, sacrificed to the need to assure the "legitimate" succession of a male line through monogamy and to achieve the widest dispersion of family influence and power through exogamy. Marriage became an affair between families, negotiated by male heads; women were merely tokens of that exchange.[9]

Although such an arrangement would tend to foster dependency in women and domination in men, the position of aristocratic women in feudal society was not defined exclusively by their marriages. They were also required to establish relations of patronage with their "vassals" as a means of promoting solidarity among the men at court. The twentieth century has tended to romanticize *fin' amor* as offering romantic and sexual fulfillment as a reasonable alternative to marriages that were primarily economic and political affairs. But such a characterization, it seems to me, ignores the material status of the mostly male poets who created this illusion. Marriage was primarily the means by which men at the apex of the feudal hierarchy defined their relations with one another, through political alliances or through the orderly succession of the patrimony from father to eldest son. But the disinherited second sons and other members of the lower nobility, who were often unable to marry, were largely excluded from these means of establishing social identity. They depended on the patronage of their feudal overlords, and the women worshiped in their lyrics were most likely the wives of their patrons and thus themselves powerful patronesses. While the medieval aristocracy was evolving toward a kinship system of ascribed status, the patronage networks that marked feudal relations, dominated by the exchange of "gifts," were still everywhere in evidence. These patronage networks were

---

[9]In an earlier essay, I deal with the politics of medieval marriage in terms of the courtly romance (1989, 114–15).

the primary means by which those outside the aristocracy negotiated their relations with it.[10]

Patronage is an informal means of structuring social relations. Patron-client relations, according to S. N. Eisenstadt and Luis Roniger (1984), are particularistic and diffuse, rather than legal or contractual. They are highly interpersonal relationships established between individuals or networks of individuals rather than between organized corporate groups. Yet these relations are defined within a system of finely articulated symbolic and institutional terms, involving elaborate rituals, codes, and rules. These rules are almost always unspoken or spoken only in an elaborately codified language that functions to disguise as personal and private the economic or political nature of the transactions taking place, transactions that, in a precapitalist economy, are required to keep the economy or the government functioning and to ensure the domination of the ruling class. The "euphemerization of economic power" (the words are James Scott's [1985, 307]) which marks patronage networks is required when direct physical coercion is not possible and yet the indirect domination of capitalist markets is insufficient to ensure the consolidation and circulation of wealth.

I suggest that *fin' amor* offers a codified language for "euphemerizing" the economic exchanges that take place in patron-client networks. An example from the *vida* of the troubadour Bernart de Ventadorn suggests how well feudalism accords with the descriptions of sociologists and anthropologists who study patron-client networks.[11]

Bernart de Ventadorn was from Limousin, from the castle of Ventadour. He was a man of humble origins, the son of a servant who was a baker, and who heated the oven to bake the bread of the castle. And he became a handsome and an able man, and he

[10]Eisenstadt and Roniger discuss social systems that combine elements of patronage with those of ascribed status (1984, 178–84).

[11]I should point out that I am concerned here with more than simply literary patronage. Literary patronage was a special case of a social structure that organized social, political, and economic relations at every level of society. I am grateful to my colleague Deborah Heath, who first pointed out to me the possibility of reading courtly love as a patron-client relationship.

knew how to sing and how to invent poetry well, and he became courtly and learned.

And the Viscount of Ventadour, his lord, grew very fond of him and of his inventing and his singing, and greatly honored him. And the Viscount of Ventadour had a wife who was young, noble, and lively. And she grew fond of Bernart and of his songs, and fell in love with him. And he fell in love with the lady, and composed his songs and his poems about her, about the love which he had for her, and about her merit. Their love lasted a long time before the viscount or other people became aware of it. (Egan 1984, 11– 12)

The relationships described here, including the "love" between Bernart and his patron's wife, might easily be described as part of a highly elaborate code for describing relations of patronage. Bernart's relationship with the viscount of Ventadorn enables him to rise from relative obscurity to some prominence, to become "courtly and learned," simply because his lord "grew very fond of him," a situation that would be impossible under "official" conditions that dictated the ascribed status of members of the community under feudalism. He is a valued client of the lord of Ventadorn not for his ability to bake bread—an economically "productive" role that would have been his hereditary function but would never have won him recognition—but for his ability to sing and invent poetry, a singularly nonproductive talent in purely economic terms. But in a culture in which economic activity must be disguised through the exchange of gifts and must be represented as personal and voluntary rather than impersonal and calculating, poetry itself may become a valuable medium of exchange.

A patron-client relationship such as this one is not based on a onetime exchange; rather it entails long-term obligations and credit, which also function to disguise the fundamentally economic nature of the relationship as a personal one. There is a great enough temporal gap between each "gift" to preserve at least the appearance of reciprocal generosity. Furthermore, the relationship is entered into voluntarily by both parties and can be terminated voluntarily by either. Yet, in spite of this reciprocal element of voluntarism, the relationship is nonetheless marked by extreme inequality. The distance between Bernart and his lord is great enough that when the viscount discovers the relation between his wife and Bernart he "banished Bernart from him and had his wife locked up" (Egan, 12). As the furor of Ventadorn's reaction suggests, this mutual dependency tended to promote feelings of both security and insecurity.

The diffusion of patron-client relationships was so great under feudalism that all but the most powerful men would be simultaneously both patrons and clients. The *vida* of the troubadour Bertran de Born provides a case in point. Bertran was the castellan of Hautefort and, according to one manuscript version, the patron— overlord—of one thousand men.[12] But his fortune was uncertain enough that he found himself in the service at one time or another of Henry II, the Plantagenet king of England; his eldest son, Henry Court Mantel; and Richard the Lionhearted and on different sides of the civil strife among them.[13] This diffusion of patronage networks created a web of alliances quite daunting in their complexity. Just how impossibly complex divided loyalties might become is suggested by this medieval charter, which defines the obligations of a vassal to his patron:

> I, John of Toul, affirm that I am the vassal of the Lady Beatrice, countess of Troyes, and of her son Theobald, count of Champagne, against every creature living or dead, excepting my allegiance to Lord Enjourand of Coucy, Lord John of Arcis, and the count of Grandpré. If it should happen that the count of Grandpré should be at war with the countess and count of Champagne in his own quarrel, I will aid the count of Grandpré in my own person, and will aid the count and countess of Champagne by sending them the knights whose service I owe them from the fief which I hold of them. (Hollister 1971, 95)

Perhaps the most important feature of patron-client relationships is that they involve exchanges of different types of resources,

[12]My remarks do not depend on the historical accuracy of the information contained in the *vidas*, which are highly fanciful accounts of the lives of the troubadours. What interests me here are the social relations that organized medieval feudalism, and these would undoubtedly be revealed even in the most outrageous narrative.

[13]For having promoted civil strife, he appears in Dante's *Inferno* (28.113–42) with his head separated from his body.

which are perceived as interchangeable. These resources may be economic and material (the fief); often they are political and military (support, loyalty); but they are also quite often intangible but no less vital resources such as power, influence, prestige, and status. In *Outline of a Theory of Practice*, Pierre Bourdieu uses the term "symbolic capital" to describe the means by which the wealthy convert some of their disproportionate wealth into forms of prestige, status, and social control through what are understood as voluntary acts of generosity or charity (1977, 178). This symbolic capital would be convertible into labor and services, which, in turn, would generate even more material wealth (Scott 1985, 307). In warning against an anachronistic distinction between economics and "culture," Bourdieu argues that analyses of precapitalist economies, including the feudal economy, must "extend economic calculation to *all* the goods, material and symbolic, without distinction, that present themselves as *rare* and worthy of being sought after in a particular social formation—which may be 'fair words' or smiles, handshakes or shrugs, compliments or attention, challenges or insults, honors or honours, powers or pleasures, gossip or scientific information, distinction or distinctions" (Bourdieu 1977, 178). Symbolic capital, which is convertible into material wealth, may indeed be the most valuable form of accumulation in a precapitalist economy that relies on cooperation and reciprocity and yet promotes extreme social inequality, in which public transactions—both political and economic—can be understood only as private transactions between individuals (Duby 1988, 3–8).

One outcome of this need to disguise economic relations as generosity or charity is that this "euphemerization" is always the focus of symbolic manipulation, struggle, and conflict (Scott 1985, 308). *Fin' amor* may be described as one strategy by which men belonging to the lower nobility, the so-called new men who provided administrative services for a newly emerging state, could articulate their relations of patronage to their feudal overlords, using women as a medium of exchange.[14] In many troubadour lyrics, as in the

[14]Eugene Vance has located in the poetry of the trouvère Gace Brulé just such an impulse: "These texts have little to do with the delineation of individual erotic impulses, but involve, on the contrary, the attempt of someone belonging to a restricted social group to elaborate, by writing texts 'about' erotic desire, some kind of performative epistemic model—one fashioned in a code conforming to the decorum of the noble rank—by which members of that group could perceive and

poem by Guillaume quoted earlier, the poet's relationship to his lady is figured as the relationship between a vassal and a lord, that is, as a patron-client relationship. The language of the feudal hierarchy is everywhere prominent; she will not free the lover from her bond, "son liam." She will write his name down in her charter; he will become her man, her vassal. Given his position as one of the most powerful lords of Occitania, Guillaume's claim to vassalage strikes a deliberately ironic tone. He exploits the disparity between his own position and the pose of lover/client he adopts. In "Companho, faray un vers . . . covinen," Guillaume handles the language of feudalism to much different effect, making explicit his own power as feudal overlord. Unable to decide between two lovers, na Agnes or na Arsen, he writes

> De Gimel ai lo castel el mandamen,
> E per Niol fauc ergueil a tota gen,
> C'ambedui me son jurat e plevit per sagramen.

> [Of Gimel I have the castle and the fief,
> and with Niol I show myself proud to everyone,
> for both are sworn to me and bound by oath.]

(22–23)

Guillaume's monopoly on the most important economic resources, the castle and the fief, protects his interests in the exchange of women, which are at once legal ("jurat," "sagramen"), amorous, and ironic.

But more often, the erotic relationship between the poet and his beloved repeats the participants' political relationship, as for instance in this poem by Bernart de Ventadorn.

> Bona domna, re no.us deman
> mas que.m prendatz per servidor,
> qu'e.us servirai com bo senhor,
> cossi que del gazardo m'an.

---

understand other important, and yet problematical, developments of their surrounding world, particularly that of an incipient economic revolution" (1975, 42).

Ve.us m'al vostre comandamen,
francs cors umil, gais e cortes!

[Good lady, I ask you for nothing
but to take me for your servant,
for I will serve you as my good lord,
whatever wages come my way.
Behold me at your command, a man to rely on,
before you, o noble, gentle, courteous, and gay.]

(128–29)

The lover here asks for his lady's patronage, promising to serve her
in exchange for a reward, for "whatever wages come my way." The
discourse of economic exchange (service, wages) structures the
erotic exchange, but the direction of the metaphor is ambiguous. It
may be that economics is simply being evoked as a metaphor for
love, but it is just as likely that courtly love is a highly codified way
of talking about economic exchanges and the investment of symbolic capital. It may be more productive to talk about a dialogical
exchange or a circulation (as money is allowed to circulate) between the discourses of desire and those of economics. Like all
patron-client relations, this one contains a strong element of interpersonal obligation, expressed in terms of reciprocity. The repetition of the grammatically derived "servidor"/"servirai" underscores this element of reciprocity and exchange, while the rhyme
"servidor"/"senhor" emphasizes the inequality of the relationship.
The *dompna*'s feudal privilege enables her to confer status, even
nobility, upon her lover/vassal, while she receives in return public
affirmation of her own courtly status and prestige—her nobility,
gentility, and courtesy (her "francs cors umil, gais e cortes").

That the beloved was the poet's superior by class is suggested by
such *senhals* (code names) as La Bel Senher and Midons, which
frequently appear in troubadour lyrics. Such androgynous terms—
the first composed of the feminine article and adjective and the
masculine noun for lord or master, the latter of the feminine possessive *mi* and the masculine *dominus* or lord [Bogin 1980, 50]—
locate in the lady the absolute power that was her privilege as a
patron within the feudal hierarchy. The coupling of male and

female in androgynous terms of address suggests the ambiguity of the noblewoman's position as a patron. Midons was, in effect, caught between contradictory ideologies of class and gender, of patronage and kinship. The feudal hierarchy granted her absolute power over the poet who sang her praises, but the sexual hierarchy, the patriarchy, limited her exercise of that power both within and outside of marriage. Patriarchy required women to be the property of their husbands, to be kept chaste to assure the legitimacy of heirs. Yet the demands of patronage required the continuing circulation of women as patrons and as markers of status. The woman's sex precluded the expression of her own desire, and in fact, her desire is beside the point precisely because it is in the withholding of her favors, in her silence, that she exercises her power. In the poem she remains a silent and passive object, represented as a thing (*res*), the object of the poet's desire. She becomes, in effect, a medium of exchange through which some of her husband's status can be transferred to the poet. That the *dompna* could be used by the poet to define his position within the feudal hierarchy explains why the object of the troubadour poets' desire was always a married woman rather than a *donzella*. The unmarried woman lacked identity and status within the feudal hierarchy, but a married woman participated in her husband's.

Entrebescar les Motz

Courtly poetry and the sentiments it conveys may strike the modern reader as clichéd, repetitive, even hackneyed, especially to the post-Romantic phenomenological sensibility, which views poetry as an expression of an individual great mind conversing with other minds. *Fin' amor* expressed itself through an elaborate and ritualized literary language and constituted one means by which members of the medieval aristocracy could articulate their relations of patronage to one another. Central to the courtly poem's function as a mode of expression is its formal construction. In challenging the formalists' claim that poetic form can be studied apart from social life, Vološinov/Bakhtin argues that the formal elements that make up a particular genre—sound, word, image, rhythm, composition—carry social and ideological meanings of their own (1976). The form of a poem is itself a complex system of signs. We cannot claim to have fully historicized the courtly lyric without understanding the kinds of meanings encoded in the elaborate forms of the courtly lyric.

Raimbaut d'Aurenga refers to the art of the troubadour as the art of *entrebescar les motz*, intertwining, entangling words. The languages of poetry and of sexual desire existed in a dialogic relationship—entangled—with the languages of economics, warfare, and politics. Both troubadours and trobairitz shared—and contested—a common language, a set of themes, vocabulary, and elaborate verse forms that required the interweaving of sounds, grammatical forms, words, images, and rhymes in ever more complicated patterns. In the courtly lyric, the sign becomes a site of ambiguous meanings that are further undermined at the level of form, where the use of homophones, repetitive voicing, and reduplication, as Julia Kristeva says, "throws doubt on meaning at its very core" (1987, 282). The polysemanticity of the sign repeats at the level of the utterance what amounts to a kind of resource polygamy. What is at stake in the courtly lyric is the power to control words and women as resources.[15]

What differences exist in the rhetorical strategies of troubadours or trobairitz in the deployment of theme, vocabulary, and form result from their different investments in the social relations of *fin' amor*, their different social positions, which are ideologically determined by the social construction of gender. Because she is positioned differently within the networks of patronage and kinship relationships that created the courtly lyric, the twelfth-century noblewoman's poetic explorations of her own subjectivity within that genre are necessarily different from those of her male worshiper. What is at stake in the substitution of a female poet for a male one in the *fin' amor* tradition is not simply a reversal of a paradigm, because, as I have suggested, the "paradigm" or hierarchy of courtly love is itself contradictory. The trobairitz's adaptations of the conventions of a genre designed to serve masculine interests—

---

[15]Bloch's analysis of medieval misogyny (1987) suggests some tantalizing links between linguistic promiscuity and sexual promiscuity.

in effect the displacement of the male subject by the female subject—as Marianne Shapiro argues, generates within the genre a whole series of displacements, both paradigmatic and syntagmatic, that threaten to reveal the power struggles the conventions of *fin' amor* were designed to repress (1978, 562). A closer examination of these displacements reveals the social dynamics of gender and class which must remain unspoken in the troubadour lyric but which are always lurking just beneath the surface.

To examine these displacements in more detail, I would like to turn now to a comparison of two lyrics—"Domna, puois de me no.us chal" by Bertran de Born, and "A chantar m'er de so qu'ieu non volria" by the countess of Dia. Inasmuch as the two poets are approximate contemporaries, both writing toward the end of the twelfth century, this comparison should reveal some of the differences between the styles of the troubadours and trobairitz. Joan Ferrante has found distinctive male and female rhetorics in the courtly lyric, which, she says, extend beyond subject matter to encompass such formal aspects of style as vocabulary, imagery, grammatical form, rhyme scheme, and sound play.[16] Because her study is necessarily preliminary and her conclusions guarded, she does not attempt to account for these differences. I believe they arise not from some essential psychological difference between men and women, or between male and female rhetorical styles, but from specific historical conditions, from the different gender roles assigned to men and women within the social systems of patronage and of courtly love. The formal differences in their poetry suggest the extent to which genre participates in the ideological making of meaning.

The poem by Bertran de Born is a virtuoso performance by one of the most colorful of the troubadours (as attested by his striking appearance in Dante's *Inferno* as a talking head). It is a tour de force of the conventional client-patron relations between the lover and his *dompna*. The poet manages to appear at one and the same time both abject and disinterested. He attempts to neutralize the power of his patron, deftly positioning her as the *object* of *his* desire by

[16]Joan Ferrante, "Notes toward the Study of a Female Rhetoric in the Trobairitz," in Paden 1989, 63; Shapiro has also noted some of the formal characteristics of trobairitz verse (1978, 565).

scattering her body into text, reincarnating her as a kind of currency by which he can purchase his desire.

> Puois no.us puosc trobar engal,
> que fos tan bela ni pros,
> ni sos rics cors tan joios,
> de tan bela tieira
> ni tan gais
> ni sos rics pretz tan verais,
> irai per tot achaptan
> de chascuna un bel semblan
> per far domna soisseubuda,
> tro vos mi siatz renduda. (236)

[And since I can find none your equal, none so beautiful and noble, or of her aristocratic body so joyful, so graceful, or so gay (courtly) or of her noble worth so true, I shall go everywhere purchasing of each lady one beautiful image, in order to make one beautiful lady until you are returned to me.][17]

In this poem Bertran "creates" his beloved as a set of precious objects literally interchangeable with one another, symbolic capital that passes from the patron to the poet and from there circulates throughout the court. The poet will "purchase" ("achaptan") from one lady her "color natural," from another "son adrech parlar gaban [her adroit and frolicsome speech]," from another her throat and hands. He will take one lady's hair, another's demeanor. He will get a "glorious young body" and beautiful teeth from still others. After creating this composite woman, this idealized fetish, the poet contemplates the enjoyment of her/it as a symbolic substitute for the woman he cannot possess.

> Bel Senher, ieu no.us quier al
> Mas que fos tan cobeitos
> d'aquesta com sui de vos; (238)

[Bel-Senher, I ask nothing of you except that I desire this assembled lady as I desire you.]

[17]To emphasize Bertran's deployment of the courtly vocabulary, I have used my own translation of this lyric.

La Bel Senher—the powerful patron—has been dispersed into words. She has been reduced to a series of signs, to "flesh made words," so that the poet can create the constant and idealized object of his desires, a woman who, unlike the real thing, will never disappoint him (Vickers, 1981; Finke, 1984). In one sense, the poem reveals the poet's painful awareness of language as a representation. It reveals the emptiness of signs, their continual deferral of presence. His verses attempt to overcome this emptiness, even as they speak to his failure. The poet cannot have the bodily woman, but he can have the textual one. Bertran de Born attempts to recreate his beloved's presence through a verbal "engine." But, at the same time, his witty manipulation of language testifies all the more poignantly to La Bel Senher's absence. It defers his enjoyment at the same time that it enables him to create, and hence possess, the image of his desire. The poet's strategy thus allows him to attain his desires at the same time as it voices his frustration.

Even as it marks one kind of failure, however, the poem creates a compensatory status for the poet which he might not acquire even if he were to possess his *dompna*. The poem allows him to accumulate symbolic capital from several patrons at once. Thus, his words contain an implicit threat. The laundry list of the names of ladies from whom he will cull the various body parts to create his beautiful composition—Cembelis, Aelis de Montfort, the vicomtesse of Chalais, Agnes de Rouchechouard, Audiart of Malamort, na Faidida—carries the warning that there are others from whom the poet might seek patronage with more success. In such a diffuse network of social relations, patronage may be sought in many quarters, multiple alliances might form, break apart, and re-form. Service without the expected reward need not continue indefinitely. The patron, the poet warns, also relies on the exchange of symbolic capital—on the accumulation of such intangible assets as prestige and "courtliness"—which drives the symbolic economy of patronage relationships and courtly love.

The countess of Dia's poem, "A chantar m'er de so qu'ieu non volria," touches on many of these same themes, but with some important differences. In Bertran's poem, the male poet wields words as a form of power. It is the poem itself, and not so much the actual woman, that becomes the means of establishing his status among his contemporaries and challenging his relationship to his lover, to whom the poem is directly addressed. What characterizes the trobairitz lyric is its reticence, its reluctance to speak for fear that the speech act itself, far from being a source of power, might constitute or signal some sort of failure. The opening line—"I must sing of things I'd rather not"—captures metonymically the sexual and political ideologies in conflict in the courtly lyric. Under patriarchy women are silenced, disempowered. To speak, to give voice to one's wrongs is a form of empowerment. This feminist view of the power of speech makes the countess's reluctance to speak seem puzzling; surely it is something more than feminine reticence. But silence is not always a sign of weakness. In the courtly lyric, the *dompna*'s silence may signify her power as a patroness. In a patronage relationship, one expects the client to address—to entreat favors from—the powerful patron and not the reverse. For the patron to dispense largess and have it refused would constitute a loss of face; to complain about it would expose the ideological contradictions not only between class and gender hierarchies but between the ideologies of reciprocal exchange and extreme social inequality as well.

This poem differs from Bertran's primarily by highlighting the unspoken vulnerability of the patron rather than that of the client. It stresses the speaker's sense of betrayal, her loss of face when her freely given gifts are rejected. That this is as much an offense against her class and status as against her person is suggested by the poet's deployment of the courtly vocabulary.

> A chantar m'er de so qu'ieu non volria,
> tant me rancur de lui cui sui amia,
> car l'am mais que nuilla ren que sia;
> vas lui no.m val merces ni cortesia,
> ni ma baltatz ni mos pretz no mos sens,
> c'atressi.m sui enganad' e trahia
> com degr' esser, s'ieu fos desavinens. (2.1–7)[18]

[18]Bogin 1980, 84–86; all trobairitz poems cited here are from this edition unless otherwise noted; translations are my own. I cite Bogin's numbering and lineation of the poems.

[I must sing of things which I'd rather not: so bitter do I feel toward him whose love I am because I love him more than anything. With him my mercy and courtesy are in vain, my beauty, virtue, and intelligence. For I've been tricked and cheated as if I were completely loathsome.]

The patron must devote considerable labor to the acquisition of clientele, to making and maintaining relationships (Bourdieu 1977, 180). In these lines, the poet reminds her lover/client of her investments in the relationship. The symbolic capital she brings to the relationship includes her mercy ("merces"), her "cortesia," her beauty ("beltatz"), her virtue ("pretz"), and her intelligence ("sens"). These are many of the same qualities which Bourdieu recognizes as symbolic capital and which Bertran builds into his idealized "lady." That these words appear with an almost monotonous frequency in the courtly lyric points to their important function in the exchange of symbolic capital. These are the *dompna*'s chief resources, her accumulation of marketable assets. They are no less significant for being intangible. Even if she is a married woman, perhaps even because she is a married woman who can use the assets that come to her through marriage to confer status on other men, these assets must be kept in circulation. When they are refused by a potential client, the poet feels cheated "as if I were completely loathsome." Her disadvantage is as great as it would be if she did not possess any significant assets whatsoever.

At several junctures in the poem the countess reminds her lover of the investments, both symbolic and temporal, she has made in their relationship. She has to remind him of the rules of a game, which are, by definition, supposed to remain unspoken, undeclared.

> e membre vos cals fo.l comenssamens
> de nostr' amor! ja Dompnedieus non vuoilla
> qu'en ma colpa sia.l departimens. (2.19–21)

[Remember how it was in the beginning of our love! May God not bring to pass that my fault should part us.]

Chief among these investments is the exchange of gifts: "e membre vos de nostres partimens" [And remember the stanzas we exchanged] (2.28). A partimen is a particular verse form structured as a debate between two persons in which the adversary is offered a choice of sides, with the proposer accepting the choice that is rejected (Topsfield 1975, 256). Poems like this might become capital, circulating within the symbolic economy of gift giving that is governed by unspoken rules. But gift giving, as Bourdieu reminds us, is slippery; it must always "retrospectively project" into its calculations the return gift (1977, 171). The giver of the gift must take into account and hence satisfy the expectations of the recipient without appearing to know what these expectations are. It is the function of the gift to cover over the elements of economic obligation involved in such transactions, to make relations of economic necessity appear elective and based on reciprocal devotion. Such a relationship will fail, as it does in this poem, when either party fails to recognize and take into account the investments of the other party, when the parties misunderstand the social meanings of the exchanges.

Such misunderstandings seem almost inevitable given the ambiguity of a courtly vocabulary that oscillates between connotations of economic and social behavior. Words such as *merces* and *pretz*, common enough in troubadour poetry, still carry their primary connotations of "payment" and "value, worth." The word *pretz*, for instance, carries a fiscal connotation that by this time had already become part of the feudal vocabulary. The word derives from the Latin *pretium* for worth or value, but also wages or reward.[19] In the fourth stanza of this poem, the countess refers to her lover's "rics pretz" which might be translated "rich worth." Such a phrase might easily refer either to his material wealth or to his great virtue. It probably must refer to both, since wealth and virtue seem virtually inseparable in the world of the courtly lyric. In the final stanza, the countess articulates the unspoken contract that underlies the courtly relationship:

> Valer mi deu mos pretz e mos paratges,
> e ma beltatz e plus mos fis coratges, (2.29–30)

[My worth and noble birth should have some weight, my beauty and especially my loyal heart.]

[19]*Merces* also carries the notions of salary and price; see Vance 1975, 48; and Shapiro 1978, 569.

The alliteration connecting the poet's "pretz" and her "paratges" and the rhyme linking her "paratges" with her "coratges" formally weave together into a single tissue the accident of being born into a class that controls the economic means of production and the virtues valued by that class; birth becomes worth, as wealth becomes virtue.

These two poems illustrate what other critics have observed about formal differences between troubadour and trobairitz poetry. The countess of Dia's poem makes use of a much less complex verse form than Bertran de Born's. Bertran's *canso* contains seven *coblas unissonans* of ten lines.[20] The poem has an elaborate strophic form in which the lines vary in length, to create the rhyme scheme and syllabic formula *a8 b7 b7 c7 d3 d7 e7 e8 f8 f8*. The lines decrease in length through the midpoint of the stanza, after which they become increasingly longer. The Countess's *canso* consists of five *coblas singulars* of seven 9-syllable lines, rhyming *aaaabab*. The rhymes differ for each *cobla*. Most critics have commented on the relative simplicity of the trobairitz poetic forms, suggesting that the trobairitz poetry is more direct, more like "natural" speech; its appeal is supposedly more to the emotions than the intellect.[21] The troubadour poem, with its elaborate intertwining of rhyme, line length, homonyms, and other sound repetition, appeals to the intellect. Complexity, then, becomes a signifier of artifice. It marks the courtly lyric as an elaborate game played in front of a sophisticated and discerning audience for the sake of publicly displaying the poet's wit, winning him preferment.

These differences illuminate the different rhetorical strategies of each poem. Note, for instance, the deployment of direct address. Both poems address the lover throughout, but the effect of direct address in each poem differs significantly. Ferrante notes that troubadour poetry uses direct address much less frequently and when it does the address is not restricted to the poet's love (Paden 1989,

---

[20]In *coblas unissonans* the same sounds are repeated in the same patterns of rhyme throughout each cobla. In Bertran's poem the rhymes are on -al, -os, -ra, -ais, -an, and -uda throughout all seven strophes.

[21]Bogin 1980, Dronke in Wilson 1984, and Ferrante in Paden 1989; the huge disparity between the number of troubadour and trobairitz poems surviving makes such comparisons shaky at best.

64). In this respect Bertran's poem is unusual in employing direct address. Yet, in conjunction with the elaborate verse form and the long list of ladies' names that occupies stanzas 3–6, Bertran's direct address gives the appearance of widening to include a larger and larger audience. There is an element of public display, of performance, in Bertran's address which is lacking in the countess's. Her address to the lover vacillates between revelation and denial, wishing to speak and, at the same time, fearing to. These differences, I would argue, result less from a difference in emotional commitment to the relationship than from the two poet's different subject positions under a male-dominated patronage system. The male poet, occupying the position of a client among many potential clients, must orient his address in at least two directions—toward the lady and toward other men with whom he must both compete and form alliances. In this regard, the poem is a homosocial exchange in which men vie with one another for status. That status derives only from the poem, from the public display of the relationship with the beloved. The male poet has everything to gain from this display because it publicizes his gift and lays an obligation upon the recipient. The female poet has everything to lose, which suggests why trobairitz poetry is marked by the poet's reluctance to speak. The shift from male subject to female subject—from client to patron—exposes yet another contradiction within the ideology of *fin' amor*. For the female poet, her public display of betrayal is a signifier of her failure as a patron to cultivate a clientele, at the same time as it affords her a means of self-representation.

Desire and Representation

The trobairitz's poetry effectively illustrates the process Louis Althusser has called interpellation, by which subjectivity is created as individuals internalize historically specific cultural representations as their own self-representation. In the slippage between the two—in the *différance* between cultural representation and self-representation—feminists can begin to uncover the cracks in the ideological facade of gender relations, the local resistances to the oppressive hierarchies of feudal patronage and kinship systems, in

short, the poaching of those silenced by official histories (de Lauretis 1987, 10). Of all the trobairitz, the countess of Dia seems to
have internalized the ideology of *fin' amor* most thoroughly. Perhaps that is the reason why her poems are most frequently anthologized. "Ab joi et ab jovens m'apais" demonstrates her commitment to the ideals articulated by the courtly lyric.

> Ab joi et ab joven m'apais,
> e jois e jovens m'apaia,
> que mos amics e lo plus gais,
> per qu'ieu sui coindet' e guaia;
> e pois ieu li sui veraia,
> bei.s taing qu'el me sia verais:
> qu'anc de lui amar non m'estrais,
> ni ai cor que m'en estraia. (1.1–8)

[I am nourished on joy and youth, and joy and youth nourish me,
because my lover is the very gayest, therefore I am charming and
and since I am true to him, it is proper that he be true to me: never
has my love for him strayed, nor do I have a heart that strays.]

This lyric celebrates all the qualities of the courtly lover: youth and
joy, courtesy and valor, intelligence and wisdom. Far from depict-
ing the cold, haughty lady with power over life and death suggested by many troubadour lyrics, this poem calls on the *dompna* to
give her affection freely to "un pro cavallier valen" (1.19), a courteous and worthy knight. Once she is sure of his merit she should
dare to love openly and faithfully (as if jealous husbands and
lauzengiers did not exist). This poem's concern with the reciprocities
of patronage, which the courtly lyric was designed both to facilitate
and to conceal, is underscored by its rhyme scheme. The two *coblas
doblas* of sixteen lines each are structured around two rhymes on
-ais/-aia and -en/-enssa in a scheme *ababbaab*.[22] In addition, the
poem employs derived rhyme (*rims derivatius*), in which the *ab* lines
in each pair of verses end on a grammatical variation of the same
word. This pattern of grammatical repetition (apais/apaia,

---

[22]*Coblas doblas* refers to two stanzas linked by the repetition of the same rhymes.

gais/guaia, veraia/verais, estrais, estraia) runs against the rhyme scheme and is used to create a variety of effects.[23]

The most consistent effect produced by derived rhyme in this poem is to generate the theme of reciprocity—the cornerstone of the patronage system—which runs throughout the poem. This reciprocity takes two forms, although the two are inextricably linked. The first is the reciprocity between the lovers or, if you will, between the patron and her client. The woman confers status on her male admirer who, on the basis of her song, becomes "un pro cavallier valen," while, in turn, the male's admiration establishes the woman's courtliness.[24] This reciprocity is reflected in the inner rhymes. Because her lover is gay, she is gay, and because she is true, her lover in turn should be true. But as in all troubadour poetry, there is an awareness that the dance being enacted between the lovers takes place within a wider social context that always dictates the participants' movements. The individual's experiences of *fin' amor* make sense only within a set of social expectations that regulate individuals' behavior. This reciprocity between individual experience and social expectation, between self-representation and cultural representation, is carried in the first and last rhymes of the stanzas, which serve as a kind of envelope for the reciprocities between individuals. The poet's joy and youth are themselves the product of a culture that values joy and youth, in which these commodities circulate and are exchanged as a means of accumulating status. The poem speaks of love not as a purely psychological state of mind but as a social institution whose function it is to facilitate transfers of power and status while concealing the true nature of those transfers. The poem exposes and enacts the repression of politics into desire.

The second set of *coblas doblas* reinforces the connection between individual and public values. Stanza 3 reads

---

[23]For a discussion of derived rhyme in "Ab joi et ab juven," see Sarah Kay, "Derivation, Derived Rhyme, and the Trobairitz," in Paden 1989, 165–69.

[24]In "A chantar" when the poet's offers are refused she complains that her courtly qualities are worthless and that she has been treated "as if I were completely loathsome" ("s'ieu fos desavinens"). In another lyric she offers her lover "mon cor e m'amor, / mon sen, mos huoills e ma vida [my heart and love, my mind, my eyes, and my life]."

Dompna que en bon pretz s'enten
deu ben pausar s'entendenssa
en un pro cavallier valen
pois qu'ill conois sa valenssa,
que l'aus amar a presenssa;
que dompna, pois am'a presen,
ja pois li pro ni li valen
no.n dirant mas avinenssa. (1.17–24)

[The *dompna* who knows about worth ought to place her affection in a courteous and worthy knight as soon as she knows his worth, and she should dare to love him openly as a *dompna* who loves openly, always those who are courteous and worthy will speak nothing but praise.]

In these lines, the derived rhymes tend to pair nouns with either verbs or adjectives. Sarah Kay has noted that medieval philosophical analyses of grammatical categories, such as those of Bernard of Chartres and John of Salisbury, describe the relation of noun to other parts of speech as that of substance to accident: "The noun contains the real substance, the adjective and the verb being subsequent attenuations of that substance through conmixture with accidental elements such as the 'person'" (Paden 1989, 160). Derived pairs like "enten"/"entendenssa," "valen"/"valenssa," "presenssa"/"presen," which set the noun against its verb or adjective, play on these philosophic beliefs. The lover's possession of such courtly values as nobility and understanding ("valen," "enten") are embedded within the public validation of "valenssa" and "entendenssa." Because of such validation, the lovers can afford to love "openly," publicly ("presenssa"). The expression of personal virtue cannot, in this poem, be separated from these public values.

The beginning of the second stanza contains a striking departure from the derived rhyme used so consistently elsewhere, drawing our attention to these two lines.

Mout mi plai, quar sai que val mais
cel qu'ieu plus desir que m'aia (1.9–10)

[It pleases me because I know he is the best, him whom I most desire to have me.]

Despite her position and power, the countess, even as a poet, conceives of herself primarily as an object of desire: she can only desire "him whom I most desire to have me." In these lines, the poet illustrates what John Berger in *Ways of Seeing* has described as a central component of a woman's interpellation of cultural representations of the feminine. Woman's "own sense of being in herself is supplanted by a sense of being appreciated as herself by another" (1972, 46). Because her success is socially defined by how she appears to men, the power of vision—of the gaze—splits her in two: "She comes to consider the surveyor and the surveyed within her as the two constituent yet always distinct elements of her identity as a woman" (46).

But the situation created by *fin' amor* is, from the woman's perspective, far trickier than Berger's account can suggest. Because the relationship she courts is both sexual and political, she must successfully balance more contradictions than just that between surveyor and surveyed. In the lyrics of the countess of Dia, the force of the poet's technical mastery holds together and balances all the contradictions. To balance the politics of marriage and primogeniture with the politics of patronage, she must remain at the same time both sexually available and chaste. She must act without appearing to act. She must be aggressive while appearing passive. The countess has mastered the technique of a sexual aggression that remains entirely passive. In another lyric, "Estat ai en greu cossirier," she fantasizes about an encounter with her lover.

> Ben volria mon cavallier
> tener un ser en mos bratz nut,
> qu'el s'en tengra per ereubut
> sol qu'a lui fezes cosseillier; . . .
>
> Bels amics avinens e bos,
> cora.us tenrai en mon poder?
> e que jagues ab vos un ser
> e qu'ie.us. des un bais amoros;
> sapchatz, gran talan n'auria
> qu'ie.us tengues en luoc del marit,
> ab so que m'aguessetz plevit
> de far tot so qu'ieu volria. (3.9–12, 17–24)

[I wish just once I could hold my knight with my bare arms, for he would be in ecstasy if I'd just let him lean his head against my breast. . . . Handsome friend, charming and kind, when shall I have you in my power? If only I could lie beside you for an hour and embrace you lovingly—know this, I'd give almost anything to have you in my husband's place, but only under one condition, that you swear to do my bidding.]

The countess insists in both of these sexual fantasies on maintaining the power to direct the relationship. Yet in both she remains traditionally passive. He would lean his head upon her breast. Her very stillness is a sign of her power. He would take her husband's position, but with one crucial difference: in marriage a woman cedes power to her husband; here the countess insists that she maintain the power that belongs to a patron.

The reference to her husband reminds us that within the system of *fin' amor* the woman must manage not only her lover/client but also a potentially jealous husband (in "Fin ioi me don alegranssa" she refers to him as "gelos mal parlan" ["evil-speaking jealous one"]) and the "nasty-worded *lauzengiers*" (called "lauzengier mal dizen" in the same poem), spies who attempt to destroy her reputation. The husband may require his wife to be sexually available to other men and yet be jealous, and the *lauzengiers* may be competing for the same symbolic capital *fin' amor* keeps in circulation. All are implicated in the same system of social relations. The kind of reciprocities achieved in "Ab joi e ab jovens m'apais" or fantasized in "Estat ai en greu cossirier" can be at best unstable poetic moments forged and held together by the poet's technical mastery. They are finally too subversive of the social and sexual hierarchies of medieval feudalism to survive, at least in institutional form, outside of the rarefied environment of the courtly lyric. The lovers are not private, cloistered individuals; they are social creatures who live in a world not only of *lauzengiers* and jealous husbands (see 4.4–11, 17–20) but of social hierarchies and economic priorities that must intrude upon and shape their private world. Poems by other trobairitz confront this fact, effectively dismantling many of the balances and reciprocities achieved in this poem. Indeed, the frequent betrayals they most often recount reveal that the private relationships between men and women in this culture remain secondary—instrumental—to the homosocial ties between men which occasion the poetry.

Only one *canso* attributed to Azalais de Porcairages survives. Unlike the countess of Dia's, her first name seems to have survived with her poem, but as with the countess, we know little more about her than the name of the town in which she lived. Yet her single poem and the impossible situation it documents is even more revealing of the contradictory ideologies—sexual, political, economic—that drove *fin' amor*.

The *canso* begins with a conventional *topos* of the courtly lyric

> Ar em al freg temps vengut
> quel gels el neus e la faingna
> e.l aucellet estan mut,
> c'us de chantar non s'atraingna;
> e son sec li ram pels plais—
> que flors ni foilla noi nais,
> ni rossignols noi crida,
> que l'am e mai me reissida. (ll. 1–8)

[Now we are come to the cold time when the ice and the snow and the mud and the birds' beaks are mute (for not one inclines to sing); and the hedge-branches are dry—no leaf or bud sprouts up, nor cries the nightingale whose song awakens me in May.]

This winter *topos*, which appears in the poetry of several troubadours, including Guillaume (see Goldin 1973, 6), Bernart de Ventadorn, Cercamon, and Giraut de Bornelh, provides an emotional counterpoint to the classical spring landscape (*locus amoenus*) that provides the other setting for the courtly lyric. Through the winter *topos*, the poet's unhappiness is projected onto the dreary landscape that surrounds her, just as in a spring setting the poet's happiness finds expression in his pleasant surroundings.[25] The

[25]Compare Azalais's opening with the following poem by Cercamon: "Quant l'aura doussa s'amarzis / e.l fuelha chai de sul verjan / e l'auzelh chanton lor latis, / et ieu de sai sospir e chan / d'Amor que.m te lassat e pres, / qu'ieu encar no l'aic en poder. [When the sweet breeze turns bitter / and the leaf falls down from the branch / and the birds change their language, / I, here, sigh, and sing / of love, whom I never have had in my power]" (96–97).

landscape becomes a lens for focusing the poet's discontent. What is striking about Azalais's invocation of the dreary landscape is her insistence on its enforced silence. The birds are mute, "for not one inclines to sing." Even the nightingale, "whose song awakens me in May," is silent, absent. The landscape's silence repeats and highlights the poet's reluctance to speak, which she shares with other trobairitz. In the second stanza, she seems to speak almost as if against her will: "e s'ieu faill ab motz verais [though I be blamed, I'll tell the truth]" (l. 13).

Azalais's reticence is further revealed in frequent circumlocutions. In the first stanza, for instance, the muteness of the landscape is conveyed negatively through the creation of absence. Negative particles abound in the stanza, five in the last half alone ("non," "ni," and "noi").[26] Her speech is hedged round with negatives that undercut straightforward, direct statement. Stanza 3 both reveals and disguises the reason for her reluctance through an elaborate periphrasis that attempts to conceal her situation by couching it in the generalized case. That situation is unspeakable precisely because it reveals the class alliances involved in the patronage networks of feudalism which *fin' amor* was designed to disguise.

> Dompna met mot mal s'amor
> que ab ric ome plaideia,
> ab plus aut de vavassor;
> e s'il o fai, il folleia,
> car so diz om en Veillai
> que ges per ricor non vai,
> e dompna que n'es chauzida
> en tenc per envilanida. (ll. 17–24)

[A *dompna's* love is badly placed who pleads with a rich man, above the rank of vassal: she who does it is a fool. For the men of Vellay say love and money do not mix, and the *dompna* money chooses has debased herself.]

[26]Ferrante argues that the trobairitz tend to employ negatives much more consistently than do troubadours to express frustration or deprivation (Paden 1989, 65). See also Shapiro, 565.

The poet's shame comes from having placed her "love" in a man of higher rank than herself, a "ric ome." This fault is represented as a major transgression. The woman is a fool who loves someone above the rank of vassal, a greedy fool who has debased herself. There is never any suggestion anywhere throughout the corpus of courtly lyrics that a man who loves a woman of higher rank is greedy or debasing himself. Indeed, that situation is presented as the norm. The language of this stanza exposes the rigid class hierarchies that dominate social relations under feudalism. It shatters the romantic illusions of *fin' amor* as an idealization of love by exposing the mercenary motives it must disguise. The language of class hierarchies dominates the stanza. The "ric ome" is "plus aut," of higher rank, although the proper object for the *dompna* is the "vavassor," the vassal. The married noblewoman's lover—the poem insists that she is a married woman; the word *dompna* is repeated twice in the stanza—should be a vassal because *fin' amor* cannot be perceived as anything other than a patronage relationship. The woman's prestige—her symbolic capital—which derives from her status within marriage, is a resource she can dispense. To bestow it upon someone higher than herself, someone not a vassal or a client, would be to take herself out of the circulation of symbolic capital required by the feudal system. Her misplaced affections work against the dissemination of resources required within a patronage system, redirecting the flow of symbolic capital upward and concentrating resources at the top of the hierarchy. It is not the man at the apex of the feudal system who requires the status that is conferred by the *dompna*; it is the man of uncertain status, the vassal or bachelor. The woman who has refused her position as patron and made herself a client has, in effect, betrayed her class. The epithet "envilanida" suggests she has made herself base, a "villein." The illogic of blaming the "woman money chooses" but not the man who chooses a rich woman exposes the collusion between love and economics, between gender and class hierarchies, which *fin' amor* conspires to conceal. The "woman money chooses" is a class traitor not because she is greedy but because she has taken herself out of circulation; her resources are not available to those men beneath her in rank who are potentially her clients.

The Dark Lady in Song

The poems of Castelloza, the last trobairitz poems I examine here, present some interesting challenges to the modern reader because in them she attempts to adapt the vocabulary and poetics of *fin' amor* to a situation they were never designed to describe. The language simply cannot be made to say what she wants it to say about feminine desire, and the energy of her poems comes primarily from this sense of having stretched the language to its breaking point. With its elaborate ritualistic language, complex syntax, and frustrated reciprocities, articulated through periphrasis, paradox, and enigmatic allusion, Castelloza's poetry dismantles all the oppositions upon which *fin' amor* depends: patron/client, male/female, joy/pain, faith/betrayal, fulfillment/longing. *Fin' amor* requires a delicate balance between gender and class hierarchies; the female who is expected to submit to her husband in marriage, retains the power of her class over her vassal/lover. This balance is primarily rhetorical, a matter of style. In Castelloza's poetry the balance is constantly upset. The *dompna* occupies the position of suffering lover usually reserved for the male poet; she has become the client forced to beg favors from a distant and more aristocratic male lover. She cannot rely, as the countess of Dia does, on her *paratges* or noble birth to ensure her *cortesia*. Pushing the courtly lyric beyond what it can say, Castelloza exposes at its breaking point the inadequacies of *fin' amor* as an ideology: its contradictions, its repressions, its hidden collusion with the politics of power.

Critics have tended to focus on the theme of suffering in love in Castelloza's poetry as if the artist and her subject matter were identical, as if content were not always mediated and distanced by form. Because Castelloza writes about suffering in love, it must be *her* suffering in love, autobiographically rendered. Therefore she is a masochist who is obsessed by and enjoys her suffering.[27] But another perspective might view Castelloza as an artist who experiments with the effects on form of displacing subject positions with-

---

[27]See Paden et al. 1981; Dronke 1984; and Siskin and Storme, "Suffering Love: The Reversed Order in the Poetry of Castelloza," in Paden 1989.

in a particular social formation. Castelloza's poems differ from other courtly lyrics primarily in their shift of class and gender roles. The male occupies the position of unresponsive patron, the distant lover of a higher class, and the *dompna* (there is no reason we *must* identify her with Castelloza herself), the married lady, occupies the position of the client, the vassal who must court patronage. In Castelloza's poetry, gender and class hierarchies coincide, upsetting the rhetorical balances required of the courtly lyric. For this reason her poems often seem a bit off-balance in comparison with the poems of other trobairitz.

In their exploration of hierarchy in *fin' amor*, Castelloza's poems make heavy use of a feudal vocabulary of rights and duties which calls attention to the operations of patronage. "Ja de chantar non degr'aver talan" employs this imagery most extensively. In the first stanza, she offers her "service," using the verb *retener* which describes the action of the seigneur or overlord in extending patronage to his vassals (Paden et al. 1981, 176).

> E s'en breu no.m rete
> Trop ai fag long badatge. (2.8–9)[28]

[And if he doesn't take me into his service now I've already made too long a wait.]

This verb reminds us that patronage relationships are entered into voluntarily by both sides. Just as her lord can accept or refuse her service, she is free to renounce her tie of vassalage. Yet she refuses to be recreant: "don no.m recre/D'amar per bona fe [Yet I don't renounce loving you in good faith]" (2.16–17). Her relationship, despite the distance of her lover, brings her "honor" (22).[29] Recognizing the multiplicity of possible patron-client relations, she can-

[28]For the poems of Castelloza, I am using the scholarly edition prepared by Paden et al. (1981) because it includes all variant manuscript readings. Paden's text differs in some significant ways from Bogin's; these differences will be discussed hereafter. I cite Paden's numbering and lineation of the poems; translations are my own.

[29]Duby (1983) reminds us that *honor* refers not only to virtue and fame in the abstract but also in feudal terms to the gifts—primarily but not exclusively the fief—that a vassal receives from his patron.

not expect, given her rank, to be the sole recipient of her lover's service.

> E sai ben que.us conve
> Dompna d'ausor paratge. (2.26–27)

[And I know well that a *dompna* of higher rank deserves you.]

Her lover seeks a much nobler patron, and if that behavior causes the speaker pain, she also recognizes that it is appropriate within the confines of courtly behavior. The description in the fifth stanza of the speaker's attempt to get the lover's glove as a love token— usually the prerogative of the knight—calls to mind the intricate rituals that accompanied feudal relations. She returns the glove because

> Pueis aic paor
> Que.i aguesetz dampnage
> D'aicella que.us rete,
> Amics, per qu'ieu dese
> L'i torniei, car ben cre
> Que no.i ai podiratge (2.40–45)

[I was afraid that you might suffer harm from the woman who retains you, friend, so I promptly gave it back, for I truly believe that I do not have any claim on it].

She seems to recognize the right of her knight to seek patronage in other places, since she doesn't have "podiratge." Paden glosses *podiratge* as "right of first mortgage," that is the primary rights over a fief that a feudal lord cedes to a vassal. At every turn, then, this relationship reenacts the rituals of feudal patronage. In describing the course of feminine desire, this poem makes elaborate use of the feudal vocabulary of *seignoratge* and *vassalatge*, suggesting the interconnections between socially mandated class and gender roles, desire, and the operations of power.

Castelloza's *dompna* is doubly oppressed, by her class and her gender. Her class makes her unattractive, at least to the knight she

wishes to "serve." Unlike the countess of Dia, she never re-
proaches her knight for ignoring either her beauty or her courtly
virtues, most likely because, given her class, she lacks the
resourses—the symbolic if not material capital -to be attractive in
a culture that inextricably links material wealth, beauty, and virtue.
Yet, her gender prevents her from courting openly, from seeking
patronage: "ben dison tuig que mout descove / Que dompna prec
ja cavalier de se, / Ni que'l tenga totz tems tam lonc pressic [people
say it is unseemly that a *dompna* pleads her own cause with a
knight, or holds him in a long sermon]" (1.18–20). That privilege is
reserved for the knight alone.

> Mout aurei mes mal usatge
> A las autras amairitz,
> C'hom sol trametre mesatge,
> E motz triaz e chauzitz (3.21–24)

[I shall have set a bad example for other women in love. It's the
man only who sends a message and words discerning and well
chosen.]

The language designed to facilitate the advancement of male vassals under feudalism cannot easily be made to serve the ends of
feminine desire.

Castelloza's appropriations of the feudal vocabulary, however,
are anything but straightforward. Her language continually contests the power of the feudal and courtly vocabulary to fix social
relations by calling into question its primary signifiers. Her poems
illustrate what Paul Zumthor has called the *mouvance* of the medieval text, its status as a text "always in the process of becoming"
(1972, 70–75). Because medieval texts circulated in manuscript,
every work would be recreated anew with each recension. In the
interests of presenting the appearance of a single authoritative text,
modern editing practices tend to erase or flatten out the differences
among multiple texts of the same work. To create the modern
printed text, textual variants have to be designated as "noise," at
best relegated to a footnote at the bottom of the page. But in the
case of the courtly lyric, this dialogism, the polysemanticity of the

signs that *fin' amor* contests (to repeat Kristeva's terms), "throws doubt on meaning at the very core of the sign" (1987, 282) by challenging the most basic principles of word formation: the relation between letter and word and the division of groups of letters into discrete words.[30] Even the most superficial glance at the textual variants in Castelloza's poems demonstrates this process of *mouvance*, whereby words oppose or interanimate one another. Two examples from "Amics, s'ie.us trobes avinen" should suffice to demonstrate the complexity of this process. Paden renders line 4 "Qu'ie.us trop ves mi mal e sebenc e ric [I find you wicked and false and haughty]" based on manuscript N. But all the other manuscripts read "tric" instead "ric" in this line, which Bogin glosses as "villainous." Both readings make sense in context; neither can be certified as more "authoritative" than the other. One might grammatically construe the string of letters "etric" as either "et ric" or "e tric." And the two interpretations illuminate each other since one might argue, and I think Castelloza does, that the lover's villainy lies precisely in his wealth and haughtiness, his higher rank.

The second example comes from line 22, which Paden, following manuscript N, gives as "Qu'ieu vueil preiar ennanz que.m lais morir [I want to pray now before I let myself die]." But manuscript A, which was the basis for the Schultz-Gora text (1888) that Bogin follows in her edition, reads "proar" ("prove") in place of "preiar" ("pray"). If we substitute "proar" for "preiar" the line reads "I want to prove now before I let myself die / that. . . " To add to the ambiguity of the line, "ennanz" can mean either "before" or "rather," so that we might construe the phrase "ennanz que.m lais morir" to mean either "before I let myself die" or "rather than let myself die."

Castelloza's poetry, then, is anything but simple and direct. Hers are perhaps the most difficult of all the trobairitz poems to read, to edit, or to translate. If we equate simplicity of structure and syntax with direct, "natural" speech, then complexity might signify either artifice on the speaker's part or her inability to say what she means,

---

[30]Medievalists are beginning to examine manuscript variants more seriously as part of the literariness of the medieval text rather than as "noise" or scribal "error." Kendrick's study (1988) of troubadour wordplay is perhaps the most persuasive attempt to apply Zumthor's (1972) notion of *mouvance* to the troubadour lyric.

either because she does not know it or because what she wants to say cannot be said within the linguistic structures available to her. The complexity of Castelloza's syntax and the difficulty of her language differ from that found in much troubadour verse. If troubadour poetry functions as a kind of symbolic capital, providing poets with a means of achieving certain socially sanctioned ends (the accumulation of patronage), Castelloza uses linguistic complexity to explore the failure of the codes of *fin' amor* to work for those whose gender or class excluded them from patronage networks. She relies heavily on hypotaxis to suggest a logical world of cause and effect and of mutual reciprocity, only to insist again and again on the failure of both logic and reciprocity. In "Amics, s'ie.us trobes avinen," she writes

> Amics, s'ie us trobes avinen,
> Humil e franc e de bona merce,
> Be.us amera—cant era m'en sove
> Qu'ie.us trop ves mi mal e sebenc e ric,
> E'n fatz chansons per tal que fass'ausir
> Vostre bon prez: don eu nom puesc sofrir
> Qu'eu no.us fasa lausar a tota gen
> On plus me faitz mal es asiramen. (1.1–8)

[Friend, if I had found you gracious, humble, open, and compassionate I would love you—since now I realize that I find you wicked and false and haughty, yet I make songs to make your good name heard which is why I cannot refrain from making everyone praise you when most you cause me harm and anger.]

This stanza is somewhat reminiscent of the opening of "Ab joi et ab joven m'apais," in which the countess of Dia uses the conditional with the subjunctive to establish a carefully balanced reciprocity between herself and her lover. But unlike that poem, this one insists on the failure of such reciprocity. As H. Jay Siskin and Julie A. Storme have argued (Paden 1989, 114), this stanza constructs an elaborate set of conditional clauses, only to abandon them halfway through. The first four lines contrast socially sanctioned qualities that define courtliness ("avinen," "humil," "franc," "bona merce") with her lover's uncourtly behavior toward her ("mal," "sebenc," "ric"), inviting the reader to imagine the consequences of each type of behavior.

> *If* I had found you courtly   I *would* love you
> *But* I find you uncourtly   *therefore* ?

But the speaker can hold no consequences out as a threat to chastise her knight's uncourtly behavior. The poet cannot complete the logical sequence she has set up. Even so, the logic does not collapse on itself, as Siskin and Storme suggest; rather, it is displaced into song. The speaker cannot punish her lover's coldness; so she displaces her desire into her poetry: therefore "I make songs to make your good name heard." There is no illogic in her praising the good name of the man she has just called "wicked, false, and haughty." She simply is not in a position to exploit the resources of her own logical argument. She doesn't command the material resources that would enable her to make good on any threat she might issue, that is, she doesn't have the patronage—or the threat of lost patronage—to hold over her lover.

Castelloza's use of the rhetorical tools of logical argument consistently exposes logic as a tool the powerful use against the powerless. Scholastic philosophy in the Middle Ages was marked by a rigorous separation of logic and rhetoric, an insistence that the rules of logic are universal and strictly separate from the dictates of self-interest. Castelloza consistently uses syntax to dismantle the philosophical separation of logic and self-interest, exposing the powerful interests served by the rules of logical argumentation. Challenges to this hegemony take the form of displacement, as in the example I have just discussed, or of non sequiturs such as the one cited earlier: "E s'en breu no.m rete / Trop ai fag long badatge [And if he doesn't take me into his service now / I've already made too long a wait]" (2.8–9). It also expresses itself in multiple contradictions in which the syntax simply implodes on itself in a *mise en abyme* of failed reciprocity, as in the following strophe.

> Ja mais no.us tenrai per valen,
> Ni.us amarai de bon cor ni per fe:

Per ver veirei si ja.m valria re,
S'ie.us mostrava cor felon ni enic.
—Non farai ja, qu'eu non vueill puscaz dir
Qu'eu anc ves vos agues cor de faillir:
C'auriaz i qualque razonamen,
S'ieu avia ves vos fait faillimen. (1.9–16)

[Never shall I consider you worthy, nor shall I love you from the
heart or with trust: in truth I'll see if ever it would do me any
good, if I showed you a treacherous and wicked heart. —I will
never do it for I don't want you to be able to say that I had the
heart to be false to you. You would have some justification if I
had committed some fault against you.]

In this labyrinthine passage, the declarative force of the first "never" is undercut by the conditional clause beginning "if," and the
possibilities engendered by that conditional are negated by the
repetition of "never." The first half of the stanza suggests that the
speaker will reciprocate her lover's coldness with "a treacherous
and wicked heart" of her own. But the futility of such a gesture
almost immediately occurs to her. Her coldness will be construed
not as power but as a fault, the failure of a vassal to render proper
"homage." The syntax alone cannot conjure up the distant, haughty *dompna* of *fin' amor* because the speaker lacks symbolic capital;
she lacks the resources that would enable her to participate in the
reciprocal exchanges demanded by *fin' amor*.

But she does have her songs, which, Castelloza seems to suggest, accumulate for her and for her family a certain amount of
symbolic capital. Her poems contain several references to the
power her songs have to create status. One enigmatic statement
even suggests that the "honor" that she gets through her relationship rebounds on her family: "Vos fai grasir mos lignage / E sobre
totz mos maritz [My lineage makes you welcome and above all my
husband]" (3.43–44). It does not seem too farfetched to argue that
the "honor" here represents the symbolic capital that accrues from
her fame as a poet, from "mos bos motz" and "mas chansos," an
honor that would be shared by her entire family as well, including,
however contradictory to the ethics of primogeniture it might
seem, her husband.

Castelloza doesn't just passively endure suffering and pain, nor does she take compensatory pleasure in contemplating that suffering, as the criticism of her poetry seems to suggest. Rather, her poems—like those of her contemporaries, both male and female— become a socially recognizable asset she can exploit as a means of self-empowerment. She can exploit the vocabulary and logic of courtly love to expose its flaws, inconsistencies, and repressions. Like all the trobairitz, Castelloza seems at once completely reactionary in the interconnections her poems forge between the political and sexual economies of her time and utterly subversive in exposing hegemonic structures of gender and class.

There are no records of any trobairitz who wrote after 1250. The network of associations among literary form, sexuality, and patronage which gave these women voice seem particular to the political life of twelfth-century Occitania, and by midcentury the conditions that created these linkages were changing. *Fin' amor* spread widely throughout Europe, but the particular forms that it took varied greatly from country to country, as political and economic conditions varied. But sexuality and the body—the female body in particular—continued to be focal points for anxieties about authority, power, and resistance. In the next chapter I turn from erotic love in the Middle Ages to spiritual love, exploring the religious technologies of the late Middle Ages which were designed to produce "docile" bodies—to control a female sexuality that was perceived as dangerous. I examine the ways in which some women were able to poach on those technologies, reconstructing their oppression as a form of power through mysticism.

3

The Grotesque Mystical Body: Representing the Woman Writer

The soul is the prison of the body.
—Michel Foucault

In "A Preface to Transgression," Foucault points to the medieval tradition of mysticism to counter the common belief that only during the modern period has sexuality been the object of anything but a murky representation: "Never did sexuality enjoy a more immediately natural understanding and never did it know a greater 'felicity of expression' than in the Christian world of fallen bodies and of sin. The proof is its whole tradition of mysticism and spirituality which was incapable of dividing the continuous forms of desire, of rapture, of penetration, of ecstasy, of that outpouring which leaves us spent: all of these experiences seemed to lead, without interruption or limit, right to the heart of a divine love of which they were both the outpouring and the source returning upon itself" (1977b, 29). Foucault's argument that mystical experience in Western Christianity conflated sexual and divine love is corroborated, in somewhat different fashion, by Lacan. Citing the example of Hadewijch d'Anvers, Lacan says that the "mystical ejaculations are neither idle gossip nor mere verbiage, in fact they are the best thing you can read." Mystics alone sense what is inexpressible—the *jouissance* "which goes beyond." Their testimony is for this very reason intensely political: "The mystical is by no means that which is not political. It is something serious, which a few people teach us about, and most often women" (1982, 146–47).

The anxiety of modernity began, according to Foucault, "when words ceased to intersect with representations and to provide a spontaneous grid for the knowledge of things" (1970, 304). What recurs at the margins of poststructuralist discourse is the figure of the mystic, and primarily the female mystic, as a sign of the failure

of representation "to provide a spontaneous grid for . . . knowledge." The contexts of these references suggest that the female
mystic represents the many manifestations of the other in contemporary thought—in sexuality (Foucault), in politics (Lacan), in discourse and madness (Irigaray), in representation itself (Kristeva, de
Certeau). For Irigaray, mysticism is a means, available primarily for
and through women, to collapse subject and other in "an embrace
of fire that mingles one term into another." It is a means to enact a
new kind of discourse, which expresses a mistrust for "understanding as an obstacle along the path of jouissance" and for "the
dry desolation of reason" (1985a, 191). Finally, Michel de Certeau
argues that mysticism is a "historical trope for loss. It renders the
absence that multiplies the productions of desire readable" (1986,
80).

These characteristics of mysticism are a product of the anxiety
and nostalgia for lost origins, for the recuperation of presence and
jouissance, so prevalent in contemporary theory. With the exception
of de Certeau, who writes about sixteenth- and seventeenth-century
mysticism, contemporary theorists who invoke mysticism—and
particularly female mysticism—as an example of *jouissance* tend to
approach it from the limited viewpoint of a psychologizing or psychoanalytic framework and therefore view it as an ahistorical, timeless phenomenon. I would like to restore a historical dimension to
the discussion of the female mystic to illuminate her role as the
locus of several kinds of cultural representation: of the female
body, of sexuality, of the unrepresentable—divinity, *jouissance*—
and finally of the woman writer, the empowered woman-as-
subject. To this end, this chapter describes as a complex network of
relations what de Certeau calls the "mystic formation." This network includes its privileged places, social categories, and forms of
labor, its concrete modes of economic and sexual relations, and
most insistently its insertion within the power relations of medieval cultures.

Foucault, in his discussion of torture in *Discipline and Punish*,
reverses one of the central beliefs of Christianity: that the body is
the prison of the soul, a miserable container that constrains the
freedom of its far more valuable contents. One lesson Christianity
since Augustine has consistently drawn from the Genesis story of

the fall is that human beings have bodies that experience pain, desire, and mortality; God does not. The body is a limit; its vulnerability and weakness impede the soul in its progress toward God.[1] Foucault challenges these beliefs by suggesting that the body has instead been constrained, been the prisoner of, the representations of it which necessarily follow from a soul-body dualism that privileges the soul. What Foucault misses in his analysis, however, is the gender component of this dualism, which guarantees that men and women experience the limits of their bodies in quite different ways. In brief, medieval Christianity construed men as spirit and women as body. Like the body, woman is accident to man's essence, despite the Church's claims of the spiritual equality of all believers.

Women in the later Middle Ages were nevertheless more likely than men to gain reputations as spiritual leaders based on their mystical experiences. Perhaps because they were in an oppressed social situation, women were especially drawn to radical forms of religious experience. Some scholars have argued that, because religion was the dominant mode of expression in medieval Europe and the Church such a powerful socioeconomic institution, political dissent almost invariably took the form of religious dissent— heresy as well as the extreme religious practices associated with even orthodox mystics.[2] Women's claims to mystical experience, then, also asserted their worthiness to appropriate the Logos in spite of the contamination of the female body; such claims enabled women to turn the dominant discourse of Christianity to their own purposes.

My concern, then, is the discourse of late medieval mysticism as it exhibits at least some women's ability to speak and be heard within a patriarchal and forthrightly misogynistic society. I make no outlandish brief for these women's anticipation of feminist concerns, nor do I intend to condemn, ahistorically, their conservatism

[1] 1977a, 3–69, cap. 30. For an important discussion of the relationships between the body and forms of divine power in the Hebraic Scriptures, especially Genesis, see Scarry 1985, esp. chap. 4, 181–243. For a useful discussion of early Christian commentaries on Genesis 1–3 see Pagels 1988.

[2] Gottfried Koch, *Frauenfrage und Ketzertum im Mittelalter* (1962), quoted in Abels and Harrison 1979, 216. See also Bynum 1982, 172.

or capitulation to patriarchal religion. Rather I wish to examine the discourse of mysticism as a site of struggle between the authoritative, monological language of a powerful social institution and the heteroglossia of the men and women who came under its sway and sometimes resisted it. Mysticism, as I describe it, is not a manifestation of the individual's internal affective states but a complex network of cultural and ideological constructs that both share in and subvert orthodox religious institutions. Furthermore, linguistic empowerment for women was tied to the social repression of the body in the Middle Ages. The discourse of the female mystic was constructed out of disciplines designed to regulate the female body, and it is, paradoxically, through these disciplines that the mystic consolidated her power. Specifically, I examine how several mystics of the thirteenth and fourteenth centuries fashioned out of cultural representations and technologies designed to contain and suppress the body a means to transcend their own secondary status as powerless members of society.

Although the women I look at in this chapter are widely separated by time, geography, and class, I wish to consider them as a single group for several reasons. These women did not live and write in total isolation. They were aware of the existence of other famous mystics and saw themselves as part of a tradition of exceptional religious women. Younger mystics often modeled their lives and writings on those of their predecessors.[3] This dialogism—this "intense interaction and struggle of one's own and another's voice" (Bakhtin 1981, 354)—is central to the visionary experience. Furthermore, these women provide yet another illustration within a particular social formation of the interactions among repression, power/knowledge, and the poaching of the repressed, and I want to emphasize the power and complexity of the cultural representations that paradoxically both confined them and enabled them to challenge their cultural figurations.

[3]In her notes to *The Book of Margery Kempe* (1940), for example, Hope Emily Allen points out many instances of intertextuality between Margery's writing and that of several continental mystics. In the book Kempe describes her visit to her contemporary Julian of Norwich, with whom she enjoyed lengthy conversations.

Sexual Linguistics

The Life of Saint Leoba, written by a monk of Fulda named Rudolph about an eighth-century Anglo-Saxon nun who participated in the Christianization of Germany, recounts a curious visionary dream that strikingly illustrates the phenomenon Sandra Gilbert and Susan Gubar call "sexual linguistics," "the creation of sex-specific fantasies of linguistic empowerment" (1985b, 515). One night the saint sees a purple thread issuing from her mouth, "as if it were coming from her very bowels." When she tries to draw it out with her hand, she cannot reach the end of it. As she pulls it out she begins to roll the thread into a ball. "The labour of doing this was so tiresome that eventually, through sheer fatigue, she awoke from her sleep and began to wonder what the meaning of the dream might be" (Petroff 1986, 108).[4] Because this is a "true vision" the dream demands an authoritative interpretation. Its meaning must be made publicly manifest by someone empowered to reveal the "mystery hidden in it." It is another woman, an older nun residing in the same monastery at Wimborne "who was known to possess the spirit of prophecy," who offers the definitive gloss on this dream.

"These things," she went on, "were revealed to the person whose holiness and wisdom makes her a worthy recipient, because by her teaching and good example she will confer benefits on many people. The thread which came from her bowels and issued from her mouth, signifies the wise counsels that she will speak from the heart. The fact that it filled her hand means that she will carry out in her actions whatever she expresses in her words. Furthermore, the ball which she made by rolling it round and round signifies the mystery of divine teaching, which is set in motion by the words and deeds of those who give instruction and which turns earthwards through active works and heavenwards through contemplation, at one time swinging downwards through com-

---

[4]I have chosen to cite the medieval mystics in translation rather than in their original Latin or vernacular because I wish to make these works accessible to general readers as well as to medieval scholars.

passion for one's neighbour, again swinging upwards through the love of God. By these signs God shows that your mistress will profit many by her words and example, and the effect of them will be felt in other lands afar off whither she will go." (108–9)

Two things strike me as noteworthy about this interpretation of the vision, a rather obscure example from the so-called dark ages of a woman's speech empowered to produce consequences in a man's world. First, it calls into question our usual stereotypes of women in the Middle Ages as either the subject of a clerical misogyny that saw woman as the incarnation of every evil or as the docile and virginal saint and martyr; it suggests that the dichotomy between Eve and Mary oversimplifies women's position in the Middle Ages. The interpretation of the dream by an older nun confers power by revealing that Saint Leoba's words will be authoritative. Her "wise counsels" will not only be spoken publicly and listened to; they will also guide actions—hers and other's. More important, her words, the ball she fashions from the purple thread, become the means by which "the mysteries of divine teaching" are realized in human and social terms; they mediate between the human and divine: turning "earthwards through active works and heaven-wards through contemplation." According to the male author of the *Life*, Leoba's speech will have powerful material effects on the social institutions of which she is a part, in this case the institutions of nascent Christianity. In Rudolph's narrative of her life, the dream's prophecy is indeed fulfilled. At the request of Saint Boniface, Leoba travels to Germany as a missionary to aid in its Christianization. She presides over a convent at Bischofsheim. Her miracles include the calming of a storm and the exposing of an infanticide. In the latter episode, her assumption of the authority of a judge in what is virtually a trial by ordeal exonerates an accused sister and saves the reputation of her convent. According to her biographer, Leoba counts among her powerful friends not only spiritual leaders such as Saint Boniface but temporal rulers as well, including the emperor Charlemagne and his queen Hiltigard.

The second striking aspect of this vision is that it locates Leoba's power to speak specifically in her body. The thread "issues from her very bowels." Leoba regurgitates her powerful words in a process that has its source in her body but seems beyond her control. This episode violates our sense of the decorum required of religious speech, which traditionally separates the disembodied voice of spirituality from the material body. It also transgresses the ideological boundaries between the classical "discursive" body—viewed as closed, homogeneous, and monumental—and the grotesque body, with its materiality, orifices, and discharges.[5] Leoba (or some other, since the dream challenges the autonomy of the individual subject), speaks the body of her text through the text of her body.

Saint Leoba is only one of a number of women throughout the Middle Ages whose mystical visions gave them an unprecedented authority to speak and write, indeed to preach and instruct, which may come as a surprise to feminists more used to proclaiming women's historical silences. Her biography suggests that the "fact" of women's exclusion from the discourses of power in any period may be more complex than it originally appeared. But although they lived in societies that shared the misogyny inherited from early Christianity, there is much that separates an eighth-century visionary like Leoba from her counterparts in the thirteenth and fourteenth centuries. Aristocratic religious women in the eighth century enjoyed more institutional power and better education and were more likely to assume duties and privileges that after the twelfth century would be reserved solely for men. Women could preside over convents and even over double monasteries, as the Saxon abbess Hugeberc did. The range of their learning was remarkable for the so-called dark ages, including, for some, Latin, the classics, Scriptures, the Church fathers, and canon law. Often they were instructed not by men but by other women. Leoba was sent to Wimborne to study under its erudite abbess Mother Tetta. Perhaps because the early Church afforded women—at least aristocratic women—a greater scope for their talents and abilities, these women were less likely than their counterparts in later centuries to indulge in abuses of their bodies. On the contrary, they preached, and practiced, moderation in all things pertaining to the

[5]On the classical and grotesque bodies, see Bakhtin 1984; Stallybrass and White, 1986.

body. Rudolph, for instance, stresses Leoba's moderation in eating, drinking, and sleeping—in everything, indeed, except her studies.[6]

The twelfth, thirteenth, and fourteenth centuries produced a large number of texts by and about women whose speech was imbued with an authority of divine origins. "This is the only place in the history of the West," Irigaray writes rather hyperbolically, "in which a woman speaks and acts so publicly" (1985a, 191).[7] While it is possible to argue that female mystics who spoke publicly merely ventriloquized the voice of a patriarchal religion,[8] it is worth asking why and how these particular women were empowered to speak with an authority that rivaled and at times seemed to surpass that of the misogynist male clerics who ruled the institutional church. Elizabeth Petroff gives a sense of the kind of social and political power women with the status of orthodox mystic enjoyed: "Visions led women to the acquisition of power in the world while affirming their knowledge of themselves as women. Visions were a socially sanctioned activity that freed a woman from conventional female roles by identifying her as a genuine religious figure. They brought her to the attention of others, giving her a public language she could use to teach and learn. Her visions gave her the strength to grow internally and to change the world, to build converts, found hospitals, preach, attack injustice and greed, even within the church" (1986, 6). Even heretical mystics

[6]See The Life of Saint Leoba, in Petroff 1986, 109–14. For a discussion of women in the early medieval Church, see Joann McNamara and Suzanne Wemple, "Sanctity and Power: The Dual Pursuit of Medieval Women," in Bridenthal and Koontz 1977, 96–109.

[7]Irigaray's psychoanalytic reading of mysticism in "La Mystérique" regards the mystical experience as belonging in some essential way to women, or at least to the female: "The poorest in science and the most ignorant were the most eloquent, the richest in revelations. Historically, that is women. Or at least the female" (192). Irigaray's somewhat romanticized idealizations place the mystical experience outside of language and representation, aligning it, ahistorically I would argue, with hysteria and madness. Irigaray's opposition of mystical discourse to the "dry desolation of reason" papers over the historical complexity of women's participation in mysticism as a public, not solipsistic, discourse, which thrived in a dialogic relationship with medieval culture.

[8]To my knowledge, no one has made this argument specifically about the medieval mystics, although it is certainly conceivable that someone might. For the dangers of feminists' appropriating medieval women writers, see Delany 1987, 177–97.

such as Marguerite Porete and more marginal religious figures such as Margery Kempe enjoyed something of this privileged status and following.[9] As Petroff's analysis makes clear, the basis of the power the female mystic enjoyed was both discursive and public, not private and extralinguistic. The mystic's possession of a public language gives her the ability to act not just within a woman's culture but in a man's world as well.

What Petroff's analysis fails to make clear, however, is how the mystic's identification as a "genuine religious figure" freed her from "conventional female roles" that mandated docility, passivity, subservience, and reticence and how her public activities came to be "socially sanctioned" by a Church anxiously guarding its spiritual and temporal power. These questions can be answered only by examining the relation of mystical discourse to institutional structures and ideologies, by taking into account not only the subversiveness of mystical discourse but also its co-optation by the institutional Church. It is, after all, not just a matter of discovering why women were turning to mysticism and other kinds of religious experiences, both sanctioned and condemned, but also why the Church in certain cases tolerated and even encouraged female visionaries, who occasionally seemed to undermine its own claims to authority. The needs served by mysticism must be understood within the context of a Foucauldian *dispositif*, or "grid of intelligibility," the nexus of social, cultural, and historical practices, both discursive and nondiscursive. This *dispositif* encompasses not only institutional morality, theological statements, and philosophical propositions but such structures and practices as architectural arrangements, the arts, regulations, laws, administrative procedures, medicine, and even hygiene. In the case of mysticism, such a *dispositif* might be constructed from three sources: the political situation of the Church after the twelfth century, which resulted

---

[9]Although Marguerite Porete was burned at the stake in 1310 and her book *The Mirror of Simple Souls* was ordered burned by the Inquisition, *The Mirror* survived her death; its popularity is attested to by the number of translations made during the fourteenth century, including one in English (Dronke 1984). Margery Kempe during her religious life was accused alternately of madness and heresy and enjoyed the patronage and support of powerful English ecclesiasts. See *The Book of Margery Kempe*.

in the institutionalization of religious women, the cultural representations of the female body, and the disciplinary technologies that attempted to realize these representations. Within the *dispositif* these three threads form a web, but for heuristic purposes it will be necessary to treat them separately in order to see each strand clearly.

Classical and Grotesque Bodies

The political situation of the Church in the thirteenth century bore little resemblance to that of its eighth-century counterpart. Concerned with consolidating its own authority by stressing the special power of the priesthood, the Catholic church, from the twelfth century on, had little use for women in official positions of either spiritual or temporal power. This jealous guarding of its prerogatives is evident in the many calls to pastoral care; the emphasis on the sacraments, particularly the Eucharist and confession, where the priest most directly exercised his authority; and in conflicts between proponents of a monastic life of contemplation and advocates of an active life of pastoral care, which often erupted into full-scale political conflict over spiritual "turf." The growing distance between the clergy and the laity coincided with a resurgence of lay piety which left both men and women searching for outlets to express their religious sentiments. The privileged status of the mystic reflected this tension between clerical centralization and lay expressions of piety. On the one hand, her claims of authority could easily be seen as subversive of clerical prerogatives; on the other, they could, when necessary, be co-opted by the Church to strengthen its own spiritual and temporal authority. Although women were officially banned from preaching or administering sacraments (for example, Penance), many orthodox female visionaries had disciples and followers whom they instructed, counseled, and even reprimanded for their sins. The line between preaching and instructing, between hearing confessions and demonstrating concern for the sinfulness and spiritual welfare of others is thinly drawn in the writings of many of the medieval mystics, as the following example suggests.

The Herald of Divine Love by the thirteenth-century mystic of the convent of Helfta, Gertrude the Great, is permeated by a sense of ministry that is articulated in specifically clerical terms.[10] Gertrude's disciples frequently questioned her about the Eucharist, specifically whether or not they dared approach communion without Penance. "She counselled those whom she thought to be in a correct intention to approach the Lord's sacrifice confidently and even constrained them to do so."

> And another time when she prayed for someone . . . the Lord replied: "Whatever anyone hopes to be able to obtain from you, so much without a doubt she will receive from me. Moreover whatever you promise to someone in my name, I will certainly supply. . . . After several days, remembering this promise of the Lord without forgetting her own unworthiness, she asked how it was possible . . . and the Lord replied: "Is not the faith of the universal church that promise once made to Peter: Whatever you bind on earth will be bound in heaven, and firmly she believes this to be carried out by all ecclesiastical ministers. Therefore why do you not equally believe because of this that I can and will perfect that which, moved by love, I promise you by my divine mouth?" And touching her tongue he said, "Behold, I give my words into your mouth." (Bynum 1982, 206)

Gertrude justifies her ministerial activities using the very same scriptural text that the Church used to establish its clerical authority (Matthew 16:19). Her exchange with the Lord has all the force of an ordination ritual; the language is ritualistic, even liturgical: "Behold, I give my words into your mouth." Caroline Bynum minimizes the subversiveness of Gertrude's claims to clerical authority, saying that they did not "undermine the structure and rituals of monasticism or the church but rather . . . project[ed] women into one of those structures, the pastoral and mediating role, which is otherwise denied to them" (207). But this analysis misses the audacity of Gertrude's claim to speak for God. If anyone—even a woman—could communicate directly with God, bypassing the prescribed forms of clerical mediation, and even claim to serve as a

---

[10]See the discussion of Gertrude in Bynum 1982, 196–209.

mediator for others, then the priesthood becomes meaningless as a special and privileged class. That the Church felt this transgression of the boundaries between clergy and laity to be a real threat to its power is attested by its struggles in the thirteenth and fourteenth centuries with lay spiritual movements such as the Beguines and heresies such as Catharism and the Free Spirit, all of which attempted to bypass clerical mediation to claim a more direct relationship between the laity and God.[11] However orthodox and conservative her religious vision, Gertrude's daring claim to speak for God challenged the hierarchies of a male-dominated clergy that jealously guarded its monopoly on religious discourse.

But if the mere existence of female mystics enjoying an unmediated relationship with the divine successfully subverted clerical authority, it could do so, paradoxically, only from within the institutional Church and only to further that institution's ends—the consolidation of its power. The Church strictly defined and controlled the nature and content of the mystical experience. It is tempting for the twentieth-century reader to see the mystic's visions as highly private and personal experiences brought on by heightened affective and psychological states, but, to repeat, in the Middle Ages, mysticism was a public discourse—not private, passive, or, despite its claims, monological but communal, active, and dialogical. The mystical experience was highly structured, and it was the Church that provided both structure and content because it controlled through various institutional disciplines the lives and learning of women in religious communities. Increasingly after the twelfth century the Church attempted through strict cloistering to bring religious women more firmly under its control, to enforce women's silence, to institutionalize their powerlessness, and most important from its own point of view, to isolate itself from women's supposedly corrupting influence.[12]

After the twelfth century, orthodox mystics were, with few exceptions, cloistered, in keeping with the Church's sense of women's spiritual role. To be sure, not all mystics were nuns. Mystics

[11]See Abels and Harrison 1979 on Catharism; Dronke 1984 and McLaughlin 1973 on the Free Spirit; and McDonnell 1969 on the Beguines.

[12]For a discussion of these changes in the twelfth-century Church, see Bridenthal and Koontz 1977, 110–16.

could—and did—express their religious ecstasies as nuns, ab-
besses, wives, mothers, tertiaries, anchoresses, beguines, or itiner-
ants. Most often, when they were not cloistered, religious women
tended to be tertiaries—like Catherine of Siena—or beguines. But
the model upon which all spiritual organizations for women were
based was the cloister. And quite clearly its primary purpose was
isolation. For example, even though she had desired to follow the
active life prescribed by Saint Francis, living and working among
the poor, the rule Saint Clair received from Pope Honorius III required that "No sister is to go out of the convent for any purpose
whatever except to found a new community. Similarly, no one,
religious or secular, is to be allowed to enter the monastery. Per-
petual silence is imposed on all members of the community, and
continuous fasting, often on bread and water" (Moorman 1968, 35).
Architecturally, the convent fostered maximum isolation from the
society outside it, and access to these communities of cloistered
women was strictly controlled. Life within the convent was structured by the liturgy and rituals of the Church, including "the seven
canonical hours of daily prayers that followed the cycle of the
liturgical year . . . [and] specific prayers for special saints days and
major feasts" (Petroff 1986, 6). The spiritual disciplines that filled
out this life included such practices as mantric prayer, flagellation,
fasting, and vigils, which, when carried to excess, as they sometimes were, seem designed to produce an emotional state con-
ducive to mystical experience.

These technologies both resulted from and fed back into medieval cultural representations of the female body. Woman had to be
enclosed, restricted, and isolated because, in the eyes of the
Church, she was the quintessence of all fleshly evil, a scapegoat—
the "devil's gateway" or "devil's mousetrap"—whose expulsion
allowed the Church to purge itself of the corruption of the body.[13]
This loathing of the female flesh, expressed in countless Church
documents, must be understood in light of its cultural meaning. To
do so, we must abandon the usual biologistic understanding of the
human "body." Ordinarily, we attribute to the body an a priori

[13]For a recent and illuminating analysis of official medieval misogyny, which sees
it as evidence of a "deep mistrust of the body and of the materiality of the sign" (14),
see Bloch 1987; on the "devil's mousetrap," see Remley 1989.

material existence without considering how our experience of our bodies is organized by cultural representations of them. These representations are not universal but historically specific.[14] Similarly, the material body can itself be one of those discursive practices. It is a sign, imbued with meaning that can be glossed. In other words, as Stallybrass and White maintain, "the shape and plasticity of the human body is indissociable from the shape and plasticity of discursive material and social formation in a collectivity." Citing V. V. Ivanov, they declare that "no absolute borderline can be drawn between body and meaning in the sphere of culture" (1986, 21).

We might conclude, then, drawing upon Mikhail Bakhtin's distinction between the "classical body" and the "grotesque body," that two antithetical representations of the body structure discursive norms in any culture.[15] In the Middle Ages, too, this opposition between classical and grotesque bodies structured those discursive practices that constituted women's understanding of their bodies. In my usage, the classical body denotes the *form* of official high culture. Medieval "high" culture was Latin, male, and homogeneous, incorporating such discourses as philosophy, theology, canon law, and liturgy, as well as art and literature. In the medieval Church, the classical body was harmonious, proportionate, and monumental; it attempted to represent a sort of disembodied spirituality, and thus, it never existed except as cultural representation. The grosser, more material aspects of "the body" were displaced onto the "grotesque body." Women—along with other marginal social groups, specifically the lower classes—were constructed by the dominant culture as the grotesque body, the low other, whose discursive norms include heterogeneity, disproportion, a focus on gaps, orifices, and symbolic filth. The grotesque body is at once feminized, corrupt, and threatening; it is a reminder of mortality, imperfection, and the wretchedness of human existence.

[14]Much recent work on the female body has illuminated this problem; see for instance Suleiman 1986. Although it appeared too late for me to address it here, Caroline Bynum's most recent book (1991) offers a fascinating account of the relationships between medieval conceptions of the body and mysticism which confirms my own argument.

[15]Bakhtin 1984, 19; see also Stallybrass and White 1986, 9–26.

This sketch describes the writings of many female mystics, whose emotionalism, intense personal involvement, polyglot mixture of genres, and open-endedness contrasts markedly to the monumental rationalism and harmonious proportion of classical theological writing by men. The emotionalism so often attributed to female piety, its so-called affective nature as compared to the rationalistic nature of male piety, is not an essential part of a feminine literary experience but a manifestation of the disciplinary technologies female mystics internalized and expressed through self-inflicted violence on their bodies—torture, screams, and howls.[16] In this passage from Angela of Foligno's *Liber de vere fidelium experientia* (*Book of the Experience of the Truly Faithful*), Angela, who was herself a notorious "screamer" ("Even if someone stood over me with an axe ready to kill me, I could not have prevented myself [from screaming]" [Petroff 1986, 259]), measures her "fire of love" exclusively in the bodily injuries she wishes to endure.

And so I disposed of myself on account of [Christ's] love that I wished that all my limbs might suffer a death unlike his passion, that is, a more vile death. And I was meditating and desiring that if I could find someone to kill me, in some way that it would be lawful to kill me, on account of his faith or his love, that I would beg him to do this favor for me, that is, that since Christ was crucified on the wood of the cross he should crucify me in a low place, or in some unsavory place or with a loathsome weapon. And I could not think of a death as vile as I desired, and I grieved deeply that I could not find a vile death that would in no way be like those of the saints, for I was totally unworthy. (Petroff 1986, 257)

Piety for Angela, as for virtually all the female mystics, is palpably physical and sexual. Images of degradation abound; Angela compares herself to a nursing baby, drinking the blood of Christ from the wound in his side. Mystical writing features representations of grotesque bodies that open up and spill forth their contents— blood, milk, excrement—bodies that endure wounding and muti-

[16]For an important discussion of the affective nature of female piety in the fourteenth century, see Kieckhefer 1984.

lation. The mystic's own body becomes a contested site of cultural discourses about sexuality and the female body. The mystic's sexuality becomes at once an emblem for her degradation and unworthiness, evidence of the forces of repression within medieval culture, and a means to transcend the physical altogether. If women in the Middle Ages were defined as sexual beings, as body, then it is only through an excessive indulgence in the body, in the mortification of the flesh, that the mystic can transcend her sex and refashion her grotesque body as a classical one.

These conflicts about sexuality and the body emerge most clearly in rituals designed to chastise the flesh. In a passage from Angela's *Liber*, for instance, we see an intense loathing for the physical body, especially the "lower-bodily stratum," expressed through the desire to inflict humiliation on it: "I do not blush to recite before the whole world all the sins that I ever committed. But I enjoyed imagining some way in which I could reveal those deceptions and iniquities and sins. I wanted to go through the squares and the towns naked, with fish and meat hanging about my neck, saying, 'Here is that disgusting woman, full of malice and deception, the sewer of all vices and evils, . . . behold the devil in my soul and the malice of my heart'" (Petroff 1986, 7). The metonymic association of the female body with the corruption of rotting meat and fish paradoxically invokes the grotesque body to exorcize it. The female mystic's only means of escaping her body is to indulge in an obsessive display and denunciation of its most grotesque features. This obsession with sexual display as a form of penance suggests the extent to which the female mystic has internalized the discursive norms of the dominant "high" culture.

We might compare this cultural construction of the grotesque female body with a very different, if related, representation of the classical body. In hagiographies of women saints, written primarily by men, the elaborate infliction of bodily pain often leaves the saint's body miraculously untouched. Unlike the grotesque body of the mystic, the classical body of hagiography is closed, miraculously impervious to wounding, invulnerable to penetration.[17]

---

[17]See Scarry's discussion of the cultural significance of wounding in the Judeo-Christian tradition (1985, 181–243).

This passage from Thomas de Cantripré's *Vita* of Christina Mirabilis indulges in a fiery spiritual purging of the female body which leaves it physically unharmed:

> Then Christina began to do those things for which she had been sent back by the Lord. She crept into fiery ovens where bread was baking and was tormented by fires just like any of us mortals so that her howls were terrible to hear. Nevertheless when she emerged, no mutilation of any sort appeared in her body. When no oven was at hand, she threw herself into roaring fires which she found in men's houses or else she thrust her feet and hands into fires and held them there for so long that they would have been reduced to ashes had it not been a divine miracle. At other times she jumped into cauldrons of boiling water and stood there immersed either up to the breast or the waist, depending on the size of the cauldron, and poured scalding water over those parts of her body which were untouched by the water. Although she howled as if she were suffering the pangs of childbirth, when she climbed out again she was quite unharmed. (Petroff 1986 , 185–86)

Several details in this passage suggest the need to discipline the flesh so prominent in Angela's writing. Although it is subtler, there is the same emphasis on what is specifically female about the saint's body. The reference to the "pangs of childbirth" calls attention to the sexual function that Christina, as a virgin, has specifically renounced, as well as to the "opening up" of the body entailed in both sexual activity and childbirth. (It is probably worth mentioning that unlike Christina, who remained a virgin, Angela of Foligno was both a wife and mother.) The immersion of her breasts and genitalia (up to the breast or waist)—the signs of her sexuality—in boiling water reminds the reader that Christina's body is a female one, subject to all the weaknesses of femininity. But Christina's chastisements differ in one significant respect from Angela's. If the torturing of the classical body produces pain, it does not wound; there is "no mutilation of any sort." Indeed, the saint's voluntary endurance of pain in imitation of Christ's bodily suffering invokes the Eucharistic miracle. The ovens into which Christina casts herself are ovens for baking bread, suggesting without explicitly stating it, her symbolic connection to the ritual of the

Eucharist. But the symbolism, in Christina's case, is reversed. In the Eucharist, the bread is transformed into the body of Christ. The central act of Christianity is Christ's assumption of a body that can be—and is—wounded, opened up by torture. Christina is transformed in the oven from body to "bread"; she escapes her body into the monumentality of a cultural symbol. She cannot be wounded. She transcends the pain of physicality—of her feminine sexuality—and emerges as an icon of religious devotion; the asexual, transcendent, because virginal, woman.

Female mystics internalized the disciplinary technologies evolved by the Church to subject and contain feminine sexuality not only discursively but physically as well. As one might guess, these technologies, misogynistic in their intent, were designed to suppress and control a female body the Church deemed disruptive and threatening. The disciplines of the most famous mystics were often spectacular examples of self-torture through extravagant abuse of their bodies. Rudolph Bell, in *Holy Anorexia*, describes Angela of Foligno's struggle to control her flesh.

> Demons filled her head with visions of her soul being strung upside down so that all her virtues turned to vices; in anger, pain, tears, desperation, she pinched herself so hard that her head and body were covered with bruises, and still the torture continued. Human vices, even ones she never had known before, tormented every member of her body. Even when these desires may have shifted away from her "intimate parts" to places where she felt the pain less, so on fire was she that until Friar Arnaldo prohibited it, she used natural fire to extinguish the internal burning. As her spiritual understanding deepened, her wish changed from instant death to a drawn out physically painful and tormenting ending, one in which she would experience all the sufferings of the world in her every limb and organ. Her love had sacrificed and so would she. . . . Earlier she had undertaken a detailed examination of each part of her body, judging them member by member and assigning to each its due penance. (Bell 1985, 107–8)[18]

[18]Although I would want to distance myself from its conclusions, Bell's book, like Caroline Bynum's *Holy Feast and Holy Fast* (1987), provides many examples of this kind of self-torture.

One can only assume that those penances would have been much like those practiced by Catherine of Siena, another Italian visionary, who wore rough clothing and bound an iron chain so tightly around her hips that it inflamed her skin and who flagellated herself three times a day with an iron chain for one and one-half hours. Angela of Foligno's obsession with the grotesqueness of the body is strikingly illustrated by another anecdote, also related by Bell: "She and her companion one Holy Thursday had gone to the local hospital of San Feliciano to wash the feet of sick women and the hands of men who were there. One leper they tended had flesh so putrefied and rotten that pieces peeled off into the wash basin they were using. Angela then proceeded to drink this mixture, it giving her almost the sensation of receiving communion, and when a bit of flesh got stuck in her throat she tried to swallow it too until against her will she choked it out" (1985, 108). In this anecdote, the juxtaposition of the putrefying rotten flesh and the Eucharist vividly recalls the opposition between the grotesque and classical bodies.[19] Indeed, it powerfully merges these two cultural representations of the body, investing the Eucharist with the power to transform the grotesque. In this way, the physical torture so prominent in the histories of many female mystics assumes an unending, ritualistic quality: its purpose is to mortify the flesh— feminine sexuality particularly—until that sexuality no longer exists. It enacts a desire to "erase" sexual difference through acts of barely repressed sexual humiliation and degradation.

Frequently, at least in legend, the mystic might seem to achieve this desire. The vitae of several mystics report the cessation of all ordinary forms of elimination. As a result of excessive fasting, many excreted neither feces nor urine, did not menstruate, never sweated, and discharged neither tears nor saliva. Some exuded sweet fragrances or oils instead, which had the power to heal others.[20] The mystic's grotesque body was transformed into a classical one, closed and monumental.

[19]Caroline Bynum writes that the drinking of pus was a common practice among female saints, see 1987, 144–45, for instance. For another argument on the "hidden alliances" between mysticism and torture, see de Certeau, "The Institution of Rot," in 1986, 35–46.

[20]See Bell 1985 and Bynum 1987 for examples. The cessation of menstruation and the diminution of other forms of elimination would be consistent with what we now know about self-starvation.

Technologies of the Self

What, one might ask, does the female mystic gain from such spectacles of abuse? My initial answer might be, like Petroff's, quite simply, power. But I would like to explore more specifically the nature of the power claimed by the female mystic, beginning with a reminder of just how audacious some of these claims were. Marguerite Porete was burned at the stake by the Inquisition for self-deification, but she was not the only woman to make such grandiose claims. Several orthodox mystics made strikingly similar statements: "My Me is God," wrote Catherine of Genoa; Hadewijch of Brabant wished "to be God with God"; Angela of Foligno wrote that "the Word was made flesh to make me God." These are not the statements of individuals who have accepted the traditional and subservient religious roles allotted to women. These women claim a virtually divine authority, which they frequently sought to exercise by preaching, writing, founding convents and hospitals, caring for the poor and sick, and occasionally meddling in Church politics. To be sure, I am not suggesting that these women "intended" in any conscious way to seek either temporal or spiritual power. Rather my analysis depends upon what Paul Ricoeur has called a "hermeneutics of suspicion." The fact that none of the mystics says her specific goal is empowerment (which in itself would be a strikingly modern statement) cannot be accepted as an indication that their utterances can be confined within a traditional rhetoric of intention; their descriptions of their intentions must be interrogated. These women were certainly capable of entertaining as part of their cultural ideology motives of which they were not fully conscious and which they could not even fully articulate. If we embed the discourses of medieval mysticism within a network of other discourses, within the Foucauldian *disposatif*, we can then interrogate the mystic's "intention" from the perspective of cultural ideology.

Mystics took disciplines designed to regulate and subject the body and turned them into what Michel Foucault has called "technologies of the self," methods of consolidating their spiritual power and authority, perhaps the only ones available to women. According to Foucault, individuals often effect, "by their own means, a certain number of operations on their own bodies, their own souls, their own thoughts, their own conduct, and this in a manner so as to transform themselves, and to attain a certain state of perfection, happiness, purity, and/or supernatural power" (in Blonsky 1985, 367). Although Foucault is describing the medieval Catholic discipline of confession, he might just as well be describing the lives of many medieval mystics. De Certeau echoes Foucault's argument about technologies of the self in his descriptions of the practices of poaching, which enable those subjected to disciplinary technologies to manipulate or evade them, or even to shape them to their own ends, by seeming to conform to them (1984, xiv–xv, 165–76). For women mystics, excess—the repression of the body, the mortification of the flesh—paradoxically becomes a revaluation of the self in relation to spiritual power.

To understand how self-torture could become a form of poaching, a means of empowerment, we must first understand the place of torture in medieval society. In the Middle Ages, torture was not regarded simply as a form of punishment. It was, as Foucault has said, a technique and a ritual, a semiotic system that "must mark the victim" (1977a, 34), inscribing on his or her body the "signs" of the ruler's power. It was one of the most visible displays of that power, an art, "an entire poetic" (45) that competed with other visual displays of theocratic rule—public spectacles, processions, coronations, and investitures. The marking of the victim's body signifies the power that punishes. According to Foucault, "in the 'excesses' of torture, a whole economy of power is invested" (35). In the excesses of her self-inflicted torture, the female mystic becomes at once both victim and torturer, she who is marked and she who marks. This duality constructs the female body as a reflexive locus of power. It is at once what seems most fascinating and most appalling about the mystic's appropriation of cultural representations of her body. The mystic's pain—her inflicting of wounds upon herself—allows her to poach upon the authority of both Church and state, enabling her to speak and be heard, to have followers, to act as a spiritual adviser, to heal the sick, and to found convents and hospitals. Her body bears the marks, the "signs," of her own spiritual power.

The mystic's spiritual progress through the various stages of mystical experience, then, is discursively organized by the disciplines authorized by religious tradition and performed on her body. She changes the meaning of the forces that oppress her, however, by usurping their power to discipline her, to chastise and purify the corruption of her flesh. She assumes for herself the power to define the authority that represses her sexuality: not man but God. Significantly, the Church at no time advised or condoned the severe fasting and self-flagellation of mystics such as Angela or Catherine of Siena. It advised moderation in all penance. In fact, the mystics themselves did not urge such extremes on others and were never seen as models to be imitated. They were considered special instances of God's grace because they chose their own suffering and thus were free to define its significance. That is why Angela of Foligno could desire such a violent and painful death, why Julian of Norwich could beg God for a terrible illness, and why Catherine of Siena starved herself to death at the age of thirty-two. Technologies that, in the hands of a powerful Church, were meant to limit severely the autonomy and authority of women became for the mystics a source of self-determination, virtually the only one available to women during this period.

It is this power to manipulate cultural representations which creates the dialogism of the mystical text, the interpenetration of its words, its signs, with other ambiguous words and signs. The mystic does not merely call upon what she has read or seen to give words to an essentially wordless experience. Instead, these "spiritual exercises," and the meanings she gives them, are constitutive of her visions. In the Long Text of Julian of Norwich's *Showings*, the fourteenth-century English mystic meditates on Christ's suffering during the Crowning with Thorns.

> And during the time that our Lord showed me this spiritual vision which I have now described, I saw the bodily vision of the copious bleeding of the head persist. The great drops of blood fell from beneath the crown like pellets, looking as if they came from the veins, and as they issued they were a brownish red, for the blood was very thick, and as they spread they turned bright red. And as they reached the brows they vanished; and even so the bleeding continued until I had seen and understood many things. Nev-

ertheless, the beauty and the vivacity persisted, beautiful and vivid without diminution. . . . The copiousness resembled the drops
of water which fall from the eaves of a house after a great shower
of rain, falling so thick that no human ingenuity can count them.
And in their roundness as they spread over the forehead they
were like a herring's scales. (1978, 187–88)

At first glance, this passage seems idiosyncratic, its metaphors
positively bizarre. What perhaps most repels the twentieth-century
reader is the disjunction between Christ's pain and suffering at the
hands of his torturers, the ostensible subject of the vision, and
the artifice with which it is conveyed. The images of the pellets, the
raindrops falling from the eaves of a house, and particularly the
herring's scales work against the impression of suffering; they de-
tach the reader from any realistic sense of pain. Instead they point
to the symbolic nature of Christ's suffering. In Julian's vision, although the torturers attempt to leave their mark of temporal power
on Christ's body, she shows that the "signs" contain messages
other than those intended by the torturers, symbols of divine
power which transcend mere physical pain, which shade over into
the decorative, into art.

Indeed, the scene reminds me of nothing so much as a painting.
Although Julian calls it a "bodily vision," suggesting a vision appearing to her eyes, reading the passage, one is put in mind of an
intense meditation upon a visual image—a picture in a book of
hours, a station of the cross, or some other church painting Julian
might have seen. As she meditates on particular details, they lose
their relationship to the whole composition and begin to remind
her of other inanimate objects. As she traces the brushstrokes,
following the change in color from brownish red to bright red,
finally vanishing from the canvas, other images—pellets, raindrops, herring's scales—suggest themselves to her, transforming
the suffering into an artistic vision, a representation that seems
self-conscious in its artifice. Hence the contradictory description of
the vision as "beautiful and vivid," "hideous and fearful," "sweet
and lovely." The mystical vision, seen from this perspective, takes
on the character less of a chance event, whether the sign of psycho-
sis or of spiritual grace, than of a calculated event, carefully pre-

pared for and highly structured by the religious experiences available to medieval women, including those designed to chastise the flesh and imitate Christ's suffering.

But women like Julian of Norwich or Angela of Foligno were not nearly as disingenuous as they had to appear in order to win the toleration and acceptance of the Church. Women could serve no ministerial or sacerdotal function within the medieval Church. They could claim no spiritual authority in and of themselves, nor could they claim it, as the clergy did, from the institutional Church. The source of the mystic's inspiration was divine; she claimed to be the receptacle, the instrument of a divine will. Hildegard of Bingen, for example, represents her authority in precisely these terms: "She utters God's miracles not herself but being touched by them even as a string touched by a lutanist emits a sound not of itself but by his touch" (Dronke 1984, 160). But any visionary experience made public is always, ipso facto, a re-visioning of that experience, an attempt to represent the unrepresentable. The doubleness of their experiences becomes a means to achieve a representational power—as both object and subject—at the very moments they seem bent on annihilating themselves. Their words, and even their bodies when necessary, became the sites of a struggle to redefine the meaning of female silence and powerlessness.

The Woman Writer?

Any attempt to celebrate medieval mystics as feminist, as self-fashioning subjects, or as the authors of themselves, however, risks applying to medieval texts feminist theories of creativity which have been developed primarily from the study of nineteenth- and twentieth-century realist fiction by women. We should be wary, in particular, of feminist readings of medieval women's writing which privilege, in Patrocinio Schweickart's words, "the manifestation of the subjectivity of the absent author—the 'voice' of another woman" (1986, 47). Of course, feminist proponents of what Elaine Showalter calls "gynocritics" are not the only literary critics who ground signification in the subjectivity of an absent author. They are merely following in a long tradition of empiricist criticism that posits authorial intention as the locus of meaning. For instance, writing recently on orality and literacy in the Middle Ages, the medieval scholar Jesse Gellrich makes the claim that "if writing does not possess the magical property of speaking for the person who wrote it, it is nothing" (1988, 468). Explorations of textuality by Derrida, Foucault, Barthes, Kristeva, and others, however, have opened up to scrutiny writing's "magical property of speaking for the person who wrote it." As my previous discussion should suggest, medieval mystics cannot be isolated from the cultural nexus—or *dispositif*—that produced them as writers, nor can they be subsumed within twentieth-century notions of authorship. In fact, these women may not have been "writers" at all, at least in the sense we use the term.

Most often when medieval women visionaries recorded their lives and works, the *writing* was done by a male amanuensis, usually a priest or confessor. This was the case with all or most of the visions of Angela of Foligno, Catherine of Siena (whose vita was recorded by Richard of Capua), and Marie d'Oignes (whose life was written by Jacques de Vitry), among others. The "scene" within which the woman mystic—often illiterate, but not necessarily uneducated—was transformed into the "woman writer" is crucial to understanding the complex nature of the mystic text, the limits imposed on that text, and the problem of determining who authorizes its final significations. The contributions of a (usually) male scribe who shaped and edited the oral accounts provided by the female mystic creates a "doubled subject" or, more accurately, a dialogic subject for the text, an "author function" resulting from the dynamic interplay between the male and female, the literate and illiterate, the clerical and lay. To investigate the gender relations that accompany the writing of these marginalized texts might deepen our understanding not only of the cultural situation of medieval women but also of the situations in which women have subsequently been empowered to write within patriarchal cultures. A critique of medieval authorship may lead to the formulation of more culturally aware (and perhaps politically powerful) feminist theories of reading and authorship which go beyond straightforward notions of "authenticity," "voice," and "experience"—all of which postulate the author as the transcendental signified of her text. These theories of authorship may enable feminists to examine the dialogic cultural activity that structures the writing of *any* text, whether medieval or modern.

I have chosen *The Book of Margery Kempe* for my analysis of the dialogic writing subject because the proem of this "autobiography" describes a scene of writing in which we see briefly figured the relationships between the female visionary and the male priest who records her visions in writing. This scene calls into question the claims of autobiography to represent the immediate expression of an authentic and authenticating "voice" and, at the same time, foregrounds the difficulties involved in preserving life stories within a culture that is still functionally oral, except for an elite that jealously guards the tools of literacy. The conflicting interests of men and women, clergy and laity, Latin and vernacular cultures, oral and written traditions intersect within visionary texts like *The Book of Margery Kempe*. An unpacking of this cultural activity may tell us much about the gender ideologies of the late Middle Ages, particularly the ways in which female "experience" gets translated into writing.

The "Proym" of *The Book of Margery Kempe* works very hard to establish Margery's credentials as the authorizing "voice" within the text, to make her "presence" felt by linking her voice to God's voice, her words to the divine Logos: "By the leave of our merciful Lord Christ Jesus, to the magnifying of his holy name, Jesus, this little treatise shall treat in part of his wonderful works" (Kempe, 1940, 1; 1985, 33). No doubt such disclaimers express a conventional piety in medieval religious works, but again and again the prologue asserts that Margery is recording her story not for self-aggrandizement but "that his goodness might be known to all the world." The anxieties surrounding female self-assertion and female speech require that this mode of textual production—the mystical autobiography—be explained, justified, and even mediated by some other authority. Like other female mystics, then, Margery does not claim to speak and write in her own name; she does not claim "authority" over her "authorship" in the same way a modern author might. But she could and did claim to ventriloquize a divine voice, to become a vessel through which God speaks.

Yet even within the short scene of the prologue, Margery dominates the text, dictating the terms on which the writing will take place, mediating between human cultural activities—like writing—and God's "goodness," creating a struggle between two concepts of the subject. Even in small details, the prologue works to establish Margery as the controlling voice, the text's authoring presence. The explanation of the autobiography's failure to keep to chronological sequence is a disarming example of the book's claims to "orality," to a successful representation of the speaking voice and its guarantee of the author's presence: "This book is not written in order, everything after the other as it was done, but just as the matter came to this creature's mind when it was to be written down, for it was so long before it was written that she had forgotten the time and the order when things occurred" (1940, 5; 1985, 36). Memory, the organizing principle of the oral culture, structures Margery's memoirs. The possibilities that writing holds out for revision, for the shaping of experience, are at the same time proffered and withheld, perhaps because of the perceived dangers these possibilities harbored: such shaping and revision might call into doubt the authenticity, the truth, of the book by transforming and deforming memory into a self-consciously literary form.

Other problems associated with writing, the circumstances that might come between the author's words and meanings—bad penmanship and spelling, poor eyesight, language barriers, fear of ostracization, punishment, and censorship—are all negotiated through Margery's powerful presence. Her demonstration of God's favor is the enabling condition of the narrative. Finally, nothing short of a miracle, mediated by Margery, will ensure the completion of the project.

> When the priest first began to write this book, his eyes failed, so that he could not see to form his letters and could not see to mend his pen. All other things he could see well enough. He set a pair of spectacles on his nose, and then it was much worse than it was before. He complained to the creature about his troubles. She said his enemy was envious of his good deed and would hinder him if he might, and she bade him do as well as God would give him grace and not give up. When he came back to his book again, he could see as well, he thought, as he ever did before both by daylight and by candlelight. (1940, 5; 1985, 37)

Even though Margery is illiterate, even in the act of writing itself, which is presumably out of her powers, the text tells us it is "she for God alone, he for God in her." She reverses the typical medieval gender relation which sees the male as essence, the female as accident. Margery attempts through this "miracle" to cancel or transcend the deferral of writing from speech, of inscription from the monological voice of God, and thereby to ensure the absolute authority of her own claims by locating her written text within an authoritative Logos that is spoken and prophetic. The text consciously strives to overcome the difference that writing necessarily preserves—the openness to interpretation and deformation—and to recuperate logocentric assumptions about the spoken word as a guarantee of access to the truth. Time and again the text self-consciously attempts to reproduce the structures of oral communication. Throughout *The Book*, Margery depends upon the spoken word as the source of her power. She preaches, confesses, narrates her life story to anyone who will listen, hears confessions (of sorts), and converses both with God and with powerful churchmen.

But at the same time that it creates Margery the visionary as the ground of the text and guarantor of its signification, the proem displays a curious anxiety about writing and its possible abuses. Writing occasionally reveals itself as an alienating technology in *The Book*; it is more closely associated with the literate clergy than with homegrown visionaries. What is interesting in the prologue is the variety of ways in which writing is shown to deform Margery's story, creating barriers between the reader and the authorizing presence of Margery's divinely inspired experience. The effect of the prologue is to make us doubt the existence in the text of a transcendent "self" whose words reflect accurately and in an unmediated way a life story.

The proem repeatedly calls attention to the difficulties involved in writing Margery's life and the distance between the actual recording of her story and the original events. Twenty years pass, we are told, between Margery's first visionary experiences and her decision to record them. When she finally finds someone to write her story down, it is a man—possibly her son; the text is unclear—"dwelling in Germany who was an Englishman by birth and afterwards married in Germany" (1940, 4; 1985, 35). He dies before the project can be finished. Margery then takes his work to a priest and asks him to read it. "The book was so ill-written that he could make little sense of it, for it was neither good English nor good German, nor were the letters formed or shaped as other letters are" (1940, 4; 1985, 35). Still, the priest promises to try to rewrite it. When a scandal arises around Kempe, the priest "for cowardice" refuses to speak with her and "avoided and deferred the writing" for four years. Finally he tells her he cannot read the book, will not finish it, and furthermore is afraid to put his life in peril by having anything more to do with her. He advises her to take the book to yet another man who had known the original scribe, "supposing that he would best know how to read the book." This man tries to write a leaf and finds it too difficult, "the book was so badly set down and written quite without reason." Finally the first priest, being pricked by his conscience, agrees to try to read and finish the book. "Trusting in her prayers," the priest begins to read the book and miraculously is able to understand it: "so he read it over before this creature every word, she sometime helping where there was any difficulty" (1940, 5; 1985, 35).

To say that this book was beset by problems of writing would be an understatement. Between Margery's experiences and the first transcription of them there is a gap of twenty years, the gap of memory. The language problems created by the first, bilingual scribe further deform these memoirs before they can be reconstructed (with Margery's help) by the priest who finally, after four or five years, agrees to redraft the text, a gap of memory, transcription, and translation. The processes of transcription and re-transciption work against the overtly stated claims to an unmediated presence of Margery's authoritative voice. She becomes a literary construct. Margery's experiences, her "self" (in the Cartesian sense of the word), recedes in the face of the "violence" of writing. The reader encounters "Margery" at three removes (at least); the presence of her voice—of mystical experience—cannot be recuperated.

There is, then, no "woman writer" in *The Book of Margery Kempe*. Instead the "self," Margery's self, is experienced as diffuse, incomplete, internally contradictory and in dialogue with other reconstitutions of herself. What is particularly interesting is the constitution and interaction of male and female "selves" in this text. Jacques Derrida has, somewhat enigmatically, described this intersubjectivity in "The Ear of the Other" when he writes, "I will even risk affirming this hypothesis, that the very sex of the addresser receives its determination from the other who will perhaps decide who I am, man or woman. And it is not the case that it is decided once and for all; but it can be decided like that some other time" (quoted in Miller 1982, 48). The text's concern with the struggle between Margery and her priest/scribe does not end with the proem, with the description of the text's transcription. Their relationship has not been given stable reference by its account of writing or by the attempt to create a subject, Margery, who can exist unproblematically on the written page. Instead, the text of her life is dialogic, a recreative process that diffuses Margery's story and shapes the narrative of events. In one sense, the priest functions as part of Margery's "self," a skeptical voice within the voice of the authoritative mystic. His faith in Margery's spiritual powers must be constantly validated. In chapter 24, for example, the priest suddenly emerges as a central actor in the narrative when he refuses to continue working on the book unless Margery shows some sign of her special grace by revealing the future to him. Reluctantly she agrees and reveals her prophetic "felyngys" to him, but in this case, he does not believe her or act on her advice. I would venture to guess (although it is impossible to verify this hunch) that it is at least partly his and not Margery's obsession with what other people are saying about her—his concern about slander, gossip, and censure—that permeates the text and makes Margery seem so self-obsessed, so conscious of how others view her. He functions at one and the same time as editor and critic. His textual space becomes that between literary transcription and the ideal of authoritative speech.

What the reader encounters in this instance and throughout *The Book of Margery Kempe* is not the "authentic voice" of a medieval woman, not a revelation of a female subjectivity that the rest of medieval history has erased, but a dialogized subjectivity, fractured and intersected by other voices. The collaboration between Margery and her scribe produces no neat synthesis, no single unified "voice," but a babel of contradictory and conflicting cultural signs—noise—which can be read only against the backdrop of the social realignments of fifteenth-century England. Besides illuminating the relations between men and women in medieval society, this collaboration also reveals, among other things, the insecurity of an "urban bourgeoisie" struggling to define itself in a world that recognized only two classes and the attempts of the religious laity to find an outlet for their spirituality within a Church monopolized by the clergy.[21] Finally, as I have suggested, this collaboration exposes the conflicts between a conservative, logocentric oral culture, in which voice and bodily presence confer meaning, and an increasingly literate and disseminated one, which challenges the authoritative claims of hierarchical models of oral communication. All these developments contribute to the complexities of fifteenth-century gender relationships. An analysis that focuses only on the relentless pursuit of the woman writer risks effacing this kind of cultural and political activity, as well as its effects on gender relations.

The more complex and diffuse notions of subjectivity that are at work (subversively) in *The Book of Margery Kempe* may help illuminate how the act of writing itself focuses the cultural as well as gender anxieties of the late Middle Ages. In the last chapter, I examined some of the ways in which writing, as a technology, accelerated political, economic, and familial changes that accompanied a redistribution of power and wealth among the aristocracy of twelfth-century France. In "The Emergence of the Individual," Georges Duby and Philippe Braunstein describe the effect of the dissemination of writing on fourteenth- and fifteenth-century life, particularly on the moneyed and propertied classes:

Writing was associated with a concern that one's property be administered well and that one's heirs inherit a capital consisting

[21]See Delany 1983, 76–92, for an analysis of the economic realignments in the late Middle Ages which created this "urban patriciate." In the economy of the early fifteenth century, she argues, money began to mediate relationships in some of the same ways it would under capitalism: "The development of industry and of mercantile capitalism meant that goods were no longer being produced for immediate use, but rather for sale in domestic and foreign markets; they were to be exchanged not for other goods but for money. Money could be accumulated then reinvested for profit or lent at interest; large fortunes could be rapidly made; the big bourgeoisie could subsidize kings and impoverished aristocrats, buy titles and estates, and successfully compete with the feudal aristocracy for political power" (85).

not only of real estate but also of spiritual precepts and memoirs. . . . It was difficult to administer or bequeath such spiritual capital if it was not organized. After 1350 an effort was therefore made to catalog and arrange the material in these family archives, stored in shops, offices, and palace studies: contracts, accounts, lists of births and deaths, remedies and potions, correspondence, family trees. Originally these records were kept on note cards, reminders which can often be seen stuck on nails in portraits of merchants and artisans. These gradually gave way to notebooks and ledgers in which debits and credits were recorded. It was some time before a distinction was made between commercial and household accounts, and between household records and personal memoirs. (in Duby 1988, 549)

This businesslike approach to writing—with its cultural construction of the self as a life, a narrative to be documented rather than assumed from orthodox religious conceptions of spiritual growth—is frequently displayed in Kempe's narrative, which bizarrely juxtaposes economic and social insecurities to religious concerns. Much at first glance might seem puzzling and even repellent in *The Book of Margery Kempe*, but in the emerging writing economy of the fifteenth century, the detail with which Margery's business ventures and losses are rendered along with her spiritual debits and credits registers the class-specific nature of the transcription of her religious experience. It suggests why her spiritual last will and testament, appointing God as executor, has about as much lyricism as a tax audit (1940, 20–21). And it explains both the niggling concern with the documentation of outlays—debt repayments, traveling expenses, and the like—and the tendency for Margery's spirituality to draw upon this same language of economics. Writing has not yet "organized" experience into neat little packets that distinguish business records from household accounts or from spiritual and visionary events; it has not yet constituted a "male experience" in the public sphere apart from a "female experience" of the private, domestic "self."

"What is an author?" Foucault asks. "What difference does it make who is speaking?" (1979, 160). Clearly, it makes a difference, a political difference, if one wants to recover something of medieval gender relations from the perspective of the powerless as well as the powerful or if one wants to understand the material oppression and resistance of real women. But the sorts of questions such an inquiry spawns also make a difference, and that too is finally a political difference. If as feminists we ask, to paraphrase Foucault (1979, 160), Who really spoke? Is it really she and not someone else? With what authenticity and originality? And what part of her deepest self did she express in her discourse? then we are perpetuating essentialist notions of the subject, of masculinity and femininity, and of the text as a closed hermeneutical totality. If instead we ask, again paraphrasing Foucault, What are the modes of existence of this discourse? Where has it been used, how can it circulate, and who can appropriate it for herself? What are the places in it where there is room for possible subjects? Who can assume these various subject-functions? then we open up our criticism to a more dialogic conception of subjectivity and gender relations, as well as to the historical and political struggles through which they are constituted and resisted. This concept of the "dialogic subject" and its effects on the formulation of gender relations in eighteenth-century England is the subject of the next chapter.

4

Style as Noise: Identity and Ideology in *A Vindication of the Rights of Woman*

The access to writing is the constitution of a free subject in the violent moment of its own effacement and of its own bondage.

—Jacques Derrida

To persuade someone to publish this book, I had first to convince several persons in authority—primarily editors and readers—that I had successfully created the illusion of a single-voiced "I" of énoncé, a speaking subject who, by virtue of the autonomy and coherence of my "voice," would authorize the autonomy and coherence of my text.[1] Drafts of chapters were met with friendly exhortations to "experiment with freeing my own voice" or to make my writing "less obsessively other-oriented," more dramatic and less dialogic. Not surprisingly, these critics read with Foucault's first set of questions in mind. Is it really "me" speaking and not someone else? Is what "I" am saying original, new? To be sure, these are the questions that publishers ask their readers to consider. They are conventions that govern the speech genre of academic publishing which we do not often think about in our work, unless we are trying to make the argument, as I am, that all language is dialogic and therefore continually interanimated by other words and other voices. If we want to challenge the illusion of a single "voice" that unifies the text, then perhaps we might want to consider how pronouns like "I" and "we" function to create seemingly unified semiotic fields—individuals, authors, readers—out of disparate linguistic materials (Benveniste 1971). In this chapter I examine how these processes operate ideologically in

[1] For a discussion of enunciation in language, see Benveniste 1971, 217–22; and Belsey 1980, 56–84.

light of recent theoretical debates—like the one to which Foucault is contributing—on the nature of subjectivity.

What happens when women publicly express their subjectivity through writing is less clear-cut, as I have tried to suggest, than many feminist accounts of female authorship might suggest. Nancy K. Miller, in a 1981 exchange with Peggy Kamuf at Cornell University, takes exception to what she sees as Foucault's "sovereign indifference" to the writer. She has in mind, of course, specifically the woman writer. In reply to his question "What does it matter who's speaking?" she writes: "What matter who's speaking? I would answer it matters, for example, to women who have lost and still routinely lose their proper name in marriage, and whose signature—not merely their voice—has not been worth the paper it was written on; women for whom the signature—by virtue of its power in the world of circulation—is *not* immaterial. Only those who have it can play with not having it" (1982, 53). In her comments, Miller expresses the anxieties of feminist critics that poststructuralist theories of authorship, which decenter and fragment the subject into a textual construction, simply reassert male hegemony in yet another guise because they foreclose feminist discussions of real female subjects' agency and resistance to dominant ideologies. If the postmodern subject, as envisioned by writers as diverse as Lacan, Derrida, Foucault, and Kristeva, is a provisional subject, a process of becoming, "suspended in a continual moment of fabrication," rather than a stable or fixed entity of being, then "woman" as such does not exist any more than "man." The "subject" of feminism simply evaporates in the free play of the text (Miller 1986, 270). But this decentering, she argues, is as much an effect of power as the assertion of stable identity. The marginal and the oppressed—those who are not white, middle-class, or male—have always experienced the self as fragmented and subjectivity as subjection. Only those who have secure and fixed identities can afford the luxury of fragmenting them. The very real danger posed by theories of the "decentered" subject, then, is that in their movement to the margins those theorists at the center of Western philosophy reinforce their own centrality by co-opting the position of those already at the margins, preventing the truly marginalized any subject position from which to articulate their exclusion.

I would not want to deny that at its most formalist and idealist the poststructuralist preference for textual production over authorial signature erases gender difference, neutralizing the female by collapsing it into the hegemonic and "universal" male. Miller's critique of Geoffrey Hartman's and J. Hillis Miller's effacement of the female subject in their appropriation of the myths of Ariadne and Arachne convincingly demonstrates this tendency (1986, 281–86). But feminist literary critics' fear of the text without an author results primarily from their ideological commitment to "gynocritics" and the assertion of an essential women's experience through the recuperation of the woman writer. We need to interrogate the investments such a program requires in a concept of stable identity and an authenticity and originality rooted in an ontological "self." Perhaps because, as feminist psychologists such as Nancy Chodorow have argued (1978), women have usually experienced their "selves" as already fragmented and the boundaries of their egos as more fluid, feminist thought has insisted upon reasserting the autonomy and coherence of the female "self." Historically, because women have been responsible for virtually all dependency relationships within the family, they have been denied the necessary independence through which white, middle-class men construct a sense of independent selfhood. Therefore, it has been the project of feminism to enable women to construct the same powerful sense of identity as men. But the search for "authentic" women's experience, for the woman writer who expresses herself authentically, grounds the female "self" in a Western mind/body dualism that ironically reinforces the very ideology of bourgeois individualism feminists wish to resist. As Nancy Armstrong has written, "If we simply assume that gender differentiation is at the root of human identity, we can understand neither the totalizing power of this figure nor the very real interests such power inevitably serves. . . . any political position founded primarily on sexual identity ultimately confirms the limited choices offered by such a dyadic model" (1987, 24). I wish to explore in this chapter the historical construction in the eighteenth century of this dyadic model of subjectivity and the powerful interests it serves.

Even Foucault does not say that it does *not* matter who speaks; he asks, "*What* does it matter?" And like Miller, he answers the question he raises. It matters, but for different reasons from those we have in the past supposed: not because a fixed, preexisting self expresses itself through discourse but because discourses—historically situated discourses—are part of the evolving, open-ended, and shifting process of becoming a subject. The contemporary theoretical concern with destabilizing subjectivity must be theorized relationally and historically rather than categorically. To dismantle the opposition between the fixed and stable self of Cartesian rationalism and the radically decentered and fragmented subject of Derridean deconstruction which has limited feminist discussions of subjectivity we need to explore the complex nexus of material, social, and historical practices through which subjectivity—and gendered subjectivity in particular has been constructed. The invention of the woman writer as the theoretical ground of her text's meaning is itself a historical process.

In other words, subjectivity does not transcend history or, as the cases of the trobairitz and the medieval women mystics suggest, the material and cultural conditions of its production. Modern philosophy and psychology have tended to take the subject out of history, to universalize subjectivity by locating it outside of the political and social in the atemporal realm of reason or the apolitical realm of the family. The specific historical practices that led to modern notions of subjectivity, particularly that of the political individual as the possessor of certain "natural rights," has, since the seventeenth century, also been the subject of feminism.[2] To theorize this process, it is necessary to examine the role of language in the historical construction of subjectivity. Following Benveniste (1971) and Vološinov/Bakhtin (1986), I argue that the individual is constructed out of the languages available to the subject in her culture; subjectivity, that is, is primarily semiotic. In the eighteenth century, during the period in which modern notions of the individual took shape, semiotic activity created a site of contention

[2]For a discussion of possessive individualism as it developed in seventeenth- and eighteenth-century political thought, see Macpherson 1962. For discussions of feminism's relationship to "natural rights" philosophy, see Eisenstein 1981; and Delmar 1986.

and struggle which redefined power relations among classes, cultures, and genders. The modern gendered individual was fashioned out of the languages that consolidated middle-class culture in Europe.[3]

By the end of the eighteenth century, those at the "center" of Western culture—primarily white upper- and middle-class men—conceived of the self as autonomous and unified, atomized and separate from other selves. Throughout the eighteenth and nineteenth centuries, this view of the subject provided the ideological legitimation for capitalism, imperialism, entrepreneurial growth, and the movement of labor from the home to the factory. The theoretical rationale for this view of the self has its origins in seventeenth- and eighteenth-century philosophy, particularly in Hobbes, Descartes, and Locke. But the success of the ideology of bourgeois individualism depended primarily upon two significant and interdependent semiotic realignments: the development of public arenas outside of the monarch's court for intellectual and cultural exchange and a reconception of the family within texts for and about women which deemphasized genealogical ties and elevated domesticity as the primary means by which the individual locates him- or herself within society.

The bourgeois "public sphere" provided one network of specific and heterogeneous sites in which individuals—men primarily—could be constituted as subjects by sharing in a consensus of universal reason.[4] The public sphere comprised many eighteenth-century social institutions—clubs, periodicals, coffeehouses, journals, salons, spas, and resorts—in which private individuals could assemble for the free and equal exchange of reasonable discourse. These institutions provided both discursive and physical spaces apart from the hierarchized, finely articulated network of genealogical relationships which marked cultural and political identities at court. In the coffeehouses, clubs, and periodicals of the early

---

[3]Felicity Nussbaum, in examining the historical situation of female subjectivity in eighteenth-century autobiography, also argues that the individual must be seen as a locus of intersection among cultural discourses (1988).

[4]For discussions of the eighteenth-century public sphere, see Hohendahl 1982; Eagleton 1984, 9–27; Stallybrass and White 1986, 80–84; also Habermas 1962.

eighteenth century, propertied men of different classes—the aristocracy, the "squirearchy," the City, and the professions—came together as equals, as "men of reason." These alliances, however, were never as homogeneous as some commentators have suggested. Nor was the public sphere simply a collection of "ideas or ideals" that articulated a new ideology of middle-class judgment and taste. The exchanges that took place within those spaces were material as well as intellectual; they produced not only the *Tatler* and *Spectator* but the stock exchange and Lloyds as well (Stallybrass and White 1986, 99–100).

Within the public sphere, identities were not preestablished but "constructed by the very act of participation in polite conversation" (Eagleton 1984, 14–15), creating a "quasi-transcendental community of subjects" (15) which laid the groundwork for modern notions of the rational, self-interested political individual. The claims made for the equalizing power of reason served to mediate, at least superficially, the conflicting interests of the landed and privileged aristocracy and the wealthy but often politically marginal middle class. Indeed, it was the function of these institutions to "negotiate cultural alliances between the gentry, the Court, and the town" (Stallybrass and White 1986, 83). Reason did not distinguish between aristocrat and commoner. At least within the spaces of the public sphere, power and position no longer conferred cultural authority. Instead, "the speech act itself, the *énonciation* as opposed to the *énoncé*, figures in its very form an equality, autonomy and reciprocity at odds with its class-bound content" (Eagleton 1984, 14). Besides temporarily suppressing class distinctions, the discursive space established by the public sphere took individuals out of history; reason assumed the status of a universalizing, transcendental ground of identity: *cogito ergo sum*.

But this account of the history of the modern individual is at best only partial. The development of the public sphere was connected to and depended upon the simultaneous development of an equally ahistorical and universalized private space. The domestic sphere of the home and the family became a site in which everyday practices performed on the body—including such things as manners, dress, and hygeine—could create new ideologies and new power relations. In *Outline of a Theory of Practice*, Bourdieu suggests the potency of these apparently insignificant practices to imbue ideological values.

> If all societies and, significantly, all the "totalitarian institutions" . . . that seek to produce a new man through a process of "deculturation" and "reculturation" set such store on the seemingly most insignificant details of *dress, bearing,* physical and verbal *manners,* the reason is that, treating the body as a memory, they entrust to it in abbreviated and practical, i.e., mnemonic, form the fundamental principles of the arbitrary content of culture. The principles em-bodied in this way are placed beyond the grasp of consciousness, and hence cannot be touched by voluntary, deliberate transformation, cannot even be made explicit; nothing seems more ineffable, more incommunicable, more inimitable, and therefore, more precious, than the values given body, *made* body. (1977, 94)

The regulation of the body through these practices becomes a means of fashioning subjectivity out of ideology. Their aim is to make "socially desirable behavior automatic, a matter of self-control, causing it to appear in the consciousness of the individual as the result of his own free will" (Elias 1978, 150). In the eighteenth century, the historically specific practices that regulated the body constructed new subjects in the privatized space of the home. The conduct books, educational treatises, and domestic fiction from which such practices emerged were designed to inculcate such middle-class virtues as neatness, industry, morality, economy, modesty, and discretion even before the middle-class ever existed (Armstrong 1987, 66).

If the public sphere was confined primarily to propertied men, the domestic sphere was presided over by women. Indeed, Nancy Armstrong maintains that "the modern individual was first and foremost a woman," that "a modern, gendered form of subjectivity developed first as a feminine discourse in certain literature for women before it provided the semiotic of nineteenth-century . . . psychological theory" (1987, 8, 14). Moreso than through the epistemological and philosophical debates of the eighteenth-century public sphere, Armstrong argues, modern notions of gendered subjectivity—of masculine and feminine identities—before they ever actually existed in social practice, were worked out semiotically through fiction, conduct books, and educational treatises written for women. A subjectivity "engendered" and shaped within the domestic sphere gave women certain powers and authority in the reproduction of bourgeois hegemony denied them in aristocratic culture. Within a privatized and naturalized ideology of the family, under the watchful eye of feminine surveillance, our peculiarly modern notions of the self became commonplace. Later, in the nineteenth century, the emerging sciences of psychology and sociology would reproduce the semiotics of domestic texts written for women, refiguring political and economic problems in terms of sexual conduct and domestic order (Armstrong 1987, 180–82). The practice of blaming poverty on the degeneration of the family continues unabated today among politicians and academics, its ideological investments masked by rhetoric about traditional family values.

Significantly, the beginnings of feminist "consciousness"—the first arguments for a uniquely female self claiming the right to equality with men—may be traced to the eighteenth century as well. Feminist discourse marks at least one point of convergence between these two discursive formations I have been describing—the public sphere and the domestic organization of the family—at the end of the century. To demonstrate this claim I turn now to examine how the eighteenth century feminist Mary Wollstonecraft constructs a female and feminist self in *A Vindication of the Rights of Woman* as a *bricolage* of the public and domestic discourses available to her—in particular, those of philosophy, the gothic novel, and bourgeois sentimentality. A close examination of Wollstonecraft's treatise illustrates, I believe, the interdependence of the public and domestic spheres in defining a uniquely modern but historically specific individual. It may also provide an opportunity to "deconstruct" modern subjectivity by revealing the cracks and fissures within this formation when the speaking subject has been gendered as a woman, when she must claim to be speaking from within the public sphere while calling upon the authority of domesticity.

A Philosophic Wanton

The publication in 1792 of *A Vindication of the Rights of Woman* provoked a predictably violent reaction. Horace Walpole, in a letter to Hannah More, described its author as one of "the philosophizing serpents we have in our bosom," and later as a "hyena in petticoats." A review of William Godwin's *Memoirs of the Author of "A Vindication of the Rights of Woman"* in *European Magazine* describes Wollstonecraft posthumously as a "philosophic wanton" (Wardle 1951, 159, 318). Although her book was not everywhere viewed with such loathing in the eighteenth century as these remarks suggest, a woman philosopher claiming to speak from within the public sphere and assuming the equality granted to "men of reason" could be dismissed as unnatural, a perversion of nature. Dr. James Fordyce in *Sermons for Young Women* writes, "You yourself, I think, will allow that war, commerce, politics, exercises of strength and dexterity, abstract philosophy, and all the abstruser sciences are most properly the province of men. I am sure those masculine women, that would plead for your sharing any part of this province equally with us, do not understand your interests" (London, 1792; quoted in Wardle 1951, 140). Just as women lacked the physical strength to wage war, so the argument went, they lacked the mental dexterity, the ability to reason abstractly, required of philosophy and of all discourse within the public sphere. Any woman who could pretend to such abilities must be unsexed, a "masculine woman." Her intellectual transgressions could easily be figured as sexual transgressions.

Philosophy, however, is exactly what Wollstonecraft set out to write in *A Vindication of the Rights of Woman* and what so many of her contemporaries vilified her for attempting to write. A philosopher, Wollstonecraft writes elsewhere, "dedicates his existence to promote the welfare, and perfection of mankind, carrying his views beyond any time he chooses to mark" (1796, v–vi). In *Rights of Woman* she claims, "Rousseau exerts himself to prove that all *was* right: a crowd of authors that all *is* now right: and I, that all will *be* right" (1975, 15). *A Vindication of the Rights of Woman* is Wollstonecraft's vision of what woman's place should be in a perfected society, her articulation of a specifically female identity within the public sphere. Her feminism, in this respect, is inseparable from the philosophy of egalitarianism which made her a staunch supporter of the ideals of the French Revolution and which, at least implicitly, also supported the rhetoric of rationality which characterized the eighteenth-century bourgeois public sphere in which Wollstonecraft tried to claim membership.

But we cannot understand Wollstonecraft's attempt to stake out a subject position from which to articulate her sense of the "wrongs of woman" without understanding the historical moment from which she speaks. In particular, it is necessary to know that the alliances forged within the discursive formation of the "public sphere" during the first decades of the eighteenth century had become fractured and divided by the end of the century. The consensus of reason and the commonality of interest was beginning to disintegrate. Terry Eagleton (1984, 30 38) cites several reasons for the demise of the "classical" bourgeois public sphere. The first is purely economic, a change in the modes of production and consumption of texts. A rapid expansion of literary production at the end of the century began to outpace the social relations that made possible the institutions supported by the public sphere— periodicals, clubs, journals. An expansion in wealth, population, and education created a larger, more heterogeneous middle class eager for reading materials, while technologies in printing and publishing made such an expansion possible, but under radically different conditions. The decline of literary patronage, for instance, increased the power of the bookseller. Thus, "as capitalist society develops and market forces come increasingly to determine the destiny of literary products, it is no longer possible to assume that 'taste' or 'cultivation' are the fruits of civilized dialogue and reasonable debate" (34). This new, more "vulgar" reading public could not be expected to participate in a reasonable and objective discourse on "taste," nor could those who had participated in the discourse of the public sphere be expected to recognize the extent to which their "reasonable and objective discourse on taste" was tinged with the values and interests of the propertied classes. The second factor that undermined the consensus of the public sphere is related. The expansion of the reading public meant that the social and political interests of the propertied classes could no longer dominate public discourse to the exclusion of all others. Once one has made the argument that the universalizing discourse of reason obliterates class distinctions between aristocrat and merchant, it is a slippery slope to the argument that other dispossessed groups must be included within the equalizing sphere of reason. During the late eighteenth century, those groups whose interests fell outside the articulated interest of the public sphere and who posed a material threat to its hegemony became increasingly vocal. Eagleton cites such counterhegemonic institutions as the corresponding societies, the radical press, the dissenting churches, and of course, feminism as examples of what he calls a "counter public sphere," a "whole oppositional network of journals, clubs, pamphlets, debates, and institutions" which "invades the dominant consensus, threatening to fragment it from within" (36).

The historical "place" from which Wollstonecraft speaks must be located within this "counter public sphere." Her argument for the rights of woman cannot be separated from this larger network of counterhegemonic discourses institutionalized in the late eighteenth century through many of the same apparatuses that served earlier in the century in the formation of the public sphere: periodicals, clubs, journals, and publishing houses. In this respect, Wollstonecraft's experience is almost paradigmatic. Upon her arrival in London, she came under the influence of the publisher Joseph Johnson, who was eventually to publish all her writing. At his house in 72 St. Paul's Churchyard, she became acquainted with a circle of intellectuals of liberal and radical leanings. These included John Bonnycastle, a mathematician; George Fordyce, a physician; George Anderson, a classical scholar; Alexander Geddes, a biblical scholar; Henry Fuseli, the Swiss painter; and later Thomas Paine, author of *Rights of Man*; the poet William Blake, and her future husband, William Godwin (Wardle 1951, 94). Wollstonecraft wrote prolifically for the *Analytical Review*, the periodical founded by Johnson in 1788. Indeed her entire literary production is bound up with her membership in Johnson's "circle"; it provided the material, financial, intellectual, and emotional support necessary for her project. Essential to her ability to assert herself as a speaking subject was her membership within a public sphere of reasonable discourse. Ironically, the very presence of people like her (i.e., women) within this public sphere created the contradictions that would eventually lead to its demise. The public sphere could survive—at least in its eighteenth-century form—only so long as those who spoke and wrote within it could maintain their pose of disinterested rationality, so long as they could mask their own interests and exclusions and suppress the contradictions upon which the public sphere was founded. Wollstonecraft's oppositional practices could not help but call this pose into question. Speaking within a public sphere designed to create male subjectivity—and a class-based subjectivity at that—Wollstonecraft had to find a language in which to express something that did not really exist within that sphere: a rational female subjectivity. The only cultural language adaptable to her purpose—outside that of rationality—was the language of domesticity. What make *Rights of Woman* such a fascinating text are the ways in which it embodies and plays out the contradictions between public and domestic identities not only in its contents but in its style as well.

Throughout, *A Vindication of the Rights of Woman* seems an argument at odds with itself, attesting to the ideological difficulties inherent in its project. Contradictions are everywhere apparent, as countless critics have pointed out. These contradictions, I would argue, are not logical flaws but productive tensions that reveal the impossibility within eighteenth-century philosophical discourse of creating a rational speaking subject who is also a woman. Wollstonecraft begins with the premise that all human beings, women included, are rational and that through the exercise of reason the lot of mankind, and womankind, can be improved. She believes that "from the exercise of reason, knowledge and virtue naturally flow" (12). In passages such as these, Wollstonecraft most clearly reveals her commitment to the eighteenth-century ideals of the public sphere, to the belief in the essential equality of individuals as rational beings. Reason, not class or sexual hierarchies, she says, provides the glue that "binds society." Wollstonecraft, mistakenly as it turns out, assumes that the abstract equality of reason promised by the classical public sphere, which generally existed to articulate the interests and culture of *propertied men*, could be extended as well to the nonpropertied and to women. But women's "state of degradation," which she sees as unnatural, has been institutionalized by the "authorities" (many of them men) who have written about women in conduct books and educational treatises. At first, Wollstonecraft's use of texts written for women and belonging more properly to the domestic sphere seems incongruous, at odds with her claims of philosophical seriousness. But it is precisely Wollstonecraft's need to call upon the language of domesticity articulated in conduct books and educational manuals to construct female identity which provides the deconstructive moment in *Rights of Woman*. Wollstonecraft's attempt to weld these two opposing discourses—the public discourse of political philosophy and the private discourse of domesticity—into a single argument creates tensions and contradictions within the text which ultimately lead to its unraveling. The "rationality" that argues for the subjugation of women cannot be divorced from the domestic institutions that by the end of the eighteenth century shaped the lives of both men and women. By the end of *Rights of Woman*, neither philosophy nor reason exists as timeless or universal, set apart from other social practices; they must develop from an "early association of ideas"—that is, from the socializing process of a largely domestic education.

With the benefit of over a century's hindsight, Virginia Woolf notes that Wollstonecraft's arguments in *Rights of Woman* are at once original and clichéd; they are, she states, "so true that they seem now to contain nothing new in them" (Woolf 1932, 176). From the perspective of the late eighteenth century, however, Wollstonecraft's difficulties seem insurmountable. She wants to make an argument for women as public agents, but she has no language out of which to construct this role except that of the masculine public sphere. The languages of female subjectivity located women exclusively within the family at the same time as they denied women public agency. The separation of public from domestic is the founding split of the bourgeois hegemony. To create the male as an autonomous independent agent in the public sphere, bourgeois ideology had to relegate all dependency relations that might undermine that independent selfhood to the domestic realm under the supervision of women. The ideology that supports separate spheres for men and women, then, is the same ideology that constructs identity, selfhood. For women to move out of the sphere assigned to them and adopt a public persona would be to expose the contradictions and exclusions the ideology of bourgeois individualism was designed to mystify.[5] Wollstonecraft continually struggles with these contradictions. She accepts without question that domesticity is the "natural" occupation for women; their primary duties ought to be nurturing children and managing their households. Women should be given rights, she argues, primarily to make them better mothers, to prepare them to exercise their domestic authority. "When I treat of the peculiar duties of woman," she writes, "as I should treat of the peculiar duties of a citizen or father it will be found that I do not mean to insinuate that they should be taken out of their families, speaking of the majority" (63). Later she writes, "As the care of children in their infancy is one of the grand duties annexed to the female character by nature, this duty would afford many forcible arguments for strengthening the female understanding, if it were properly considered" (151). These statements are characteristic of most of Wollstonecraft's argument. Women "belong" in some essential way "in" the family. The care of children is given to women "by nature." She accepts as biological facts the social imperatives that limit women (with some exceptions) to roles as wives and mothers.

Yet without making Wollstonecraft into a twentieth-century feminist, we can perceive in places a more radical tendency toward asserting the rights of women to public identities—to roles that allow her to articulate the social, political, or economic interests of women. At times she verges on promoting women's political independence *from* domesticity, frequently casting her argument in economic terms: "How many women thus waste life away the prey of discontent, who might have practised as physicians, regulated a farm, managed a shop, and stood erect, supported by their own industry, instead of hanging their heads surcharged with the dew of sensibility, that consumes the beauty to which it at first gave lustre" (149). Passages such as this one work against the ideology of domesticity that Wollstonecraft generally accepts. In this re-

[5]For a discussion of the political ramifications of bourgeois individualism and the split between public and domestic spheres, see Eisenstein 1981, esp. 55–112. For a discussion of the formation of gendered identity within the domestic sphere, see Armstrong 1987.

spect, at times her argument is often forthrightly egalitarian and feminist. But these moments also reveal the contradictions that the emerging ideologies of bourgeois egalitarianism and feminism created for women. Wollstonecraft has to argue that if women are to be better mothers and wives, they must have at least the choice of alternative ways of living.

Nowhere are the contradictions between the bourgeois and the radical in Wollstonecraft's thinking more evident than in her penultimate chapter on the reform of national education. She argues for an equality within marriage which hinges on equality of education for both sexes: "If marriage be the cement of society, mankind should all be educated after the same model, or the intercourse of the sexes will never deserve the name of fellowship, nor will women ever fulfill the peculiar duties of their sex, till they become enlightened citizens, till they become free by being enabled to earn their own subsistence, independent of men; in the same manner, I mean, to prevent misconstruction, as one man is independent of another" (165). The implication of her argument is clearly radical: women must be given greater political and economic freedom to exercise their rights in new and, at least for her critics, potentially disruptive ways. Education becomes inseparable, in Wollstonecraft's mind, from equality of opportunity for the sexes. As she explains, her notion of equality is based on eighteenth-century, particularly Lockean, notions of selfhood which envision individuals as atomized and disconnected from social relations. But she is careful to subsume "education" within the framework of bourgeois gender roles that dictate a division between public and domestic identities. She is unable to see how this ideology of the subject rests on the recuperation of social connectedness in the domestic sphere. If women are to preside over all dependency relationships, they will obviously be unable to participate in the ideology of individualism which requires agents free from social dependency.

Style as Ideology

Even though the critics, both her contemporaries and ours, have perceived in *Rights of Woman* well-defined speech genres—history, politics, education, philosophy—the work has frequently been attacked for its stylistic transgressions precisely because of these contradictions. Wollstonecraft's husband, William Godwin, calls it "a very unequal performance and eminently deficient in method and arrangement" (1974, 83). Mary Hays notes in her memoirs of Wollstonecraft that "in perspicuity and arrangement it must be confessed to be defective" (quoted in Wollstonecraft 1975, 212). Even its more recent critics, while admitting the text's undeniable power, harp on the same flaws its original critics were so fond of pointing out. Ralph Wardle writes condescendingly of it: "The book is tedious. Did she write it in six weeks? Then would she have spent six years on it! . . . Its worst fault is its lack of organization" (1951, 156). Eleanor Flexner says that Wollstonecraft's "lack of education is also shown in her inability to organize material, to follow a consistent train of thought, or to avoid digressions when they are largely irrelevant and in her habit of loose organization. She is incapable either of the coherent organization of ideas or of avoiding repetition" (1972, 164)

This criticism, however, faults Wollstonecraft for her disregard of philosophical authority and for not conforming to what most would acknowledge as the rhetorical rules of the public sphere: a commitment to a coherently expressed and logical argument, the dispassionate weighing of alternatives, and the objective observation of the world.[6] The charges that *Rights of Woman* lacks a coherent, rational organization criticize it, paradoxically, by the very standards of rationality her treatise ultimately contests. Preoccupied with her breaches of philosophical and stylistic decorum, her critics largely fail to identify the alternatives posed by her writing because they have not done justice to the more subversive elements of her argument. A more sympathetic critic notes that the "unevenness of the book, its unclear organization, its repetition or arguments, have less to do with Wollstonecraft's lack of formal education—she can be formidable in argument when she allows herself to be—than with her attempt to bring about a bloodless revolution" (Vlaspolos 1980, 462). As Anca Vlaspolos suggests, the stylistic idiosyncrasies that have been criticized in the past can be

---

[6]For a critique of this notion of philosophical rhetoric, see Bordo 1982; Rorty 1979; and Richetti 1983, 4–32.

seen as a set of rhetorical strategies by which Wollstonecraft attempts to forge out of a hostile philosophical tradition an alternative language that can represent—and even create—a subject position from which a woman can effect political change.

Wollstonecraft's style wavers between strategies of assimilation and strategies of rebellion, between conservative philosophical language and a radical attempt to call its assumptions and values into question.[7] This stylistic instability reflects the tensions in her argument between traditionalist and revolutionary views of the nature of women, as well as the rhetorical difficulties she faces in trying to redefine the "nature of woman," while moving between the public and domestic spheres. Stylistic analysis, then, may provide a lens through which to examine the relationships in the text between ideology and subjectivity.

Wollstonecraft herself, in keeping with eighteenth-century beliefs about philosophical decorum dismisses style as "noise," reaffirming her commitment to "objectivity," which, she claims, inheres in a view of language as transparent which dismisses rhetoric and concerns itself with "things."

> Animated by this important object, I shall disdain to cull my phrases or polish my style;—I aim at being useful, and sincerity will render me unaffected; for, wishing rather to persuade by the force of my arguments, than dazzle by the elegance of my language, I shall not waste my time in rounding periods, or in fabricating the turgid bombast of artificial feelings, which, coming from the head, never reach the heart.—I shall be employed about things, not words!—and, anxious to render my sex more respectable to members of society, I shall try to avoid that flowery diction which has slided from essays into novels, and from novels into familiar letters and conversation. (10)

This passage accomplishes two purposes. First, it distances Wollstonecraft's writing from the "noise" of women's writing—novels, letters, and the like—and identifies it more closely with masculine writing, with the purposeful writing of the public

[7]For a perceptive discussion of the conflict between radical and conservative ideologies in Wollstonecraft's political thought, see Eisenstein 1981, 89–112.

sphere; it purports to be forceful, not flowery. Second, and more important, it does what most philosophical writing since Plato has attempted to do: it creates the fiction that its rhetoric—the rhetoric of rational discourse—does not really exist, that the prose is simply a vehicle, a "mirror of nature," which conveys unmediated truth. Wollstonecraft's sincerity and hence the truth of her argument are assumed by her concern with things, not words. She rather ingenuously disdains "rounding periods," "the turgid bombast of artificial feeling," and "elegant" language as so much noise. Her claims are intended to prevent the reader from considering the role that style—language and rhetoric—must necessarily play in shaping "truth" and hence the possibility that "truth" is more subject to the writer's perspective and position within a particular historical and social context than many philosophers would like to believe.[8]

As Robert Markley has noted, style implicates the individual in a complex dynamic of history, culture, and hence ideology: "Style records the writer's struggle against convention and towards an elusive individuality that is itself bounded culturally. It is a dynamic record of the pressures created by a vocabulary simultaneously demonstrating and rebelling against its conventional nature. Style constructs a dynamic and historical rather than a static and ideal self, forcing us to reassess constantly the relation between the internal and external, between idiosyncratic utterance and anonymous replication" (1988, 26). This kind of dialogical analysis conceives of style not merely as an expression of essentialist notions of the self—"style is the woman"—or as an abstract system of generic classification but as a historical arena of conflict, a dynamic interplay among individuals, genres, conventions, and ideologies in which style functions as both a producer and a production of social meanings. In Wollstonecraft's case, the confrontation between radical and conservative styles—between philosophical reason and a radical assertion of women's political rights—is played out as a dialogical rather than dialectical process. *Rights of Woman* offers no third term to transcend the ideological contradictions with which it wrestles. Rather than a dispassionate, objective treatise, it is the record of a struggle.

[8]On the relationship of truth and rhetoric in philosophic writing, see Richetti 1983, 6–8; and Rorty 1979.

The conservative elements of Wollstonecraft's argument reveal her conscious stylistic decision to write about women's inequality from within the public sphere. This was, after all, not the only stylistic option open to Wollstonecraft, who did not limit her writing to those speech genres belonging exclusively to the public sphere. Before *A Vindication of the Rights of Woman*, she wrote prolifically in several domestic genres, including children's stories ("Lessons for Children"), educational treatises (*Thoughts on the Education of Daughters*), conduct books (*Original Stories*), and domestic fiction (*Mary* and the posthumous *Maria*).[9] She justifies her stylistic choices in *Rights of Woman*: "Because I am a woman, I would not lead my readers to suppose that I mean violently to agitate the contested question respecting the inequality or inferiority of the sex; but as the subject lies in my way, and I cannot pass it over without subjecting the main tendency of my reasoning to misconstruction, I shall stop a moment to deliver, in a few words, my opinion" (8). The apologetic tone of these remarks (and many like them) reveals the anxieties Wollstonecraft experiences as a woman writing publicly for a living. She must avoid the appearance of being too radical; she must not appear violent or overly passionate or she risks being pigeonholed as an emotional woman who cannot master the rhetoric of philosophical discourse. Instead, to gain her audience's acceptance, she must appropriate masculine models of writing while effacing her sexual identity. Characteristically, Wollstonecraft attempts to outdo her male counterparts in their own style, to demonstrate her rationality, objectivity, and evenhandedness. She identifies herself with men, in this passage referring to women as "the sex" and in others simply as "them." She distances herself throughout *Rights of Woman* from her "despised femininity" by dismissing "pretty feminine phrases" (9), "pretty superlatives," and "false sentiments" (10) from her self-consciously masculinized style.

These decisions reflect Wollstonecraft's belief that she is writing for an unsympathetic audience: she conceives of and addresses her readers primarily as men, not as other women (Vlaspolos 1980,

[9]Mitzi Myers examines Wollstonecraft's exploration of subjectivity in her pedagogical texts. "Wollstonecraft's pedagogical exercises," she writes, "try out a plurality of selfhoods" (1988, 206).

462). She also writes within a paternalistic philosophical tradition
that excludes women as both writers and subjects. To enable herself to write, Wollstonecraft adopts the objective and therefore
powerful rhetorical pose of patriarchal discourse, even as she simultaneously subverts it. She must work within the confining
strictures of a rhetoric that, while aggressively masculine, presents
itself as transparent and unproblematic, as uninterested in anything except the true representation of reality. As a woman,
Wollstonecraft could not hope to be taken seriously without appropriating the trappings of this rhetorical pose, however incongruous
it might seem for her sex. For this reason, she is stridently argu-
mentative in asserting her thesis: "In this work I have produced
many arguments, which to me were conclusive, to prove that the
prevailing notion respecting a sexual character was subversive of
morality, and I have contended, that to render the human body
and mind more perfect, chastity must more universally prevail"
(4). And again: "I have repeatedly asserted, and produced what
appear to me irrefragable arguments drawn from matters of fact, to
prove my assertion, that women cannot, by force, be confined to
domestic concerns" (5). She "contends" and "proves" arguments,
drawn from "fact," which are "irrefragable" and "conclusive." The
first four chapters are full of such self-conscious references to her
argument: she speaks of disputes and proofs, of "simple truths," of
"unequivocal axioms," and of "reason," a word that can be found
at least once on virtually every page of *Rights of Woman*. The mili-
tant tone of her language is partly the result of the political purpose
with which she writes, but it is also calculated to establish her
credentials as an aggressive, even masculine reasoner, and to enlist
the sympathies of heretofore hostile or indifferent male readers by
proving herself one of them and not merely a woman. The value
Wollstonecraft places on such a "masculine understanding" is evident in her praise of Catherine Macaulay, who for Wollstonecraft
was "an example of intellectual acquirements supposed to be incompatible with the weakness of her sex. In her style of writing,
indeed, no sex appears, for it is like the sense it conveys, strong
and clear" (105).

Like Macaulay, Wollstonecraft, in appropriating the rhetoric of
the public sphere must efface her sexual identity and her historical

perspective as a speaking subject along with it. Again and again she tries to ensure her objectivity by creating a fictional vantage point that allows her to stand outside the particulars of her time and place as a disinterested observer: "Let me now from an eminence survey the world stripped of all its false delusive charms. The clear atmosphere enables me to see each object in its true point of view, while my heart is still. I am calm as the prospect in a morning when the mists, slowly dispersing, silently unveil the beauties of nature, refreshed by rest" (110). In dedicating herself to describing the "truth," she assumes what one critic has called an "ideal, disembodied state" that allows her to transcend her femininity (Poovey 1984, 80). Her "Miltonic disinterestedness" creates the illusion that she speaks from outside the "false delusive charms" of the world, from beyond the historical circumstances that led her to compose *A Vindication of the Rights of Woman*. In assuming this philosophical stance, she adopts the pose most favored by the bourgeois public sphere, that of the "spectator," who sees more clearly because he does not participate actively in the "human show" around him, who sees, as Addison and Steele's *Spectator* argues, "as Standers-by discover Blots, which are apt to escape those who are in the Game."[10] On the surface, therefore, Wollstonecraft's treatise attempts to conform to the rhetorical rules of logical argument, rules that historically excluded women from philosophical discourse. It asserts and supports a thesis, attacking its opponents by rational argument. Its prose attempts to be, like Catherine Macaulay's, "strong and clear."

Wollstonecraft's insistence on the disinterestedness of her prose, and hence its truth, is one reason she is so often criticized when she fails to live up to her standards. Yet this rhetorical strategy proves much more problematic for a woman writing within the public sphere than for her male counterparts. It is not entirely clear that Wollstonecraft recognizes the problems inherent in adapting these masculine models to her purposes. For her "philosophical project," the illusion of objectivity is necessary, but it does not suit her purposes beyond establishing her ability to reason as effec-

[10]For a discussion of this pose of objectivity, see Straub 1989, 855; Poovey 1984, 80; and Bordo 1982, 181–85.

tively as a man, because it reinforces as truths masculine notions of women as irrational, thereby ensuring their intellectual subservience. Her attack on patriarchy requires that she question any "artificial structure" (78) that represses women as subjects; one of the most powerful of these structures is writing. She must appropriate the apparently disinterested rhetoric of masculine authority for her own purposes because there is no other language in which she can write; but she must simultaneously subvert it, exposing it as an arbitrary fiction, a prejudice that keeps women in their place. She must fashion out of patriarchal discourse a language in which to inscribe her subjectivity and experience as correctives to the masculine authorities on women she has read.

The Dialogics of Style

Wollstonecraft's solution is to interweave the languages and genres of public rationality and domestic feeling in a dialogue that allows her to create an oppositional stance within public-sphere discourse and reveals the extent to which writing had become an arena of sexual conflict in the late eighteenth century. The opening paragraph illustrates this productive tension between what becomes in *Rights of Woman* two kinds of rhetoric: that of philosophical authority and that of domestic authority.

> After considering the historical page, and viewing the living world with anxious solicitude, the most melancholy emotions and sorrowful indignation have depressed my spirits, and I have sighed when obliged to confess, that either nature has made a great difference between man and man, or that the civilization which has hitherto taken place in the world has been very partial. I have turned over various books written on the subject of education, and patiently observed the conduct of parents and the management of schools; but what has been the result?—a profound conviction that the neglected education of my fellow-creatures is the ground source of the misery I deplore; and that women, in particular, are rendered weak and wretched by a variety of concurring causes, originating from one hasty conclusion. (7)

The first sentence is a microcosm of Wollstonecraft's style. The tone of the first clause is judicious. Words such as "considering" and "viewing" create the impression of a thoughtful observer, while "anxious solicitude" gives just the right sense of distanced objectivity. The speaking subject, if not totally suppressed, stands outside of and apart from the situation she surveys. "Historical page" imparts weight and authority to the prose, both because it is a circumlocution for "books" and because it invokes "authority." The rationality and disinterestedness of the first clause, however, give way in the second to a personal emotion of gothic intensity, conveyed by words and phrases such as "melancholy," "sorrowful indignation," "depressed," and "sighed." In the second clause, Wollstonecraft invokes the language of feeling prominent in domestic and sentimental fiction and conduct manuals. The second sentence repeats the same pattern. The dispassionate phrases "turned over" and "patiently observed" are followed in the second clause by "profound conviction," "neglected education," "misery," and "weak and wretched," all of which she "deplores." The contradictions of Wollstonecraft's life—her belief in the Enlightenment ideal of reason as opposed to the passionate intensity of her life (which often reads like a domestic novel)—are embedded in her prose. Each sentence begins objectively, but the facade is quickly dropped, replaced by a prose of subjective and emotional involvement. The pose of objectivity itself is called into question. The reader is drawn with the writer into a rhetorical and ideological reconstruction of the subjective experience of womanhood. The paragraph climaxes in an extended simile describing woman as created—and perverted—by man, a hothouse flower "planted in too rich a soil," whose "strength and usefulness are sacrificed to beauty" (7). Wollstonecraft's strategy in this introductory paragraph enables her to consider herself—a woman—as both subject and object and to dismantle the opposition between them. It enables her to adopt the masculine rhetoric of eighteenth-century philosophy and at the same time to subvert it by invoking the rhetoric of domestic authority, questioning all truisms about women.

The clash between public and domestic rhetorics or strategies of writing repeats itself throughout *A Vindication of the Rights of Woman*. The effect is less that of a single style (however various), than of a variety of competing styles, each of which makes different claims on the reader's attention. The extremes of Wollstonecraft's styles testify to the perspicuity of Mary Hays's remark that "the high masculine tone, sometimes degenerating into coarseness, that characterizes this performance, is in a variety of parts softened and blended with a tenderness of sentiment, an exquisite delicacy of feeling, that touches the heart, and takes captive the imagination" (quoted in Wollstonecraft 1975, 212). As Wollstonecraft appropriates and experiments with various kinds of rhetorical strategies, she demonstrates just how difficult it is to construct a language capable of empowering female desire and subjectivity. Because the personae established by the discourse of the public sphere frame the questions Wollstonecraft can ask, she is necessarily limited in the kinds of answers she can offer.

In *A Vindication of the Rights of Woman*, as I have been arguing, Wollstonecraft strives for stylistic effects appropriate to the philosophical seriousness of her argument. Thus, her language, because it adopts the language of philosophical rationalism, is often elaborately structured, even ponderous, given to rhetorical flourishes that are intended as much to create a tone of weighty disinterestedness as to further the specifics of her argument. Consider, by way of example, the following passage:

> The stamen of immortality, if I may be allowed the phrase, is the perfectibility of human reason; for, were man created perfect, or did a flood of knowledge break in upon him, when he arrived at maturity, that precluded error, I should doubt whether his existence would be continued after the dissolution of the body. But, in the present state of things, every difficulty in morals that escapes from human discussion, and equally baffles the investigation of profound thinking, and the lightning glance of genius, is an argument on which I build my belief of the immortality of the soul. Reason is, consequently, the simple power of improvement; or, more properly speaking, of discerning truth. (52–53)

Both diction and syntax contribute to the impression of philosophical authority which Wollstonecraft tries to create in this passage. She relies heavily on largely abstract, Latinate nouns such as "stamen," "immortality," "perfectibility," and "dissolution" to create a solidity and stasis. Her first sentence delays, through a long series of dependent clauses, her main point that perfection logically precludes existence since the purpose of existence is to strive for perfection. The reader is asked to follow the movement of the sentence, and indeed the whole passage, hypotactically through a series of logical connectives: "if," "for," "when," "but," and "consequentially." The passage as a whole attempts to command assent by convincing the reader of the objectivity, the orderliness, and hence the truth of its argument. The characteristics often associated with philosophical discourse—seriousness, abstraction, logical connection through subordination and cause and effect—all figure prominently here in Wollstonecraft's style.

Yet even in this passage, so thoroughly serious about itself as philosophy, Wollstonecraft characteristically undercuts its fictions of objectivity and certitude. Many of the dependent clauses create seemingly unnecessary hedges: "if I may be allowed the phrase," "I should doubt," "I build my belief," and the subjunctives "were" and "did." The author, in one sense, heaps qualification upon qualification, creating a rhetoric that both asserts and questions its stated beliefs. The result is a language that reveals its distrust of the authority of philosophical discourse and of the ability of language to proceed logically to a discovery of truth. Her philosophical style, in this regard, insists not merely on its own authority but on the ambiguities that inhere in the assumptions eighteenth-century philosophy makes about its claims to authoritative and objective discourse.

Wollstonecraft's distrust of the language she employs results in radical shifts in style and tone. Her prose is experimental, given to pushing the decorum of philosophical language to its extremes by incorporating stylistic conventions from other speech genres. Chapter 7, "On Modesty," begins with an exaggerated apostrophe that recalls the worst stylistic excesses of the domestic fiction she rejects at the beginning of the treatise.

Modesty! Sacred offspring of sensibility and reason!-true delicacy of mind!—may I unblamed presume to investigate thy nature, and trace to its covert the mild charm, that mellowing each harsh feature of character, renders what would otherwise only inspire cold admiration—lovely!—Thou that smoothest the wrinkles of wisdom, and softenest the tone of the sublimest virtues till they all melt into humanity;—thou that spreadest the ethereal cloud that, surrounding love, heightens every beauty, it half shades, breathing those coy sweets that steal into the heart, and charm the senses—modulate for me the language of persuasive reason till I rouse my sex from the flowery bed on which they supinely sleep life away! (121)

This passage is often counted among the inflated excesses of Wollstonecraft's style. Mary Poovey, for instance, discusses it at some length, noting that the "artificial and abstract rhetoric" enables Wollstonecraft to distance herself from her more volatile emotions, in this case from her sexuality (1984, 78). For Poovey, Wollstonecraft's "dematerialization" of her subject is proof of her ideological commitment to the repression of female sexuality. No doubt Poovey is right; others have commented on Wollstonecraft's almost pathological denial of female sexuality.[11] Yet the excesses of this passage border on parody, and considered in the context of the chapter's style, they have the quite different effect of paradoxically calling attention to—and hence constructing—sexual difference.

The language of this passage is a parody of the rhetoric of domestic fiction. It mocks the docile, acutely feminine voice of countless gothic heroines, echoing and representing women's culturally enforced weakness and dependence. To lend some authority to the prose, Wollstonecraft borrows an archaic and nearly biblical phraseology, replacing the more common "you" and "your" with "thou" and "thy" and employing the verb ending -est in "smoothest," "softenest," and "spreadest." Her abstract diction forgoes the pursuit of philosophical truth for the clichés of domestic bliss: "mellowing," sublimest," "wrinkle of wisdom," "ethereal cloud," "coy sweets," and "flowery bed." The climax of the paragraph conjures up the image of a Sleeping Beauty or a gothic heroine passively, even docilely, awaiting the arrival of the man who will be at once her savior and her despoiler.

[11]See, for instance, Miriam Brody, "Mary Wollstonecraft: Sexuality and Women's Rights (1759–1797)," in Spender 1983, 40–59.

Wollstonecraft underscores the ironic mockery of her prayer to Modesty to "modulate for me the language of persuasive reason" when in the next sentence she does exactly that: she "modulates" her style to a different kind of language: "In speaking of the association of our ideas, I have noticed two distinct modes; and in defining modesty, it appears to me equally proper to discriminate that purity of mind, which is the effect of chastity, from a simplicity of character that leads us to form a just opinion of ourselves, equally distant from vanity or presumption, though by no means incompatible with a lofty consciousness of our own dignity" (121–22). The straightforward language of this sentence is as serious as the previous one is purplish. Despite its length, it has a "plainness" lacking in the previous passages, and even in the more philosophical sections of Wollstonecraft's prose. Its insistence on logical divisions and classifications coincides with its comparatively straightforward diction and style. It must be read, then, as the antithesis of the preceding paragraph, even as it implicitly asks the reader to compare rhetorical strategies. Taken together, these two passages define the difference between what Wollstonecraft sees as a domestic feminized "style" foisted upon women by their culturally defined subject position and what she sees as a truly denotative style, which, in effect, subsumes the differences between masculine and feminine in its pursuit of general, transhistorical truths.

Wollstonecraft's attempts to rewrite philosophical discourse, to move from a prose characterized by its reliance on the models of public-sphere discourse to one that can accommodate her own interests and observations, are the basis for her efforts to create a style free from the tyranny of both masculine and feminine ideologies. But her success at circumventing—or subverting—the ideologies of patriarchy and middle-class morality is necessarily mixed. To criticize the system, Wollstonecraft must write from within it; she must borrow from various cultural languages in order to create a new one. Her attempts to deal with "women's experience" as something immediately accessible, unmediated by language, ideology, and cultural representations, are undermined by a style that frequently verges on bourgeois sentimentality.

One long passage suggests the difficulties all feminists since Wollstonecraft have encountered when trying to talk about some essential "woman's experience":

Cold would be the heart of a husband, were he not rendered unnatural by early debauchery, who did not feel more delight at seeing his child suckled by its mother, than the most artful wanton tricks could ever raise; yet this natural way of cementing the matrimonial tie, and twisting esteem with fonder recollections, wealth leads women to spurn. To preserve their beauty, and wear the flowery crown of the day, which gives them a kind of right to reign for a short time over the sex, they neglect to stamp impressions on their husbands' hearts, that would be remembered with more tenderness when the snow on the head began to chill the bosom, than even their virgin charms. The maternal solicitude of a reasonable affectionate woman is very interesting, and the chastened dignity with which a mother returns the caresses that she and the child receive from a father who has been fulfilling the serious duties of his station, is not only a respectable, but a beautiful sight. So singular, indeed, are my feelings, and I have endeavoured not to catch factitious ones, that after having been fatigued with the sigh of insipid grandeur and the slavish ceremonies that with cumberous pomp supplied the place of domestic affections, I have turned to some other scene to relieve my eye by resting it on the refreshing green every where scattered by nature. I have then viewed with pleasure a woman nursing her children, and discharging the duties of her station with, perhaps, merely a servant maid to take off her hands the servile part of the household business. I have seen her prepare herself and children, with only the luxury of cleanliness, to receive her husband, who returning weary home in the evening found smiling babes and a clean hearth. My heart has loitered in the midst of the group, and has even throbbed with sympathetic emotion, when the scraping of the well-known foot has raised a pleasing tumult. (142–43)

In this passage, Wollstonecraft confronts a subject of almost exclusive concern to women—breast-feeding. Whereas this subject might occupy the attention of, say, a medical book on obstetrics, in the context of a philosophical work such as this one purports to be, its inclusion appears ludicrously incongruous, even tasteless. Yet Wollstonecraft's treatment of the subject is less tasteless than overly sentimental, less radical than fraught with the values of a conservative and bourgeois ideology of domesticity. This passage would be appropriate for an eighteenth-century conduct book intended to socialize a young daughter to her domestic duties. It employs a clichéd poetic diction to defuse a potentially embarrassing subject, one perhaps too closely allied with female sexuality. Women's sexuality, which Wollstonecraft generally prefers to ignore in *Rights of Woman* as potentially dangerous or highly disturbing, is thus displaced onto a description of maternal duty. Her choice of imagery, euphemisms, and circumlocutions in this passage disembody her subject, rendering it nonsexual and therefore safe. Nowhere is there any hint of the physical suggested by the word "breast-feeding." Instead, "the child" is "suckled by its mother." Such images as "stamp impressions," "snow on the head," and "chill the bosom" distance the writer from her own body—both as a material and a symbolic object—and perhaps from her own unsanctioned desires as well. The entire passage basks in the kind of sensibility and flowery diction of which she has earlier been so critical and which she had hoped to excise from her writing: "virgin charms," "maternal solicitude," "caresses," "smiling babes," "throbbed with sympathetic delight," and "pleasing tumult" create a safe emotionalism that allows the writer to assume a position of both superiority to and alienation from her own sexuality. This passage, rather than confront women's physical emancipation as a potentially creative and liberating, although disturbing, force for change, endorses the middle-class virtues of economy and cleanliness which created the domestic slavery of women Wollstonecraft deplores. While sentimentalizing the breast-feeding (middle- or upper-class) mother, she quickly dismisses the "servant maid" to take care of the "servile part of the household business."

Wollstonecraft's failure to offer any real alternatives to women's confinement in the domestic sphere is instructive. In this passage she demonstrates just how distorting it is to refract female identity through the stylistic conventions of a philosophical discourse that was created to treat only a masculine subjectivity. Her choices are circumscribed by the cultural representations available to her. She can appropriate either the vocabulary of the medical textbook or that of the sentimental novel, but either way she offers an ideological representation of the experience which is at odds with the one she desires. Breast-feeding was a subject Wollstonecraft felt very strongly about. It symbolized for her one way in which women could be at once creative, powerful, and nurturing without violating middle-class standards of propriety. For her, breast-feeding and the celebration of femininity that it symbolizes must become fit subjects for philosophy if philosophy were ever to be truly egalitarian. Yet the philosopher's insistence on reason and detachment must deny the emotional and connected nature of the mother-child relationship, leaving only the flowery diction of sentimentality—of domestic fiction—to describe these emotions. The stylistic dilemma this passage creates for Wollstonecraft is crucial to understanding the so-called flaws of *A Vindication of the Rights of Woman.* Wollstonecraft must constantly move between two poles, between a public posture of confrontation which is troped as masculine and a strategy of indirection and feeling which is troped as domestic and therefore feminine. In short she must move between reason and emotion.[12]

The Passions Should Unfold Our Reason

"We reason deeply, when we forcibly feel," Wollstonecraft writes in *Letters Written during a Short Residence in Sweden, Norway, and Denmark* (1976, 160). As my analysis suggests, reason and passion, for Wollstonecraft, cannot exist as mutually exclusive modes of thought. She attacks the eighteenth-century bifurcation of emotion and reason and the concomitant devaluation of emotion as feminine.[13] Emotions are not the sole prerogative of the female. Indeed, in their present state, she argues, women do not experience true emotion: "Women are supposed to possess more sensibility, and even humanity, than men, and their strong attachments and instantaneous emotions of compassion are given as proofs; but the clinging affectation of ignorance has seldom any thing noble in it, and may mostly be resolved into selfishness" (188). Nor are men purely rational creatures, like Dean Swift's "insipid Houyhnhnms" (58). Their so-called rational arguments slide as easily into sentimentality and emotion as a woman's. According

[12]For a discussion of the "masculine" and "feminine" in Wollstonecraft's prose, see Poovey 1984, 68.
[13]See Bordo 1982, 192–93.

to Wollstonecraft, Rousseau's errors all arise from "sensibility": "When he should have reasoned he became impassioned" (90). Neither reason nor emotion can be the exclusive province of one sex, nor can the two function independently: "the passions should unfold our reason" (14).

Accustomed as they are to the elegant dialectics of eighteenth-century philosophy—in which reason opposes passion, slavery tyranny, power powerlessness, body spirit, and male female—it is little wonder that Wollstonecraft's critics feel so ill at ease with her prose and have accused her of pointless digressions. Central to her critique of patriarchal culture is her challenge of a rhetoric that can so neatly dispose of contradictions by creating rigid dichotomies, often in the service of oppression. All such oppositions imply the valorization of one term to the exclusion of the other; the powerful are privileged over the powerless, objective knowledge over the subjective passion, reason over emotion, and male over female. Generally, the lesser of each pair is ideologically typed as feminine and devalued accordingly. *A Vindication of the Rights of Woman* attempts to forge a new rhetoric to counter the oppressive power of this confrontational rhetoric by conflating oppositions, collapsing one term into the other. This strategy has the effect of robbing the "higher" term of its privileged masculine status and revaluing the other.

Elissa Guralnick has pointed out that in *Rights of Woman* "oppressed womankind serves . . . not merely as a figure for oppressed and impoverished mankind, but as a figure for all men, high as well as low, who are implicated in social and political contacts which condone inequality of wealth, rank, and privilege" (1977, 159). Woman is at once a figure for both oppressed and oppressor, for in Wollstonecraft's mind, woman is *both* tyrant and slave. Women, "sometimes boast of their weakness, cunningly obtaining power by playing on the *weakness* of men; and they may well have more real power than their masters" (40). Her strategy, throughout *Rights of Woman*, exposes the neat dialectics of patriarchy as tools of oppression. The long digressions in chapter 1, for example, on the monarchy, the army, and the clergy, illustrate for many critics Wollstonecraft's tendency to lose track of her argument. In their minds, the abuses of power she finds in these institutions have nothing to do with her argument about the rights of women. For Wollstonecraft, however, the association between women's oppression and patriarchal institutions is precisely the point; these are examples of that "arbitrary power" (15)   social convention—which keeps women from exercising their rights and duties as citizens. She attacks all institutions "in which great subordination of rank constitutes its power" (17).

> It is impossible for any man, when the most favorable circumstances concur, to acquire sufficient knowledge and strength of mind to discharge the duties of a king, entrusted with uncontrouled power; how then must they be violated when his very elevation is an insuperable bar to the attainment of either wisdom or virtue; when all the feelings of a man are stifled by flattery, and reflection shut out by pleasure! Surely it is madness to make the fate of thousands depend on the caprice of a weak fellow, whose very station sinks him *necessarily* below the meanest of his subjects! But one power should not be thrown down to exalt another—for all power inebriates weak man; and its abuse proves that the more equality there is established among men, the more virtues and happiness will reign in society. (16)

Central to Wollstonecraft's argument, which anticipates the Hegelian master-slave dialectic, is the belief that power is powerlessness and tyranny is slavery. This passage suggests that the institution of monarchy is a figure for this paradox. It oppresses not only the "common mass of mankind" (37) but the monarch as well, who becomes enslaved to flatterers and sycophants. By usurping all power for itself, the monarchy becomes powerless. By tyrannizing over others, a king is himself enslaved; his "very station sinks him *necessarily* below the meanest of his subjects." Repeatedly in *Rights of Woman*, Wollstonecraft attacks the divine right of kings along with the divine right of husbands (41). But women, too, are like kings: their power springs from their weakness and their weakness springs from their power. "A king is always a king—and a woman always a woman" (56); both exercise their right to enslave others to the detriment of their own freedom. Wollstonecraft, at some level, recognizes that the political system is implicated in the oppression of women, despite the eighteenth-century project of isolating women within a universalizing domesticity that masks the exercise of political power.

The clergy and the military provide Wollstonecraft with two more analogies for the woman who is both slave and despot. "Blind submission" (18) is the lesson of the clergy, and the army is "a chain of despots, who, submitting and tyrannizing without exercising their reason, become dead weights of vice and folly on the community" (17). Soldiers become feminine in their tyrannical servility: "As for any depth of understanding, I will venture to affirm, that it is as rarely to be found in the army as amongst women; and the cause, I maintain, is the same. It may be further observed, that officers are also particularly attentive to their persons, fond of dancing, crowded rooms, adventures, and ridicule. Like the *fair* sex, the business of their lives is gallantry.—They were taught to please, and they only live to please" (24). The language in this and in similar passages (17) emasculates army officers, exposing them as vain, trivial, and sentimental. Officers, far from being virile and masculine, love fine clothes, dancing, flattery, and idleness—the vices of women. This passage works to reduce the distinctions between male and female, showing them to be not biologically innate but the result, at least in part, of social prejudices and early training. In this respect, Wollstonecraft's argument is clear: gendered individuals are not born, they are made, historically and culturally constructed.

As Wollstonecraft's argument develops, the oppression of women attaches itself to so many other social issues that eventually it encompasses all forms of political inequality. Wollstonecraft intuitively understands how various forms of oppression—by gender and class—operate in relation to one another. Yet, as Elissa Guralnick has pointed out, she rarely compares women to the "truly abject" (1977, 161). Instead, Wollstonecraft links women to the powerful and privileged, arguing that "wealth and female softness equally tend to debase mankind" (51). Repeatedly, the rich, like military officers, are emasculated:

The whole female sex are, till their character is formed, in the same condition as the rich: for they are born . . . with certain sexual privileges, and whilst they are gratuitously granted them, few will ever think of works of supererogation, to obtain the esteem of a small number of superiour people. (57)

Women, in general, as well as the rich of both sexes, have acquired all the follies and vices of civilization, and missed the useful fruit. (60)

The comparison [of women] with the rich still occurs to me; for, when men neglect the duties of humanity, women will follow their example; a common stream hurries them both along with thoughtless celerity. Riches and honours prevent a man from enlarging his understanding, and enervate all his powers by reversing the order of nature, which has ever made true pleasure the reward of labour. (64)

Wollstonecraft so frequently reiterates the comparison between women and the rich that it becomes an essential element in her argument rather than a pointless digression or tedious repetition, as some of her critics have contended. She realizes that the edifice of male privilege has been built upon the bifurcation of masculine and feminine virtue between the public sphere, where monarchs, the wealthy, soldiers, and clergy contend for power, and the domestic, where women wield power. Metaphoric emasculation, the collapsing of the dichotomy between male and female, is one of the tools she uses to dismantle these "artificial structures" of power, exposing them as ideological formations and not the natural order of things.

By collapsing this distinction between male and female forms of power, Wollstonecraft defines power in ideological terms. Underlying and uniting all the digressions and repetitions in *Rights of Woman* is an attack on an ideology of power which has hardened into absolute authority: "Power, in fact, is ever true to its vital principle, for in every shape it would reign without controul or inquiry. Its throne is built across a deep abyss, which no eye must dare to explore, lest the baseless fabric should totter under investigation" (150). Ideological power is all the more difficult to question precisely because its foundations are nearly invisible. For Wollstonecraft, power inheres not in any single institution or individual but in what Foucault calls its "deployment" or in the discursive formations of language and belief. Therefore, her attack on masculine preroga- tives is an attack on the language in which they are cast. The rhetorical tools of eighteenth-century philosophical discourse—its fictions of dispassionate objectivity and rational oppositions— support the conservative ideology upon which both aristocratic and masculine privilege are based. Wollstonecraft's efforts, like those of her predecessors, the architects of the French Revolution, to con- struct a counterideology of the rights of man and woman necessi- tates a counterdiscourse. The "flaws" in Wollstonecraft's style, in this context, become the vehicles for her philosophical program, which embraces the so-called feminine values of subjectivity and emotionalism and looks forward to romanticism with its valoriza- tion of intuition, passion, and the imagination over reason.

Wollstonecraft's poaching takes the form of a confrontation—a dialogue—with her philosophical fathers, the authorities on wom- en she has read and to some extent internalized. While drawing on the tradition of philosophical reason, she realizes that the authority of books, of the written word, powerfully perpetuates the myths of male superiority and female weakness precisely because it is a discourse controlled by—and for—men: "I must therefore venture to doubt whether what has been thought an axiom in morals may not have been a dogmatic assertion made by men who have coolly seen mankind through the medium of books" (110). Ralph Wardle has noted that in *A Vindication of the Rights of Woman* Wollstonecraft alludes to more works by other authors than in any of her other books, and although she refers to a few works by women, includ- ing Catherine Macaulay and Anna Laetitia Barbauld, the majority of the texts she discusses are by men. The list is extensive. She refers to authorities on women's education—Rousseau, Talleyrand, Vicesimus Knox, Dr. James Fordyce, Dr. John Gregory—and to works on political theory, linguistics, philosophy, and literature. She cites or quotes passages from the Bible and works by Shake- speare, Milton, Pope, Locke, Hume, Richardson, Swift, Johnson, Lord Monboddo, Adam Smith, Butler, Gay, Boswell, Dryden, Cowper, and Edward Young. This list suggests not so much the extent of her indebtedness to other writers (or the alleged gaps in her education) as the freedom she exercises in appropriating and recasting the voices of her "fathers." Because she has less at stake in perpetuating the voice of reason than in subverting and reconstructing it, she is relatively free to experiment with the dialogic power of the speech act. Without feeling constrained to prove the "authenticity" and "originality" of her "voice," Wollstonecraft is able to permit her words to become entangled with other, "alien" words in complex relationships of attraction and repulsion, alliance and struggle, intersection and merger.

In *Marxism and the Philosophy of Language*, Vološinov/Bakhtin argues that the processes of citation involved in both direct and indirect quotation are not passive and mechanical but active and dialogic (1986, 125–40). Wollstonecraft's method of extensive citation demonstrates how masculine discourse has created and perpetuated the weaknesses of women. She devotes her entire fifth chapter to writers who, in her words, "have rendered women objects of pity, bordering on contempt." She insists that it is not the power of individuals, or even institutions, which has kept women from assuming equal citizenship with men but the power of the written word. Two writers who particularly epitomize for Wollstonecraft the power of masculine discourse to exclude and silence women as subjects, the power of the father to stifle his daughters, are Rousseau and Milton. Both represent the ideological work of the public sphere as a discursive formation that creates and enforces and even naturalizes the dichotomies of gender that degrade women. Her critique of these influential authors demonstrates how the hegemony of the public sphere depends on a network of exclusions upon which the powerful ideological formation of the male subject as whole, autonomous, and unified is based.

Rousseau represents to Wollstonecraft the masculine deployment of discursive power against women in education and philosophy. She devotes almost half of chapter 5, "Animadversions on Some Writers," to her argument with Rousseau's ideas on the education of women. On the surface, the education of children—whether boys or girls—does not seem an issue weighty enough for philosophical debate; but Wollstonecraft recognizes in Rousseau's comments on the education of Sophia the subtle ways in which the unequal relationships inherent in such institutions as schools underlie and undercut the theoretical equality of men claimed by philosophy.[14] She examines and questions the disciplinary "technologies" of education advanced by Rousseau—the separation of children from their parents (158), the separation of the sexes (79, 165), and the physical constraints imposed upon schoolgirls (82, 162)—which constitute the modern "individual" and invisibly perpetuate the unequal relationships between the sexes. Rousseau attempts to argue from biological necessity that because men and women are not "constituted alike in temperament and character," they should not be educated alike: "The education of the women should always be relative to the men. To please, to be useful to us, to make us love and esteem them, to educate us when young, and take care of us when grown up, to advise, to console us, to render our lives easy and agreeable: these are the duties of women at all times, and what they should be taught in their infancy" (79). This version of the domestic ideal, Wollstonecraft argues, constitutes an arbitrary distinction that Rousseau claims is "the natural order of things." But if this domesticity is so natural, one wonders why it need be so thoroughly inculcated "from infancy": "The effect of habit is insisted upon as an undoubted indication of nature" (81). Such trivial activities as a young girl's playing with dolls, her fondness for dress, even her capacity for needlework form the basis of Rousseau's system of female education, providing at the same time both the proof of woman's unfitness for masculine subjectivity and the means of her exclusion from it. As Bourdieu has argued, "The whole trick of pedagogic reason lies precisely in the way it exhorts the essential while seeming to demand the insignificant." This is the "hidden persuasion of an implicit pedagogy, capable of instilling a whole cosmology, an ethic, a metaphysic, a political philosophy, through injunctions as insignificant as 'stand up straight'" (1977, 94–95). The very triviality of the activities recommended for young girls allows Rousseau to maintain social conventions and "narrow prejudices" (92) more powerfully than any tyrannic authority imposed from above because they are so thoroughly and invisibly inculcated in young girls as "habits of thinking" at an early age that they seem "natural." As Bourdieu notes: "The con-

---

[14]In this connection see also Dreyfus and Rabinow 1982, 184–88.

cessions of politeness always contain political concessions" (1977, 95).

Wollstonecraft perceptively grasps the problems inherent in Rousseau's thoughts on the education of women for his vision of a perfected society. His ideas, which Wollstonecraft discusses at length, support rather than subvert the unequal distribution of power throughout society. In this regard, Rousseau is a "partial moralist" (84) whose notions endorse and perpetuate the very vices he wishes to correct. Wollstonecraft protests: "I now appeal from the reveries of fancy and refined licentiousness to the good sense of mankind, whether, if the object of education be to prepare women to become chaste wives and sensible mothers, the method so plausibly recommended in the foregoing sketch, be the one best calculated to produce those ends? Will it be allowed that the surest way to make a wife chaste, is to teach her to practise the wanton arts of a mistress, termed virtuous coquetry?" (90). Far from being a rationalist and an egalitarian whose first wish is to perfect mankind, Rousseau is a sensualist whose licentiousness supports the status quo under the guise of rationality. For Wollstonecraft, Rousseau is not a philosopher but a "poetic writer" who "skillfully exhibits the objects of sense, most voluptuously shadowed or gracefully veiled—And thus making us feel whilst dreaming that we reason, erroneous conclusions are left in the mind" (91). As this passage suggests, Wollstonecraft attacks not Rousseau so much as the ideology he presents—the fiction of sexual inequality disguised as philosophical disinterest.

Yet it is Milton, the philosophical poet, even more than Rousseau, the poetic philosopher, who represents for Wollstonecraft the co-opting of creative energy by men. Sandra Gilbert and Susan Gubar note that *A Vindication of the Rights of Woman* "often reads like an outraged commentary on *Paradise Lost*."[15] If Wollstonecraft's domineering "poetic father" troubles her imagination—and incites her rebellion—more than her "philosophical father," Rousseau, it is because of the mythic power of "the institutionalized and elabo-

[15]Gilbert and Gubar 1979a, 205. I am indebted to Gilbert and Gubar's discussion of Milton's influence on women writers. For discussions of Milton's influence on Wollstonecraft specifically, see Poovey 1984, 72–80, and on eighteenth-century women writers in general, see Wittreich 1987.

rate metaphoric misogyny Milton's epic expresses" (Gilbert and Gubar 1979a, 189), buttressed by the full weight of biblical authority, by "Moses's beautiful poetical cosmogony." Indeed, Gilbert and Gubar find that most women writers have been all too aware of Milton's intimidating presence. Virginia Woolf, they note, remarks in *A Room of One's Own* that literate women had to "look past Milton's bogey, for no human being could shut out the view" (188). If *Paradise Lost* is more incapacitating for Wollstonecraft than Rousseau's "wild chimeras" (39), it is because the book itself "constitutes the essence of what Gertrude Stein has called patriarchal poetry" (Gilbert and Gubar, 188). So intimidating is Milton's presence for Wollstonecraft that she cannot confront him directly as she does Rousseau, but only indirectly, through allusions and footnotes. Her reading of *Paradise Lost* suggests that to assert her independence and the possibility of her creativity requires the ultimate act of rebellion against masculine authority: "I will simply declare, that were an angel from heaven to tell me that Moses's beautiful, poetical cosmogony, and the account of the fall of man, were literally true, I could not believe what my reason told me was derogatory to the character of the Supreme Being: and, having no fear of the devil before mine eyes, I venture to call this a suggestion of reason, instead of resting my weakness on the broad shoulders of the first seducer of my frail sex" (79). In the end, Milton's "bogey" is his theology, his cosmology. Although he did not create the myth of origin which is the heart of Western patriarchy, he gave it a poetic force that has, as Harold Bloom has said, made *Paradise Lost* an inhibiting text for all his successors. It is particularly intimidating for the woman writer since the eighteenth century. For Wollstonecraft, *Paradise Lost* not only represents, but coalesces the invisible network of authorities—both religious and cultural—which have traditionally claimed the power to define female nature, female identity. His history defines woman as secondary—"he for God only, she for God in him"—and other, a "fair defect of nature." By making the ultimate act of creation the sole act of a father, Milton defines creativity itself as a masculine act (Froula 1983). Therefore, to be able to write, Wollstonecraft must rebel against the poem's definition of the feminine in the submissive Eve—"for softness she and sweet attractive grace"—and identify her creative energies with the usurper of God's creative potential, Satan. "Similar feelings has Milton's pleasing picture of paradisiacal happiness ever raised in my mind; yet, instead of envying the lovely pair, I have, with conscious dignity, or Satanic pride, turned to hell for sublimer objects" (25, n.3). Milton's "paradisiacal happiness" deprives woman of soul, reason, and creativity. More important, it denies her authority and subjectivity. Like her literary daughters in the nineteenth century (including her biological daughter, Mary Shelley), Wollstonecraft, as both writer and woman, can overcome the anxieties created by Milton's specter only by identifying with his rebel, by opting not for paradise and order but for chaos and noise.

Wollstonecraft's rebellion against the central text of Western patriarchy and her rejection of the fictions of authority which structure its philosophy reveal the dilemma posed by her writing. The more she struggles to rid her language of the ideologies of her bourgeois upbringing, the more they strangle her creativity, denying her a subject position from which to speak. Because she constructs her rhetorical self to conform to the strictures of male-dominated philosophical discourse, her solution to the problem of feminine dependence must be cast in a language tainted by that dependence. Feminine creativity in *A Vindication of the Rights of Woman*, then, is experienced as a problem, a tension between the text as a creative act, the forging of a new rhetoric, and the text as necessarily parasitic, the site of a struggle with masculine authority. The great achievement of this book is that as Wollstonecraft strives to "make human conventions conform more closely to human need" (Woolf 1932, 176), she reveals just how profoundly those conventions—writing in particular—shape and define human needs and identity. Her text articulates a revolutionary critique of the cultural authorities that have defined woman's "nature," but it also shows how difficult resistance can be. In the final chapter I turn from this inaugural text of Western feminism to examine the dynamics of cultural authority which contemporary feminism must resist and revise, to the processes by which cultural values are created and deployed.

5

Theories of Value and the Dialogics of Culture

> To describe what you mean by a cultural taste you have to describe a culture. What belongs to a language game is a whole culture.
>
> —L. Wittgenstein

Wollstonecraft's rejection of the cultural and religious authority of *Paradise Lost* returns me to the questions with which I began in Chapter 1 about the complex mechanisms by which societies historically reproduce and refashion themselves and their structures of authority. All the texts I have examined in the previous chapters have, at one time or another, been excluded from the "canons" of literature, religion, and philosophy; they have been devalued as cultural noise, as information that has not been a part of the "messages" about our culture "we" wish to preserve. In this final chapter, I would like to examine the processes by which cultures distinguish between those kinds of knowledge that are valued and those that are excluded as irrelevant noise, looking at the largely invisible network of social relations and institutions that create and deploy cultural value. These processes, I argue, are not static and unchanging but dynamic and shifting.

I would like to begin to describe these dynamics with an allegory of enculturation and resistance drawn from one of my own classes. A few years ago, two students (both women) in my Introduction to Shakespeare class chose to write final papers on a subject that had been of concern to them throughout the term—Shakespeare's representations of gender and sexuality. After "sophisticated and insightful" analyses that demonstrated they had internalized the appropriate critical discourse (mine), both students arrived at strikingly negative conclusions about their responses to Shakespeare's plays. The first student wrote:

Women are portrayed negatively [in the plays], which can only lead me to believe that Shakespeare was a misogynist and the views in the plays were related to his own personal views. Perhaps he couldn't have been a staunch misogynist because he was married, but I'm sure his wife obeyed his every command if these plays reflect his views on women at all. I realize that I have only read a few of his plays, so perhaps it is narrow-minded of me to make these statements, but they are only based on these plays and what I have found in them, not conclusive ones.

The other concluded:

I am left with a sour impression from Shakespeare as he depicts gender relations only in the framework of perpetuating the traditional ideologies— maintaining the dominance of males while publicly denouncing the empowerment of women. But then these traditional gender ideologies seem to be presented in such an obnoxiously conspicuous manner that perhaps our friend Mr. Shakespeare is attempting a little subversive drama. I suppose we will never know.

These students' awakening feminist thinking created a frustrating dilemma for me, one that I am sure is familiar to most feminist teachers of the canon: although their resistance to the cultural authority of the Shakespeare canon struck a familiar and indeed sympathetic chord in me, in both instances, my first impulse was to defend Shakespeare, while deploring the cultural values his plays are frequently made to serve. But because I was reluctant to attack their hard-won and fragile sense that this "great author" was not exempt from critical evaluation, I was stopped in midcomment. If these students' desire to "blame" the individual writer—in this case Shakespeare—for the cultural representations that inhabit his plays strikes the English professor or cultural critic in me as naïve or unsophisticated, my feelings do not necessarily invalidate their responses or make them in some absolute sense "wrong." It seemed to me at the time, and still does, that their responses might be probed as a means of posing some questions about how cultural values take shape and perpetuate themselves, more specifically about how feminist literary critics articulate and pass on cultural and political values to their students. These students were acting out (as students often do) the role of Terry Eagleton's "child-as-theorist," who is forever asking "impossibly fundamental questions" that "interrogate the whole form of social life" (1986, 171), in this case the social life of literary criticism, which structures both the meanings and the values we find in Shakespeare's plays. Questions of this nature create several dilemmas for feminists, who, while challenging traditional systems of value, must deal with the institutional authority conferred upon them as "custodians of a discourse" on values.[1]

My students, of course, are not children and are not naïve. Both have some familiarity with the kinds of "language games"[2] required by both literary criticism and feminism, and both have, to some extent, internalized rhetorical strategies and analytic biases that they have learned from me and their other teachers. Indeed, the second student's comment might serve as a possible response to the first student, who wants to see the playwright as a "bad man," a misogynist. The second student, a senior English major, has more successfully internalized the language games of criticism. She realizes there are alternatives to questioning the poet's individual motives, and she can rely, at least implicitly, on the intentional fallacy to buttress her argument. Her two "rationalizations" of Shakespeare's misogyny are totally contradictory; yet she feels compelled, at least in the last paragraph, to include both possibilities. She first tries to see Shakespeare as perpetuating the "traditional ideologies" of his own time which disempower women, contrasting that unconscious bias with our own, more enlightened views. The poet is the victim of his own "false consciousness"; so his shortcomings result more from ignorance than from viciousness. Her second ploy is to recuperate Shakespeare for modern feminism by seeing his representations of gender relations as ironic: by presenting such distasteful gender relations so obvi-

[1]Eagleton 1983, 201; see also Froula 1983, 322.

[2]The term is Wittgenstein's way of describing how various categories of utterance (such as literary criticism) can be defined in terms of rules specifying their properties and the uses to which they can be put. In this regard, a language game is not much different from what Bakhtin calls a "speech genre."

ously, Shakespeare is really subverting them. In short, the second student has internalized critical orthodoxies the first student is still resisting, to wit: the critical orthodoxies of the New Criticism, in particular the intentional fallacy and the primacy of irony.[3] The second student knows that because the great masterworks of literature are the vehicles of our cultural ideals—the best that has been thought and said—they cannot be seen as promoting vicious doctrines such as sexism, racism, or anti-Semiticism (all, by the way, beliefs Shakespeare has at one time or another been accused of promoting). Critics have conventionally disposed of the problems created by such skewed values in exactly the same somewhat contradictory and ahistorical way: either Shakespeare is the product of his own culture and could not have resisted such widely held cultural values, or he is the astute observer of the human condition who managed to remain aloof from—or even ironically to subvert—what we in the twentieth century regard as immoral prejudices.

Although feminist literary critics have for at least two decades been questioning the ways in which traditional histories of Western literature have created the canon—the " 'great tradition' of the 'national literature' " (Eagleton 1983) which constitutes the content of the syllabi and anthologies used in most literature courses and which therefore determines what our students learn about the Western humanist tradition—they have also been prone to the same kind of confusion about literary value which my students and I experienced in this instance. Attempting to negotiate divided loyalties to feminist politics and the humanistic and liberal values of literary criticism, they have more often than not tried to forge some sort of dialectical synthesis between these two often conflicting ideological positions. Elizabeth Meese's remark in *Crossing the Double-Cross* seems paradigmatic in this respect: "Obviously, certain writers such as Chaucer and Shakespeare enjoy permanence [in the canon], but there are numerous others whose reputations remain in a state of flux, waxing and waning in accord with the prevailing interests of the critical moment" (1986, 6). If the canon

[3]For a fascinating study of the ways in which college students begin to internalize the epistemologies of the disciplines they are studying, see Belenky et al. 1986, especially their chapter on procedural knowledge.

allows for some flexibility, some rise and fall of literary reputations, while maintaining a hierarchy of indubitably great writers, then there must be some values that transcend the local politics and fluctuations of reputation. But for Eagleton's child and for my students, it is crucial to ask why it is obvious that Shakespeare and Chaucer enjoy permanent and unquestioned membership in the canon of Western literature. If Shakespeare and Chaucer cannot be questioned, does that mean that their work embodies fundamental and transhistorical aesthetic values that cannot be questioned? If we answer "yes" then we risk reducing the feminist critique of the canon to a debate over literary fashion, over who's in and who's out this year. The questions my students' responses intuitively, if tentatively, raise are the same two questions I. A. Richards asked in 1925: "What gives the experience of reading a certain poem [today we would say text] its value? Why is one opinion about works of art not as good as another" (5–6). Any inquiry into the nature of literary value which begins with these two questions, however, must be structured around a historical understanding of the various social and political contexts in which these questions are asked and answered.

The feminist argument about literary value is by now familiar. The canon—the tradition of "great literature" which constitutes Western culture—has been an exclusive and almost entirely male club; it has also been predominantly white, first-world, European, and ruling-class, but this fact, if it is mentioned at all by feminists, usually rates only a parenthesis (at least until recently). The very few women who have been admitted to the club (Austen, Dickinson, Woolf) are often subjected to backhanded compliments and miniaturization, if not withering scorn.[4] But this criticism leaves unchallenged the fundamental assumptions about value which have created this oppression because it does not, in itself, suggest a historically and politically based theory of value to replace traditional accounts.

[4]Mark Twain's dismissal of Jane Austen ("It seems a great pity they allowed her to die a natural death") is among the most spectacular examples of the scorn heaped on canonical women writers, but it is by no means unique; see Gilbert and Gubar 1979a, 109. Mary Ellmann (1968) and Joanna Russ (1983) have also documented the ways in which male writers have belittled the accomplishments of writing women.

During the 1970s and 1980s, when feminist critics raised the issue of how women's texts might be evaluated—and valued—four responses dominated. Throughout the 1970s, most feminist critics argued for the inclusion of newly recovered female writers in the canon, usually on a case-by-case basis, claiming that their works meet the existing criteria of aesthetic excellence. In a 1976 review essay, Annette Kolodny criticized this approach as ineffective. By 1980 several critics, including Nina Baym (1981) and Kolodny (1980a), were calling for the canon to be expanded to accommodate a larger number of female voices. Both of these arguments reinforce the imperialistic pluralism of the canon: newly recovered works can be subsumed—even co-opted—by the humanistic values represented by the canon, but traditional notions of literary excellence remain unexamined. A third position, best represented by Gilbert and Gubar's 1985 *Norton Anthology of Women's Literature*, maintains that feminists should create a countercanon of women's texts, thus rejecting androcentric values for gynocentric ones. Only a few radical feminists suggest we altogether abandon the idea of a canon as outmoded and elitist, but without suggesting what might fill the void. All these responses tend to reproduce the dialectical circularity of traditional theories of value. Challenges to the canon issuing from both liberal and radical feminists have tended to fall back on simple dialectics—good versus bad literature and oppressive versus liberating values—instead of inquiring into the dialogic nature of utterances about value. While these arguments have been instrumental in what Showalter has called "gynocritics," the rediscovery and reevaluation of women writers, none directly examines the aesthetic or ideological judgments that underlie and legitimate the canon, and none makes explicit what standards of judgment are necessary to any "revision" of the canon. Both traditionalists and radicals assume that value is transparent, that aesthetics or the correct politics can speak for themselves. This reluctance to discuss the theoretical principles that govern canon— and value—formation reveals a fundamental uncertainty among both liberal and radical feminists about the relationship of feminist critiques of literature to both traditional theories of value and to the political agenda of feminism. Feminist critics have found it easier to write about their resistance to traditional canons of taste than to "articulate what a radical feminist politics of literary judgment" would look like (Meese 1986, 5).

But "a radical poetics of judgment" is beginning to coalesce around yet another possible feminist approach to the canon, articulated in the work of such critics as Lillian Robinson (1983), Christine Froula (1983), and Jane Tompkins (1985). These critics contend that any feminist challenge to the canon must be rooted in an interrogation of the traditional aesthetic and cultural values that create the canon. Why, to cite only one example, are irony and complexity valued over sentimentality and simplicity? Feminist criticism must interrogate the processes through which such values are produced, given authority, and disseminated within a particular historical and social formation, and the "feedback mechanisms" through which those values help to reproduce the social formation that created them. This final chapter, then, examines the cultural work required to make value judgments seem natural, timeless, and self-evident through the suppression of cultural noise.

Value-For

Since 1987 the debate about literary value has become, if anything, more heated. Calls for reforming the canon have issued from several constituencies, only one of which is feminist, while the "institutional guardians of literature and the humanities" have called just as vehemently for a return to the "great books" of the Western tradition (Veeser 1989, ix). The stakes involved in canon revision are suggested by several salvos, including a special issue of *Critical Inquiry* published in 1987 titled "Politics and Poetic Values," the solicitation of papers for a special issue of *PMLA* on the canon, and a response by Hazard Adams to the 1983 *Critical Inquiry* issue on the canon, not to mention popular jeremiads (by Allan Bloom, E. D. Hirsch, and William Bennett) that denounce our collective cultural illiteracy.[5] As the urgency of these well-known arguments either for opening up or for maintaining the traditional

---

[5]Adams 1988. *PLMA* issued a call for papers for a special issue on the canon in volume 103 (1988). See also Hirsch 1987, Bloom 1987, and Bennett 1985.

canon suggest, these debates go beyond intramural discussions about which writers to include in courses and textbooks. They demonstrate that canon formation and value formation are serious political debates about authority, about who decides what values— what political norms—we will teach our students.

But the debate, as it has been formulated, is simply unresolvable. Literary critics have usually thought of value as either an objective property of texts or a subjective projection of emotion, and the either/or nature of this kind of dialectical thinking has characteristically obscured other possible perspectives. Critics such as E. D. Hirsch (1976a, 1976b), Charles Altieri (1983), and Hazard Adams (1988), who have been concerned with establishing criteria to allow us to distinguish "good" literature from other forms of discourse, often simply conclude (albeit drawing upon philosophically dense arguments about aesthetics, "contrastive frameworks" [Altieri 1983, 47], and "antithetical criteria" [Adams 1988, 755]) that value is "intrinsic" or "essential" and that, in effect, "good" literature is canonical because it is good. Others, Northrop Frye, for instance, have dismissed evaluation as so much literary gossip, as subjective, emotive, and essentially personal: "This sort of thing cannot be part of any systematic study, for a systematic study can only progress: whatever dithers or vacillates or reacts is merely leisure-class gossip."[6] But literary criticism, and feminist literary criticism in particular, does not need to invoke unexamined and circular notions of universality or timelessness or the transcendental and transhistorical qualities that all good literature supposedly shares as criteria of value. Nor does it need to abandon evaluation altogether as so much gossip. Just because we cannot make value judgments that are timeless and universal, just because we cannot invoke a single standard of taste, we do not have to abandon the study of literature to a kind of aesthetic quietism in which no value judgments can be made at all. If value is not an inherent property of objects, neither is it merely an "arbitrary projection of the subject." One might argue, as Barbara Herrnstein Smith has, that value is radically contingent, the product of cultural forces that are often dismissed as extrinsic to the text (1983, 11–19).

[6]Frye derides "all the literary chit-chat which makes the reputations of poets boom and crash in an imaginary stock-exchange" (1957, 18).

Contingency is not the same thing as relativism, although some more traditional-minded critics would have us believe it is.[7] Contingent, from the Latin *con* + *tangere*, "to touch together" (*OED*), means literally that a thing does not exist of itself but is dependent upon, "touches," something else. If value is contingent, it is not intrinsic to an object (or text) but depends upon something else. The logical next step is to ask *what* value depends upon. As recent debates indicate, even those critics who argue that value is intrinsic evoke extraliterary ideals—culture, literacy, democracy, humanism, tradition—to buttress their claims that literary knowledge is significant. Any value judgment is an utterance, and as such, it is noniterable, unique (Vološinov 1976). But even though the value judgment as an utterance cannot be reiterated, it is not doomed to languish in complete isolation or relativity. Every value judgment exists in dialogue with other value judgments. Each value judgment responds to previous value judgments; it also anticipates a response, a dialogical antagonist. In this respect, every utterance about value forms part of a discourse on value, forming a class of judgments, a speech genre governed by rules that determine the authority (or lack thereof) of the speaker or the receiver and the particular historical, social, or institutional context in which an utterance is given force—the classroom, a book review, a literary journal, a conference.

Debates about the objective or subjective nature of literary value obscure a more fundamental uncertainty about what value is and the intellectual, social, and political agendas it embodies. The "canon," as opposed to the single value judgment, is a collection of utterances, a speech genre or discourse about value, and the primary means by which we institutionalize literary value judgments. One way—the idealists' way—of defining the canon is as "the unquestioned 'great tradition' of the 'national literature'" (Eagleton 1983, 11), a "fixed body of literature whose greatness has been taken to be self-evident, whose meanings have been deemed timeless, and whose alleged cultural centrality has been used to marginalize other literature" (Zagarell 1986, 274). Here is the all too

[7]Adams, for instance, describes Smith's position as "hardheaded relativism that once and for all rids us of what Smith regards as humanistic fantasies of transcendence, universality, endurance, and the like" (1988, 751).

familiar list of "great books." But such traditional definitions imply that the canon can be defined dialectically—the ins versus the outs, great books versus "rubbish," literature versus popular culture, the central versus the marginal. All these differential assumptions about literary value which the canon both confers and embodies are hierarchical; furthermore, they presuppose literary value instead of defining a means to investigate or assess it. Significantly, when theorists attempt to define what a "canon" might be, they favor abstract, even circular, rhetoric to finesse the problem of the political nature of both the canon and the values it supposedly transmits. Charles Altieri, for instance, maintains that "For a work to play canonical roles it must exhibit qualities which define it as a significant distinctive entity. Canonical works are expected to provide knowledge of the world represented, to exemplify powers for making representations that express possible attitudes or produce artistic models, and to articulate shared values in a past culture that influence the present or to clarify means of reading other works we have reason to care about" (1983, 54). It is safe to say that there is hardly a word in this statement whose meanings are not currently being contested. The abstract language enables Altieri to beg several highly political and volatile questions about what constitutes significance or distinction, about whose attitudes and whose values will be represented and articulated, and about what kind of knowledge and what kind of history canonical works will provide. What is missing from Altieri's description is an account of exactly who is assessing and legislating value and what interests they might have. His disarming "we" glosses over the conflicts of interest that characterize any heterogeneous sociocultural group, the centrifugal energy of its heteroglossia and the centripetal powers of its cultural institutions, which order those interests hierarchically and decide what parts of our past "we have reason to care about."

Any theory of the canon which presupposes a dialectical contest between the ins and outs, the canonical and noncanonical, is, I believe, doomed to engage in precisely this zero-sum game of power politics: new hierarchies can replace old hierarchies, the stock of individual authors can rise and fall, but the canon itself remains an imperialist construct that seeks to legitimate its politics—its values—by conquering, subsuming, and disarming radical challenges to its hegemony. Women writers, black writers, Hispanic writers, third-world writers, lesbian writers can all be painlessly absorbed into the canon—co-opted—without fundamentally altering the cultural or institutional powers that direct the process of canon formation and whose interests are served by it.

As I demonstrated in the first chapter, such dialectical formulations of the "problem" of women's literature and feminist theory lead to new forms of authority rather than an anti-authoritarian reformulation of the politics of value. Instead of a dialectical view of the canon, what I have in mind is a *dialogical* view of both the canon and canon formation. Rather than view the canon as an ideal, as critics from T. S. Eliot to Altieri and Nina Baym (1980) have done, we need to view the canon as a dialogical site of political contention which, given its very nature, can never be stabilized, depoliticized, or idealized. The question that we need to ask ourselves is not how to "open up" the canon to marginal groups of writers—women, blacks, and so on—but how to ensure that their works are not simply assimilated into "ideas and ideals" of the canon. A radical transformation of the canon depends on a radical questioning of the values by which literature has traditionally been defined.

This historical, contextual approach to value requires a frankly materialist definition of the canon, one that takes into account the material practices that create both literature and the canon. Consider, for example, Paul Lauter's definition: "I mean by the 'American literary canon' that set of authors and works generally included in basic American literature college courses and textbooks, and those ordinarily discussed in standard volumes of literary history, bibliography or criticism."[8] The canon is forged in the classroom, in syllabi, anthologies, textbooks, literary journals, and reviews in a process that seems decidedly circular. Literature, in this view, is what gets published, taught, written about, and kept in print. This definition is materialist precisely to the extent that it deals with the means of literature's production and consumption, a process de-

[8]Paul Lauter, "Race and Gender in the Shaping of the American Literary Canon: A Case Study from the Twenties," in Newton and Rosenfelt 1985, 19.

scribed by Richard Ohmann as "saturated with class values and interests, . . . inseparable from the broader struggle for position in our society, from the institutions that mediate that struggle, as well as from legitimation of and challenges to that social order" (1983, 200).

This shift toward describing the historical processes that create value and that valorize literary texts necessarily focuses attention on the conditions that create value. If, as I argued in Chapter 1, citing Lévi-Strauss, history is always "history-for," then value is always "value-for" because it is through selection, classification, and ordering (hierarchies) that we confer value upon objects. "Value-for" enables us to reevaluate objectivist theories of intrinsic value by requiring us to pose questions that in traditional terms are unposable "nonquestions." If value is value-for, then we must ask of any valued object, value for whom? under what circumstances and conditions? and for what purpose? These questions have the decided advantage of bringing the rather abstract language of value down to specific cases. Any value judgment, Smith argues, can be unpacked as a statement of value-for, that is, as "the evaluator's observation and/or estimate of how well that object, relative to others of the same implied category, has performed and/or is likely to perform certain particular (although taken for granted) functions of some particular (though only implicitly defined) set of subjects under some particular (unspecified but assumed) set or range of conditions" (1983, 20).

A dialogic theory of value ceases to take for granted those functions value is measuring. It explicitly defines the set of subjects for whom value functions. And finally, it specifies the range of conditions under which the value judgment applies. This kind of dialogical theory also enables feminists to describe a "dynamics of value" that goes beyond traditional concepts of the canon as a homogeneous, timeless, and static array of monuments. A dialogical conception of the canon allows us to see it as continuous interaction and debate, a field of intersecting and often conflicting interests, including those of writers, publishers, critics, readers, teachers, and students. It enables us to examine the roles institutions, particularly the university, play in shaping the desires and expectations of the readers and consumers of literature.

Rubbish to Art

Any dialogic or dynamic theory of value must be able to describe the social processes by which a work negotiates the boundary between art and nonart, the ways in which *both* positive and negative value are conferred upon objects and texts. Classical descriptions of the coming into being of a work of art, such as the one T.S. Eliot offers in "Tradition and the Individual Talent," frequently suppress the operations of negative valuation—the category of rubbish, nonart, or trash—in defining the work of art, just as they suppress the operations of agency, of value-for. According to Eliot, "The existing monuments form an ideal order among themselves, which is modified by the introduction of the new (the really new) work of art among them. The existing order is complete before the new work arrives; for order to persist after the supervention of novelty, the whole existing order must be, if ever so slightly, altered; and so the relations, proportions, values of each work of art toward the whole are readjusted; and this is conformity between the old and the new" (Davis and Finke 1989, 588–89). Eliot describes not so much a relationship between art and non-art as a boundary between what is art—a monument—and everything else, a boundary between durability and transience and a method by which transfers are made across that boundary. Note, however, that the transfer involves no agents. "Existing monuments" form the "ideal order" by some miraculous and unexplained mechanism that doesn't require the intervention of mere mortals. A new work "arrives," but where it arrives from or how is never hinted at. The passive voice dominates in Eliot's description—order must be altered, values are readjusted—as indeed it must in this profoundly conservative world view in which "timeless" aesthetic value takes precedence over both human and social or cultural agency.

Eliot's idealist theory of value is unable to explain transformations in the value of a literary text over time because he posits a blind evolution of value, a ceaseless movement without discernible cause or agents. Eliot might have explained this ceaseless movement in much the same way that Saussure, writing only a few years earlier in *Course in General Linguistics*, explains alterations in the sign; the tradition "is exposed to alteration because it perpetuates itself" (1966,74). However stretched this comparison might seem, it does shed some light on the authoritarian ideologies of modernism as they asserted themselves at the turn of the century, as well as on the necessary invisibility of the power relationships that create both linguistic and literary authority. In *The History of Sexuality*, Foucault declares that invisibility and mystification are essential to the operations of cultural authority: "Power is tolerable only on condition that it mask a substantial part of itself. Its success is proportional to its ability to hide its own mechanisms. . . . For it, secrecy is not in the nature of an abuse; it is indispensable to its operations" (Foucault 1978, 86). In "Tradition and the Individual Talent," Eliot suppresses diachronic and historical transformations of value in favor of a synchronic stasis. He erases the network of transactions required to create the "monument," setting up a local, contingent authority as universal.

Eliot's account of value and canon formation has heavily influenced twentieth-century discussions of value and has helped suppress those very concepts of agency, function, and condition central to any dynamic theory of value. We might examine the repressed diachronic operations in Eliot's account by looking at how literary and cultural institutions and agents shape the transformation of a text from nonart to art. We can then see how determinations about the "monuments" of great literature depend upon the construction of a complementary category that we might call rubbish.[9] This discussion, however, cannot take place in a vacuum, outside a specific historical context, because such transformations are diachronic and so must take place within history. Our analysis requires that a time and place specify the situation within which any discourse about the value of a particular text will occur. An analysis of the movements of a specific text across Eliot's hypothetical boundary requires that we specify the times and places in which such movements take place.

I have chosen as an example of this transfer Kate Chopin's 1899 novel *The Awakening*. Although now recognized as an "American classic" as well as a feminist classic (according to the *Norton Anthology of Literature by Women* it is "a shadowy story about female erotic

[9] I am indebted to Michael Thompson and his writing on rubbish theory (1979) for this idea.

freedom and even about feminist emotional independence" [Gilbert and Gubar 1985a, 993])—this book was out of print for half a century following its highly controversial initial reception. I have set out side by side for comparison some excerpts from two contemporary reviews of the novel which demonstrate how the language of the "ideal order" is constructed out of complex and dynamic dialogues in which conflict, contradiction, and opposition, particularly in the social realm, are ultimately smoothed over as the text is "swallowed up" by the canon.

There may be many opinions touching other aspects of Mrs. Chopin's novel "The Awakening," but all must concede its flawless art. The delicacy of touch of rare skill in construction, the subtle understanding of motive, the searching vision into the recesses of the heart—these are known to the readers of "Bayou Folk" and "A Night in Acadie." But in this new work power appears, power born of confidence. There is no uncertainty in the lines, so surely and firmly drawn. Complete mastery is apparent on every page. Nothing is wanting to make a complete artistic whole. In delicious English, quick with life, never a word too much, simple and pure, the story proceeds with classic severity through a labyrinth of doubt and temptation and dumb despair.

Miss Kate Chopin . . . has put her cleverness to a very bad use in writing "The Awakening." The purport of the story can hardly be described in language fit for publication. We are fain to believe that Miss Chopin did not herself realize what she was doing when she wrote it. With a bald realism that fairly out Zolas Zola, she describes the result upon a married woman who lives amiably with her husband without caring for him, of a slowly growing admiration for another man. He is too honorable to speak and goes away; but her life is spoiled already, and she falls with a merely animal instinct into the arms of the first man she meets.

"The Awakening" is not for the young person; not because the young person would be harmed by reading it, but because the young person wouldn't understand it, and everybody knows that the young person's understanding should be scrupulously respected. It is for seasoned souls, for those who have lived, who have ripened under the gracious or ungracious sun of experience and learned that realities do not show themselves on the outside of things where they can be seen and heard, weighed, measured, and val-

The worst of such stories is that they will fall into the hands of youth, leading them to dwell on things that only matured persons can understand, and promoting unholy imaginations and unclean desires.

ued. . . . No the book is not for the young person, nor, indeed, for the old person who has no relish for unpleasant truths. For such there is much that is very improper in it, not to say positively unseemly. A fact, no matter how essential, which we have all agreed shall not be acknowledged, is as good as no fact at all. And it is disturbing—even indelicate—to mention it as something which, perhaps, does play an important part in the life behind the mask.

It is sad and mad and bad, but it is all consummate art. The theme is difficult, but it is handled with a cunning craft. The work is more than unusual. It is unique. The integrity of its art is that of well-knit individuality at one with itself, with nothing superfluous to weaken the impression of a perfect whole. (C. L. Deyo, St. Louis *Post-Dispatch*, May 20, 1899)

It is nauseating to remember that those who object to the bluntness of our older writers will excuse and justify the gilded dirt of these latter days. (*Providence Sunday Journal*, June 4, 1899)[10]

The value of Chopin's novel, for each reviewer, is unequivocal. For C. L. Deyo, the novel is "flawless," even "consummate art." For the *Providence Sunday Journal* reviewer, the novel is garbage; it "can hardly be described in language fit for publication." Deyo constructs the novel as art by drawing exclusively upon a positively charged set of literary and aesthetic criteria that stress the author's control (her "complete mastery," "cunning craft," "delicacy of touch of rare skill in construction," "searching vision," and "subtle understanding"), the unity of the work (its "integrity of art," it is a "perfect," a "complete and artistic whole"), and its simplicity. The *Providence Sunday Journal* reviewer constructs his review out of a negatively charged language of disapprobation which draws almost instinctively on rubbish imagery. The novel is "nauseating," "gilded dirt"; it can promote only "unholy imaginations and unclean desires." His attack focuses on the presumed social effect of

[10]Both reviews, along with several others that demonstrate the controversy surrounding the reception of *The Awakening*, are reprinted in Margaret Culley's edition of the novel (Chopin 1976, 147–50).

the novel, to the exclusion of its artistic form. These two reviews are diametrically opposed. Yet each writer is certain of his judgment. In both reviews, the indicative "is" dominates the verbal forms. There are no modal constructions—ought, should, might— to undercut the certainty of either judgment.[11] This is particularly true for Deyo, who, after conceding the possibility of other "opinions" of the novel, uses the indicative construction "A is B" seventeen times in the three passages quoted. Both reviewers attempt to give their evaluation of the novel the status of ontological fact, to make it seem transparent, natural, inevitable. To reply glibly that one person's art is another's garbage is to beg the question, to ignore the certainty with which each reviewer evaluates the novel. How could the novel's readers negotiate between two such radically opposed utterances about value, utterances that call attention to their own facticity?

To understand the dynamics of this conflict as more than just a difference of "opinion," we must recognize the conventions of the review as a speech genre. The book review is an important part of the apparatus by which literary value (and with it the literary canon) is constructed. It is ideally (that is, within the framework of the assumptions T. S. Eliot offers) designed to give its readers enough information about a book, along with an evaluation of it, to enable them to make an informed judgment about whether or not to read it. Because the reviewer must speak with an authoritative voice, she must assume the right to speak objectively and dispassionately about literary value and to speak for some particular cultural community that shares her values. However authoritative or objective this process may seem, it is always, as Richard Ohmann has demonstrated, saturated with class values and interests, always part of a struggle to legitimate or to challenge the social, as well as the aesthetic, order (1983, 200–204). The reviewers of *The Awakening*, in this respect, write from specific sociohistorical and political positions, not from the Olympian vantage point that their rhetoric is meant to imply. Knowing that C. L. Deyo was a friend of Chopin's might incline traditionalists to doubt the "objectivity" of

---

[11]See Hodge and Kress 1988, 120–28, for a discussion of the grammatical function of modality in determining the relationship between facts and opinions.

his review. Within any idealist theory of value, Deyo must appear the more "biased" reviewer, whose "objective" evaluation is tainted by "special interests," by his friendship with Chopin and perhaps also by his regional biases since his review appeared in a St. Louis newspaper. But the second, anonymous reviewer is really no more "objective" because he did not know Chopin personally. Despite the disembodied anonymity which seems a mark of its authority, implying it speaks disinterestedly, presumably for "all" readers, the review appeared in a Providence, Rhode Island, newspaper, and one could argue that it speaks for an eastern literary and intellectual elite that largely controlled the apparatus by which value in literature and culture was conferred. Both reviews represent the communities for which they speak, and perhaps they embody, on a small scale, an ongoing conflict between a powerful and authoritative northeastern literary establishment and an emergent midwestern center of "provincial" culture.

One procedure for validating the community's established taste is to co-opt and neutralize assumptions and values that differ from the hegemonic norm. The two reviews I have quoted are ostensibly about two different sets of issues, drawing upon very different criteria. Deyo praises the novel, calling for a judgment based solely upon what he sees as literary or aesthetic criteria—the novel's "art." The Providence reviewer condemns the impropriety of the novel's subject matter. But this apparent form/content split is more illusory than real. Central to the strategy of each is the discrediting of alternative sets of assumptions and values by which the novel might be judged. Each anticipates and neutralizes the other's point of view. Deyo admits that the novel contains "much that is very improper in it, not to say positively unseemly," The *Providence Sunday Journal* review grudgingly allows the novel's literariness: its "cleverness" and its "bald realism," which "out Zolas Zola."

Both reviewers, however, recognize at some level that the issues at stake in the novel are ideological. Deyo casts his approval in the language of aesthetic value; the anonymous reviewer his disapprobation in the language of moral value. But both ultimately collapse moral *and* aesthetic judgments into hegemonic assumptions about the socio-ideological function of art. Deyo, for instance, argues that the novel is only for "seasoned souls," not for the young or for those who have "no relish for unpleasant truths." The assumption behind this polemical defense is that the novel is both artistic *and* moral because it is true; it reveals the complex intermixing of pleasant and unpleasant realities that are part of life. He attempts to neutralize opposition by arguing that those who cannot perceive the novel's vision of morality cannot properly read it. But although Deyo briefly notes some of the novel's ideological contradictions and conflicts—"Her children did not help her, for she was not a mother woman and didn't feel that loving babies was the whole duty of a woman"—he trivializes them by treating them as aesthetic details, robbing Chopin of her awareness of sexual politics: "This [the preceding quotation] sounded clever because it was paradoxical, but she didn't quite know what it meant" (148). The second reviewer is as astute a polemicist as the first. He recognizes and recoils in horror from the novel's threat to late nineteenth-century patriarchal hegemony. He discusses more overtly what he perceives as the novel's moral and ideological faults. But these social and moral criticisms edge over into the aesthetic when he argues that Chopin's "bald" realism entails the uncovering of unpleasant realities that one expects to be "masked" in polite society. Chopin's primary fault (one Deyo recognizes as well, but defends) is that she reveals "indelicate" things that good "taste" would have left unsaid.[12] "Taste," then, far from being a timeless, aesthetic quality, as Edmund Burke thought, or an arbitrary projection of idiosyncratic preferences, as I. A. Richards and Northrop Frye thought, is an ideological construct that conflates social, moral,

---

[12]The conflict between these two reviews provides an illuminating example of the problems inherent in what Harriett Hawkins (1983, 103–7) has called the "example theory" of literature. Since Plato, literary critics have assumed that literature must ultimately serve some moral agenda. Literature represents not only the good, beautiful, and true, but also the wicked, ugly, and cruel. And sometimes the latter manage to capture readers' sympathies and imaginations more effectively than the former. To this dilemma, Hawkins notes two characteristic responses. The Platonic response, the basis of virtually all attempts to censor literature, argues that because literature often makes evil seem attractive, it ought to be somehow restrained, if not banned; most defenses of literature respond to this argument on its own terms, invoking the same assumption that literature will serve some moral agenda. They argue that literature can be recuperated for moral ends. Evil is as much a part of life as good and so must be represented, but as part of a larger vision in which good is ultimately rewarded and evil punished.

ethical, and ideological values while disguising the processes by which such values, painted as universal givens, are socially and historically constructed and negotiated within heterogeneous communities.

The Awakening was disturbing for its contemporary audiences not only in its portrayal of the socioeconomic condition of women at the turn of the century but also in its frank portrayal of female eroticism, which, at least according to most of the reviewers, threatened to destabilize conventional sexual roles.[13] The novel's aesthetic value for its original audience was inextricably tied up with the sociopolitical conditions that were part of its reception, in particular contemporary controversies over the position of women in society. Apparently neither "female erotic freedom" nor "feminist emotional independence" (the qualities of the novel praised by *The Norton Anthology of Women's Literature*) was highly valued by readers at the turn of the century. Indeed these qualities were seen as a dangerous threat to sociopolitical order.

During the last decade of the nineteenth century social tensions within American life seem to have been particularly acute. According to one historian, "America in the late nineteenth century was a society without a core" (Wiebe 1967, 12–13). By the 1890s the structure of American industry was changing dramatically. Economic power was becoming centralized in a few large cities, and as a result, urban populations grew rapidly, fed by massive immigration as well as by migration from small towns and rural communities. Cities were unprepared to meet the growing number and complexity of social problems that accompanied urbanization, immigration, and industrialization. These included transportation of raw materials and workers, the delivery of educational and medical services, disease control, lighting and gas, police and fire protection, sewage disposal and water purification. Communication and transportation in many cities threatened to collapse under the

---

[13]Another reviewer of the novel wrote, "A woman of twenty-eight, a wife and twice a mother who in pondering upon her relations to the world about her, fails to perceive that the relation of a mother to her children is far more important than the gratification of a passion which experience has taught her is, by its very nature, evanescent, can hardly be said to be fully awake" New Orleans *Times-Democrat*, June 18, 1899 (Chopin 1976, 150).

strain; there were labor riots; child mortality among the poor became alarming; disease was rampant. Alarm seemed to run particularly high among those economically defined as middle class. As historian Robert Wiebe notes, some of the anxiety that one reads in the documents from this period seem generated by the bourgeois fascination with and loathing of the city: "Once roused the sense of emergency was self-generating. Matters that previously would have been considered separate incidents or even ignored, were seized and fit into the framework of jeopardy, each reinforcing the other as a proof of imminent danger."[14] The characteristic response of the bourgeoisie to this growing sense of alarm was, as I suggested in the last chapter, to place the blame for social disorder on the degeneration of the traditional nuclear family.

These anxieties and fears accentuated class divisions and strained traditional values, particularly those that centered on the family. Traditional gender roles that limited women primarily to the domestic sphere seemed to some in danger of disappearing altogether, while to others they seemed increasingly confining. During this time women could not vote (that right was still three decades away) and they had few legal rights. In some parts of the country—most notably in Louisiana, the setting of the novel—women could not sign contracts, initiate a lawsuit, hold office, or witness testaments. Upon marriage, a woman's property became her husband's, and her husband was legal guardian of any children they might have. In the event of a separation, the husband would be granted custody; the wife would have nothing, not even, technically, the clothes on her back.[15]

The "woman question" was much debated during the 1890s. On the one hand, there were repeated attempts to expand at least bourgeois women's public roles and to recognize their rights as citizens. There were demands for equality in education, employment, and wages. There were even demands for the vote. The movement of bourgeois women away from marriage and domes-

[14]Wiebe 1967, 45. See also Stallybrass and White 1986, 125–48. For this discussion of late nineteenth-century social unrest, I am also indebted to Smith-Rosenberg 1985, 167–81; Newman 1985; Eisenstein 1981, 145–49; and Culley in Chopin 1976, 115–40.

[15]For a discussion of the position of women at the turn of the century, see Culley in Chopin 1976, 115–40; Smith-Rosenberg 1985, 218–96; Newman 1985.

ticity was represented by the phenomenon of the "New Woman," which Carroll Smith-Rosenberg describes as a specific sociological and educational "cohort" of women born between the late 1850s and 1900. They represented the trend among bourgeois women toward later marriages, college education, and often professional careers: "The New Women, rejecting conventional female roles and asserting their right to a career, to a public voice, to visible power, laid claim to the rights and privileges customarily accorded to bourgeois men" (1985, 176). The successes of the New Woman predictably resulted in reactionary calls for a return to traditional family values, which could be disregarded only at the risk of undermining the moral fabric of decent society. In the words of one physician, "The gradual disappearance of the home, which any thoughtful observer must deplore, is, to a large extent, the result of the discontentment of the educated woman with the duties and surroundings of wifehood and motherhood, and the thirst for concerts, theaters, pictures and parties, which keeps her in the public gaze, to the loss of her health and the ruin, very often, of her husband's happiness."[16] The reaction to the threat of women's growing independence, symbolized by the figure of the New Woman, was the creation and institutionalization of a medical discourse about sexuality which functioned as an agent of social control.

Debates about female sexuality were particularly acrimonious during the last decades of the nineteenth century, and these debates almost certainly fueled the controversy surrounding the reception of Chopin's novel. The popular and scientific press was full of anxieties about the declining birthrate among bourgeois women. Part of this anxiety was no doubt racist and xenophobic in origin; the 1880s and 1890s saw a huge upsurge of immigration into this country.[17] But part of it must also have been a response to changes in the power relations within the bourgeois family which resulted from social and economic change. The falling birthrate was attributed to the increased education of women, later marriages, and the availability of effective birth control (the mass production of vulcanized rubber in the 1870s added the condom to more primi-

[16]A. Lapthorn Smith, *Popular Science Monthly* (1905), quoted in Newman 1985, 151.

[17]See Gould 1981; and Newman 1985, 105–21.

tive forms of birth control such as coitus interruptus and absti-
nence) and of abortion before the 1880s.[18] All these developments
increased bourgeois women's sexual freedom and their power
within the family, at the same time as they highlighted their dangers.

The development of American sexology (a medicoscientific discipline dealing with sexual deviance) at the turn of the century is
almost a textbook example of Foucault's thesis in *History of Sexuality*
that sexuality—discourses about sex—once institutionalized, unite
power and knowledge in ways that enhance the social control and
political aims of the dominant class, in this case the control of
women and an increase in the birthrate among middle-class wom-
en to offset population increases from immigration. "Technologies
of sex" led to the production of "docile bodies"—women's bodies
whose "normal" functioning emphatically required that women
not use their minds. The discourses of American sexology as described by Smith-Rosenberg (1985) display all the technologies articulated by Foucault in *History of Sexuality*. The sexualization of
women's bodies was accomplished by defining the female body as
its reproductive system. Women's brains, wrote Havelock Ellis, are
"to a certain extent in their wombs" (Smith-Rosenberg 1985, 278).
In the words of one physician, "Not only does wifehood and motherhood not require an extraordinary development of the brain, but
the latter is a decided barrier against the proper performance of
those duties" (A. Lapthorne Smith, quoted in Newman 1985, 147).
Energy directed away from the reproductive organs, say, toward
the mind, led to medically defined and carefully classified
diseases—neurasthenia, hysteria, insanity, sterility, cancer. The
control of procreation was accomplished by the criminalization of
abortion, the medicalization of birth control, and the increasing
hegemony of university-trained obstetricians and gynecologists
over midwives and other medical practitioners. Finally, the creation of a psychology which defined anomalous sexual behavior as
perversion was accomplished through the development of a scientific discourse on homosexuality and lesbianism in which taxon-
omy, measurement, classification, and control figured heavily.

[18]Smith-Rosenberg 1985, 217–44; Newman 1985, 105–21.

The foregoing data do not merely constitute "historical back-ground" or "context" for Chopin's novel. Reactions to the political and social instabilities of the late nineteenth century interpenetrate the "values" of both the reviewers and the readers of *The Awakening*. The fact that the position of woman became increasingly tied to her role within the family was clearly recognized on both sides of the debates about the novel. One reviewer of *The Awakening* wrote of the novel as a threat to the order of civilized society precisely because it undermined the traditional family: "In a civilized society the right of the individual to indulge all his caprices is, and must be, subject to many restrictive clauses, and it cannot for a moment be admitted that a woman who has willingly accepted the love and devotion of a man, even without an equal love on her part—who has become his wife and the mother of his children—has not incurred a moral obligation which peremptorily forbids her from wantonly severing her relations with him, and entering openly upon the independent existence of an unmarried woman" (New Orleans *Times-Democrat*, June 18, 1899, quoted in Chopin 1976, 150). On the other side, Charlotte Perkins Gilman, in the same year *The Awakening* was published, sardonically attacked the narrowness of this ideology of the traditional family in *Women and Economics*: "Since we hold that our home life, just as we have it, is the best thing on earth, and that our home life plainly demands one whole woman at the least to each home, and usually more, it follows that anything which offers to change the position of wom-an threatens to 'undermine the home,' 'strikes at the root of the family,' and we will none of it" (quoted in Chopin 1976, 135). Gilman's "we," here used ironically to distance her from the senti-ments she is expressing, suggests her frustration with the re-sistance to proposals for changes in women's social and economic position. Clearly, the 1890s had seen enough of a challenge to the rigid Victorian morality that kept women tied to the role of the "angel in the house" that such a novel as *The Awakening* could be written and that such a desire for female freedom could be con-ceived by Chopin and Gilman. But equally clearly, given the recep-tion of the novel, there was not enough sentiment in favor of female sexual freedom for it to be deemed "acceptable" literature for a broad spectrum of readers.

The *Post-Dispatch* and *Sunday Journal* reviews of *The Awakening*, then, are not just "opinions." They represent entire world views— political, social, cultural, and intellectual ways of viewing the world which exist in dialogical tension with one another. In them we can more closely view the workings of social authority because the two views can be negotiated only through a complex political dynamic of authority. There is nothing intrinsic to the text of the novel which can "choose" between these two positions. They exist in dialogue with each other and, as I have demonstrated, are mutually intelligible. What separates them is not a cognitive gap but a social one, in this case, beliefs about gender differences that have been given social meaning. A patriarchal and largely eastern literary elite was able to impose at least the illusion of temporary closure to the debate, so that its value judgments seemed neutral and self-evident, while others appeared politically motivated. It is to the advantage of the dominant cultural community to elide the kind of dialogue I have been describing and to impose a monologic sense of closure on debates that reveal the complicity of "high" culture in politics, sexism, and racism. In an idealist theory of value, both views can not become part of the novel's history, and it is the group with the power to enforce and standardize "agreed-upon values" which has the power to write this history and marginalize competing viewpoints. Its evaluations have consequences, both for the subsequent history of *The Awakening* and for the history of American literature. Chopin languished in relative obscurity, marginalized as a "local colorist," a provincial writer who may have illuminated the character of a region but who could hardly claim to have unfolded the great universals, which somehow seemed never to be found west of Philadelphia. Of course it was not entirely coincidental that *The Awakening* was denied "universality"; it is a "fact" of cultural hegemony, part of the logic of marginalization, that whatever group is constructed as the "other," the marginal—local colorists, women writers, black writers, third-world writers—will always be perceived as writing about less universal themes than those of the culturally dominant group. This criterion is characteristically evoked as an aesthetic ideal, which can then be used to deny marginal groups representation in the canon. If Deyo's point of view had endured—and it did not, at least initially—the book would have been reprinted, kept in print, housed in libraries, and read compulsorily by schoolchildren or at the very least by college students and their professors. But because the *Providence Sunday Journal* reviewer's judgment of the novel (and several others like it) proved more durable, the book was condemned as trash. Like other trash it became disposable, the unwanted by-product of the consumption of popular literature, and was thrown away. In the aftermath of controversies over *The Awakening*, the novel was removed from libraries and remained out of print for nearly half a century before it was "rediscovered."

The processes by which the novel was "rediscovered," transformed from trash to art,[19] are crucial to the formulation of a dialogic theory of value. The idealist who believes that value is intrinsic to a text might argue that the true classic must withstand the "test of time" and that Chopin, if she is good enough to be read today, must be either a "misunderstood genius" whose true value awaited a more perceptive audience or the darling of bra-burning, fire-breathing feminists whose demands for "women writers" to teach and write about threaten to contaminate the purity of aesthetics with their special-interest politics. Both of these views ignore the very mechanisms by which texts like *The Awakening* are preserved; the material practices by which they cross the boundary between transience and durability—publication, reprinting, library collections, and compulsory education—are largely created and controlled by a dominant cultural apparatus similar to the one that originally determined their value. The process is circular. Texts that stand the test of time do so because people and institutions with the power and means to keep them available deem them valuable enough to preserve and publicize; it is this very preservation and promotion that continues to confer value on these texts.

But the process is not nearly as seamless and inflexible as this description might make it sound; otherwise it would be impossible for a text like *The Awakening* to be rediscovered after fifty years of

---

[19]It is a curious sidelight to my discussion of rubbish or trash as a covert category for the construction of value that one critic who participated in its rediscovery expressed surprise that the novel had not "been picked up today by reprint houses long on lurid covers and short on new talent" (Kenneth Eble, quoted in Chopin 1976, 166).

neglect. The interests of the dominant cultural group—which is, after all, heterogeneous, not homogeneous—are always contradictory and conflicted; the dialogues that have been repressed are always threatening to reassert themselves. Nor are the dominant group's the only interests represented in the processes of cultural preservation. The canon cannot be construed simply as a list of books or, as Eliot saw it, an array of monuments, static and unchanging except for the addition of the occasional new classic. Rather, the canon, as the repository of literary value, is a dynamic process in which many material practices interact and in which the interests of different sociopolitical classes (including racial and gender classes) intersect and conflict. Even the briefest consideration of compulsory education—which constitutes only one of the practices that contributes to the perpetuation of literary value— suggests the complexity of the model required to describe this dynamic. What is compulsory reading for schoolchildren will not be the same as what is required of undergraduates at elite liberal arts colleges. Graduate students and their professors read and conduct research on a much larger array of valued texts, both major and minor, than either of these two groups, and the results of their research, in turn, contribute to the formation of value.

Still, a book that is out of print and not easily available in libraries cannot be read by anyone except perhaps the academic specialist reading in rare book collections that may have preserved a copy. *The Awakening* survived in obscurity during the first half of the twentieth century, although it was the subject of only sporadic academic interest, much of it negative (Percy Pollard made fun of it in his *Their Day in Court* [1909]) or concerned with it as an example of local color. In a 1932 biography, Daniel Rankin called Kate Chopin an "original genius" but still seemed somewhat shocked by a book he called "exotic in setting, morbid in theme, and erotic in motivation." Only in the late 1960s did *The Awakening*, along with other "regional" works from the turn of the century, experience something of a revival. That decade produced a biography of Chopin, a complete edition of her works, and several critical reassessments of her novel. Kenneth Eble's 1956 essay, aptly titled "A Forgotten Novel," illustrates this transformation of value. He calls *The Awakening* a "first-rate novel" that "goes beyond the limitations of regional material" and insists, "Having added to American literature a novel uncommon in its kind as in its excellence, [Chopin] deserves not to be forgotten. *The Awakening* deserves to be restored and to be given its place among novels worthy of preservation."[20] This is a version of the familiar idealist argument. Chopin, misunderstood in her own time and undeservedly neglected since, deserves to be resurrected from her oblivion because of her novel's general "excellence." As one might expect, given the date of his essay, Eble's analysis of the novel is thoroughly New Critical in its insistent formalism, its privileging of aesthetic form over social content. His article deals almost exclusively with qualities of language and style, and relations of image and experience; he praises Chopin's "complete command of structure" and her use of "unifying symbols." He dismisses the content that earlier readers had found so shocking: "Quite frankly, the book is about sex." Gone is the sense one feels in reading the early criticism of the novel that its contents were profoundly disturbing because they challenged and undermined existing social and sexual relations. It is replaced by a concern with establishing the novel's pedigree, placing it in a direct line with the great "masters" of nineteenth-century realism—if not Flaubert, Zola, James, and Tolstoy, then Crane, Dreiser, and Norris. For the New Critic, the very specific and local problems of women's oppression and sexual freedom articulated in *The Awakening* are replaced by more easily digested "universal" and philosophical platitudes about the limits of the individual's freedom and the dangers of absolute freedom. The thornier issues of women's oppression and the role of the family as a social institution in perpetuating that oppression would not be seen as central to the novel until the rise of academic feminism in the early seventies.[21]

The collision between the New Criticism and a newly emergent feminist literary criticism in the 1970s ensured the reputation of *The Awakening* as both an "American classic" and a "feminist classic," highlighting the material practices that led to its resurrection, in particular the differences between publication and teaching as discourses on value. Although *The Awakening* suited New Critical as

[20]Quoted in Chopin 1976, 170.
[21]For a discussion of the effects of New Critical hegemony in postwar American universities, see Eagleton 1983, 48–51; and Tompkins 1985, 192–95.

well as feminist agendas, Chopin remained for critics and scholars of American literature a minor writer, the subject of mostly scholarly interest. It was the pedagogical needs of feminist criticism for women writers to teach in classes on Literature by Women which brought the novel into larger numbers of classrooms in the 1970s. Margaret Culley's 1976 Norton Critical Edition of *The Awakening*, which provided an easily accessible teaching text as well as a history of its controversial reception and its then-favorable literary reputation, marked the novel's final assimilation into the canon of American literature.

The new literary scholarship on women, increasingly prominent after 1975, required its own critical reevaluation of literary reputation, which served its own distinctive ends. As Smith has noted, any theory of value must take into account the "interactive relation" between classification of an entity and the function it is expected to perform (1983, 13). By locating a text within a particular category—literature as opposed to journalism or history, the novel as opposed to the epic or the travel narrative—we foreground certain possible functions, and the value of that text becomes contingent on its success in fulfilling those functions. If *The Awakening* is classified as an American realist novel, then what will be valued in the novel is the authenticity of its representation of "reality," its expression of some peculiarly "American character" or some set of shared "American" values,[22] and its satisfactory manipulation of the conventions we have come to expect from the genre we have called the novel. But the process also works in reverse. Sometimes under conditions that produce a new "need," certain other functions and properties of a text may be foregrounded and both classification and value will change accordingly. *The Awakening* is a case in point. Feminist literary criticism created a need for new literary functions—women's issues, women's perspectives, women writers. *The Awakening* was able to serve all those ends; it could be appropriated for feminist purposes and become a major text in a new feminist canon. *The MLA International Bibliography* might serve as a kind of crude index of these interactive relations among literary reputation, classification, and value. Kate Chopin was not even

[22]See Baym 1981.

listed in the *MLA Bibliography* until 1965. In 1965 she has one entry, an edition of *The Awakening*. By 1975 the scholarship on Chopin runs to twenty-one entries, including a bibliography and the *Kate Chopin Newsletter*. After 1975 the titles of the articles begin to change as well, reflecting the new feminist agenda that Chopin's novel was being asked to serve. Such New Critical topic markers as "the tragic imperative," "ironic vision," "narrative stance," and "ambiguity in art" give way to markers more identifiably feminist such as "sexuality," the "woman question," "female identity," and "motherhood."

It begins to look from this single example as if literary value, far from being intrinsic to the text or self-evident, and thus either static or progressive, is marked by radical discontinuity and rupture. This observation would seem to validate several recent historiographic theories of discontinuity, including the account of literary history propounded by Stanley Fish, who says that no reading of a literary text, "however outlandish it might appear, is inherently an impossible one" (1980, 347). For Fish, any function might be foregrounded in a reading of a text; therefore none is intrinsically necessary to the text's value and none can be excluded on the grounds that it is unthinkable. At any given time, we may be unable to appreciate the value of certain functions because of our commitment to others; the revolutions projected by these readings have not yet occurred. Fish's account may be useful, as far as it goes, in explaining such phenomena as the transformations in Chopin's literary reputation in terms of crises or revolutions like the revolution in feminist literary criticism.

His explanation of the transformation of literary value in terms of discontinuity or breaks with the past, however, tends to mystify the process at work in such transformations. Fish cannot explain how such ruptures occur; he merely states that they "project a revolution." As Robert Hodge and Gunther Kress have said, however, "'To see periods of art or culture as monolithic blocks divided by deep fissures of incommensurability and incomprehension . . . repeats the hegemonic act whereby history is rewritten by a dominant group, which attempts to elide the very opposition which completes its meaning" (1988, 185). Fish's problem is rather like that of the structural linguist who argues that languages inevitably change but cannot explain the mechanism by which they change. Value judgments of literary texts change, Fish asserts, because the functions these texts serve change, but he can articulate no process that will describe how these changes occur, and so they appear to happen mysteriously, as "revolutions." Fish sees both the literary text and its reader as complex but static sign systems, isolated from the larger "social text," which creates the literary text and governs how it can be received by its readers. Even his notion of "interpretive communities," which has the advantage of explaining how readings and judgments about literary texts are valued and authorized within the profession, still tends to treat these communities as operating in isolation from all other social and historical processes. Membership in interpretive communities remains for him largely a matter of individual taste and education. As such, interpretive communities alone cannot explain how transformations in value occur except through the somewhat mystifying agency of "revolutions."

I have maintained that the elements of the New Critical appreciation of *The Awakening* were already present, if suppressed, in the dialogues, debates, and controversies surrounding the novel's initial reception. So too, feminist reappraisals of the novel are intelligible only insofar as they respond to and, indeed, are dialogically anticipated in earlier evaluations of the novel. Feminist critics did not really create radically "new" readings of *The Awakening*; they only seemed to. What feminist criticism said about the novel was already present in the novel's own history of production and reception, but it was present as "noise." Feminist critics exposed *The Awakening*'s history of conflict, the dialogic interplay of voices which had been temporarily suppressed by the monologic account offered by the dominant (and predominantly male) high culture, by the "tradition." Nor were previous discussions of the novel, particularly New Critical discussions, unintelligible to feminist literary critics. They did not abandon the vocabulary and methodologies of New Criticism or indeed of other critical paradigms that had gone before. If feminist critics distinguished themselves from the New Criticism that preceded them in terms of a major transformation, it is not because they did not understand what came before but because they did understand and repudiated its major premises, just as feminist criticism was perfectly intelligible—if abhorent—to traditional critics, who resisted it.

If the process I am describing sounds suspiciously like T. S. Eliot's notion, articulated in "Tradition and the Individual Talent," that "the past should be altered by the present as much as the present is directed by the past," I would maintain that my attempt to create a transformation within theories of value must be no less dialogic than the transformations I have dealt with in this chapter, no less rooted in the controversies and debates about value which have preceded it. I have attempted to transform Eliot's account of value formation by restoring to it its own history of dialogue and conflict. Feminism, I would argue, entered literary criticism as a "work" enters the "tradition," not as a rupture, a break with the past, and not mysteriously by some unknown agent but as a dialogue among various groups with conflicting and intersecting interests, a dialogue that can be recovered. This dialogue continues still and depends on mutual intelligibility, on a language shared by all the participants. Value is one site of this dialogue. A feminist dialogic theory of value will attempt to uncover opposition—the noise—and restore it to the debate, thereby adding a third set of terms to the dialectic between objectivity and subjectivity which has thus far limited discussions of literary value.

Shakespeare's Weeds

In the previous section I concluded that a literary text designated a classic succeeds by effacing the dialogue that constitutes the history of its reception so that its artistic merit seems self-evident. My analysis of *The Awakening* examines some of the methods by which the dialogic activity of cultural exchange is replaced by monologic, "authoritative" pronouncements about value. This process, I would contend, corresponds to the oft-cited "test of time," articulated by Samuel Johnson in the eighteenth century: "What has been longest known has been most considered, and what is most considered is best understood." Once a great author has outlived his century, Johnson writes in *Preface to Shakespeare*,

> Whatever advantages he might once derive from personal allu-
> sions, local customs, or temporary opinions, have for many years
> been lost. . . . The effects of favour and competition are at an end;
> the tradition of his friendships and his enemies has perished; his
> works support no opinion with arguments, nor supply any fac-
> tion with invectives; they can neither indulge vanity nor gratify
> malignity; but are read without any other reason than the desire of
> pleasure, and are therefore praised only as pleasure is obtained;
> yet, thus unassisted by interest or passion, they have past
> through variations of taste and changes of manners, and, as they
> devolved from one generation to another, have received new
> honours at every transmission. (Davis and Finke 1989, 407)

For Johnson, time has the effect of transforming what is personal,
local, and contingent, particularly "variations of taste" and
"changes of manners," into the impersonal, universal, and permanent. That is, it represses history-for, conceived of as the record of
the cultural activity that has preserved the text, in favor of self-
justifying statements about the transhistorical nature of its value.
But as Jane Tompkins has argued, value is not, as Johnson thought,
"a natural fact; it is constantly being produced and maintained by
cultural activity" (Tompkins 1985, 193), the very cultural activities
that have been the subject of the other chapters in this book. In
order to investigate this "cultural activity," it is necessary to interrogate the motives that lie behind Johnson's attempts to formulate
an aesthetics in which all truths are general and value transcends
culture. We must, in other words, uncover the history of sociopolitical conflict that underlies and the interests that buttress—
and continue to legitimate—Johnson's claims that nothing restricted to specific circumstances of time and place can last as a
work of art.

During the eighteenth century, literary criticism was one of several discourses that served as an arena for the conflicts between a
landed and privileged aristocracy and a wealthy but politically marginalized middle class, of which Johnson was a member. Although
the middle class grew increasingly powerful economically, political
influence did not necessarily accompany that wealth. By midcentury criticism, no longer the preserve of the aristocrat, had become

one means by which middle-class writers and readers could claim to share cultural authority by asserting the moral superiority of notions of individualism and self-determined worth to aristocratic claims that value is solely a function of birth. But that cultural authority was not without its attendant anxieties for middle-class writers like Johnson. As Frederick Bogel has suggested, "The assumption of authority was both necessary and necessarily guilt-ridden . . . [and] he sought ways to assume and disclaim that authority in a single gesture."[23] Middle-class claims to share power with the aristocracy rested on a network of ideological pronouncements about the benefits of middle-class industriousness, hard-working devotion to the enrichment of the country, prudence, moderation, common sense, temperance, stability, and virtue—in short, about the *moral* superiority of the middle class to the profligate aristocracy. This ideological argument underlies much of eighteenth-century literary criticism, including Johnson's. Eighteenth-century criticism, in this regard, was primarily concerned not with formal questions of aesthetics but with the sociocultural implications of identifying the moral value of literature with class-based assumptions about virtue.[24] Johnson's position on value was worked out within an intensely partisan political climate. His statement that a work of art transcends customs, manners, and politics is an attempt to translate his own political positions, and those of his class, into "timeless" assessments of what literature and taste should be, an attempt to insulate literature from politics by claiming the ideological high ground—a move that would later be repeated in different historical circumstances by his successors, from Wordsworth, Coleridge, and Arnold in the nineteenth century to T. S. Eliot and Cleanth Brooks in the twentieth century.

[23]Frederick Bogel, "Johnson and the Role of Authority," in Nussbaum and Brown 1987, 205. This discussion is also indebted to Eagleton 1984; Markley, "Sentimentality as Performance," in Nussbaum and Brown 1987, 210–30; and Cannon 1984.

[24]The third earl of Shaftesbury, Anthony Ashley Cooper, articulates some of these assumptions early in the eighteenth century when he writes, "To *philosophize*, in a just Signification, is but to carry *Good-Breeding* a step higher. For the Accomplishment of Breeding is, To learn whatever is *decent* in Company, or *beautiful* in the Arts: and the Sum of Philosophy is, To learn what is *just* in Society, and *beautiful* in Nature, and the Order of the World" *Characteristicks of Men, Manners, Opinions, Times*, quoted in Markley 1987, 147.

The *Preface to Shakespeare*, with its insistence on the "test of time" as a criterion of value, illustrates the process by which the mono-logical impulse of the dominant culture—or, more accurately, the culture that would become dominant—can subsume and delegiti-mate dialogues about value which reveal the conflicting invest-ments of various classes and cultural groups. This monologue helped to constitute the canon of statements about value. Certain ways of talking about value—certain statements—have been au-thorized by hegemonic practices and have been shaped into a "his-tory" of literary criticism. Once this history is written and pre-served, primarily through the cultural practices I described in the previous section—textbooks, anthologies, compulsory educa-tion—the conflicts, debates, and struggles that were part of its construction are marginalized and the statements stand alone as unassailable "facts" or "truths." Alternative voices are lost, al-though not, as we shall see, irrecoverably.

Although feminist critics in the 1980s rediscovered previously "lost" female writers in almost every period of literary study, the history of literary criticism is one canon from which women remain almost totally excluded. In fact, Lawrence Lipking notes that the history of literary criticism, best represented by Hazard Adams's standard anthology, *Critical Theory since Plato*, "does not find room for a single woman in its 1249 double-columned small-printed pages."[25] The implication is that presumably until the second half of the twentieth century women had nothing to say about the formation of the canons of taste by which literature has historically been valued. Furthermore, women's exclusion from the history of literary criticism seems to have gone almost unnoticed by femi-nists. To my knowledge, the only study of the subject is Lipking's 1983 essay "Aristotle's Sister: A Poetics of Abandonment." Lipking's figure for the forgotten female literary critic is Aristotle's sister, Aristemne, who was never allowed to record her thoughts about literature because she was never allowed to write. For Lip-king, she stands for centuries of women's silence on "theory," a silence that, he argues, may not be a bad thing after all: "In another

[25]Lipking 1983, 61; Adams 1971. Lipking writes, "Adams assures me that any future edition of this anthology will contain at least one woman" (79 n. 2).

respect the silence of Aristemne might be considered a rare piece of good fortune—at least for her later sisters. No dead hand of tradition grips feminist literary theory. Its time is the present. During the past decade more and better criticism has been written by women than in all previous history" (62). Lipking makes two assumptions here which merit examination. First, he assumes that feminist literary criticism has no "history" before the twentieth century. He has presumably never read or perceived as criticism the writing of Christine de Pizan, Mary Astell, Aphra Behn, Anne Finch, Eliza Haywood, Fanny Burney, Mary Wollstonecraft, and George Eliot, to name only a few. Second, he assumes that feminists are really better off without such a "tradition" because any such history would only stifle creativity by chaining feminism to a dead past. In one respect, Lipking may be right. The monologism of literary criticism in "the tradition" from Plato to Eliot has narrowly constrained what can allowably be said about literature. But Lipking assumes that any feminist history of theorizing by women would be equally monologic. He fails to consider that, rather than simply accept that women were historically silent on the subject of theory before the twentieth century, feminists might expose the processes by which women who did speak about value were silenced. They might challenge the monologism that marks the history of literary criticism, uncovering in particular the processes that marginalize challenges to cultural hegemony. This approach might restore to all literary criticism the history of its production along with its accompanying noise—its conflicts, contradictions, political debate, and turbulence. This history would certainly be messier than the one currently in fashion, but it would also be more interesting, less "dead."

In 1986 I had the opportunity to fashion such a history when I agreed to collaborate with Robert Con Davis in compiling a new anthology that would cover the history of criticism from the Greeks to the present. I was somewhat reluctant to take on the task, primarily because the history of literary criticism had never seemed a particularly interesting subject. It always struck me as rather like an all-male *Dinner Party*. As I ran down the names in the table of contents of Charles Kaplan's *Criticism: The Major Statements*—Plato, Aristotle, Horace, Sidney, Dryden, Pope, Johnson, Wordsworth,

Coleridge, Keats, Shelley, Arnold, Pater, Eliot, Brooks—I envisioned graybeards sitting around some cosmic table holding forth on metaphysics, the imitation of nature, and morality in poetry: all male and all representative of cultural privilege and authority.

But both of us were also intrigued by the possibility of rewriting the history of criticism and creating in that history some sense of the dialogues that had been suppressed, of the challenges to critical orthodoxies in every period. We wanted to create a dialogic history-for of criticism which would restore to "the tradition" (the *major* texts) the historical debates of which they were a part and which would not gloss over or erase our own cultural investments and biases. We soon discovered conflicts other than the ones we expected to find among literary critics of various theoretical persuasions—New Critics versus structuralists, deconstructors versus feminists, traditionalists versus oppositional critics—together with imagined conflicts between ourselves and a whole array of august and humanistically minded adversaries. There were also conflicts within our culturally constructed notions of what literary criticism is as a discipline, what its purposes are or should be. In our desire to rewrite history, we quickly found ourselves struggling with the economic necessity of producing a volume with enough familiar texts to make it marketable. Do we substitute George Eliot, or even William Morris, for Schlegel? Eliza Haywood for David Hume? Christine de Pizan for Scaliger? In what ways would the inclusion of Aristophanes' *Frogs* change the ways in which we read Plato or Aristotle's *Poetics*? Would the inclusion of Saint Augustine's *De Doctrina Christiana* challenge how we read Derrida? How would these selections affect course adoptions and sales? How would they change—or fail to change—the history of literary criticism? Despite our high ideals, we found ourselves continually caught between our desire to rewrite history and the need to consider marketability, always within the constraints of a fixed number of pages.

At the same time, we were frequently surprised by the answers to our questions and in particular by the extent to which women had contributed to the history of literary criticism and by the importance of those contributions. We didn't have to dig very hard to find substantive statements by women challenging the seemingly monologic discourse of critical canon formation. *Literary Criticism and Theory: The Greeks to the Present* illustrates that women, far from being silent, have been voicing their thoughts on the nature of literary value all along. A careful scrutiny of the critical record left behind by women in literary theory before the twentieth century suggests that not only have women been writing about value, the stories they have to tell us about women writing and about the value of what is written force us to revise radically our histories of particular periods in literary criticism. It is not enough simply to position women within the field. The inclusion of women theorists in the *history* of criticism will require changes in our perspectives of what constitutes that history. In particular we need to rethink the comforting stories literary theorists since Plato have been telling themselves about literature's transcendence of the petty squabbles of economic necessity and its efficacy as a transmitter of transcendent *moral* value.

One of the oldest statements in Western literary theory about the value of literature may be found in Horace's *Art of Poetry* and it reminds us of the central orthodoxy of classical Greek and Roman thought on value: "The aim of the poet is to inform or delight, or to combine together in what he says, both pleasure and applicability to life" (Davis and Finke 1989, 99). This statement—that the purpose of literature is to delight and instruct (*dulce et utile*)—has been repeated so often in the history of Western criticism from the Middle Ages through the eighteenth century that it has come to be known as the Horatian platitude. It is called a platitude because it has attained the status of an unexamined axiom in the criticism of value. It seems so commonplace that one has to wonder if it has not been entirely emptied of meaning. Nothing struck me so forcibly in the history of criticism as the repeated assertion—from fifth-century Athens to late twentieth-century America, in writers as diverse as Chaucer, Boccaccio, Sidney, Dryden, Pope, and Johnson—that literature is somehow "good for us." The question of a literary text's aesthetic value all too frequently gets answered by assertions about its moral value, which, like aesthetic value, is conceived of as transcendent and universal. Indeed, versions of this argument are alive and well today in polemics like those of E. D. Hirsch and Allan Bloom as well as in recent theoretical texts bearing such titles as *The Ethics of Criticism* (Siebers 1989).

Commonplaces about the moral utility of literature obscure their own complicity in defining what "morality" is and how it is de-ployed. It is worth noting that Horace was more forthright about the economic and material basis of his advice than most of his followers. In a less well known passage from the *Art of Poetry*, a few lines after the platitude, he writes that a book that both instructs and delights "is the sort of book that will make money for the publisher" (100). But it took a seventeenth-century Britishwoman to expose the economic underpinnings of the seemingly simple and presumably inoffensive statement that literature should in-struct and delight. In her "Epistle to the Reader" attached to her play *The Dutch Lover*, Aphra Behn takes on the dogma of poetry's moral utility as part of her "defense" of her writing: "I am myself well able to affirm that none of all our English Poets, and least the Dramatique (so I think you call them) can be justly charg'd with too great reformation of men's minds or manners, and for that I may appeal to general experiment, if those who are the most assiduous Disciples of the Stage, do not make the fondest and the lewdest Crew about this Town" (Davis and Finke 1989, 294–95). She con-tinues, "I will have leave to say that in my judgement the increas-ing number of our latter Plays have not done much more towards the amending of men's Morals, or their Wit" (295). In this indict-ment of the men who hide behind the emptiness of the Horatian platitude rather than acknowledge their political interestedness, Behn exposes, with characteristic wit, the reliance of seventeenth-century criticism on the imitation and appropriation of received authorities, particularly the "master texts" of classical antiquity. These texts presented arguments about literature and morality which buttressed the ideologies of the educated and ruling elite, an elite from which Behn was excluded because of her sex and to which she desired access. Knowledge of Greek and Latin was a mark of membership in this class. As a woman and a socially marginal professional writer, Behn was barred from the classical education which would give her an investment in the Horatian argument about the moral utility of literature. She was, however, able to see the political purposes "instruction" could be made to serve and to expose the contradictions within its ideology.

Aphra Behn occupies a position within seventeenth-century so-ciety and theater that could best be described as ambiguously (non)hegemonic.[26] Behn was the most outspoken of a new group of writers—women—who had traditionally been excluded from both literature and literary criticism, and she wrote vociferously against the unfairness of that exclusion. She was a "middle-class" woman forced to turn to writing professionally to support herself. As a result, she suffered from a tarnished reputation. A later generation of critics would refer to her as "a harlot who danced through uncleanness and dared others to follow" (Behn 1984, i). Although she was all her life a staunch royalist (she even spied for Charles II during the Dutch Wars) and politically conservative, much of her critical writing, particularly the prefaces to the plays written before the Exclusion Crisis (1678–1681), exposes the aristocratic and elitist ideologies underpinning the debate over poetry's moral utility and the imitation of nature. As a successful playwright she had more than a little self-interest in the newly emerging avocation of criticism and the proliferation of critics, "whose Business it is to find Fault." Her defense of *The Dutch Lover* undermines every commonplace of seventeenth-century criticism by setting her practical experience as a playwright against the "rules" of neoclassical orthodoxy. More than any other critic of the seventeenth century, Behn reveals the difficulties faced by a practicing dramatist in the Restoration theater, particularly one who must operate outside of "proper" society while striving to gain a place in it. Her essays are peopled by theater managers and licensors who threaten to suppress her plays, audiences who shout them down, directors who rewrite her lines, and actors who mangle them.

In Behn's preface to *The Dutch Lover*, the theater emerges as a cultural activity, full of energy, conflict, collaboration, and even gossip. It is an agent of both social and cultural behavior, a producer of—as well as a production of—social meanings. Her depiction of the theater contrasts with the more static view of "dramatic poesy" articulated by her contemporaries, in whose work drama

---

[26]The term "(ambiguously) nonhegemonic" is used by Rachel Blau DuPlessis to describe women's ambiguous participation in patriarchy. Women remain "outside of the dominant systems of meaning, value, and power." Yet, because of the nature of hegemony, women are frequently internally oriented toward hegemonic norms in what DuPlessis calls a "painful double dance." See "For the Etruscans: Sexual Difference and Artistic Production," in Eisenstein and Jardine 1980, 148–49.

seems almost disembodied. Dryden in particular seems more concerned with such abstractions as the "imitation of nature" or the poet, conceived of as the lone producer of meanings in his poetry, struggling with the classical rules of the three unities. Value, for Dryden, is transcendent, a result of an author's successful negotiation of the rules of classical decorum. Although an astute observer of political and religious contention, an effective polemicist, and an accomplished satirist, he characteristically suppresses historical contingency in his accounts of literary value and the imitation of nature. Behn, by contrast, exposes the cultural work that enables and perpetuates values, work that is as much economic and political as it is artistic.

As a means of foregrounding perspectives on value which are most often marginalized as noise, I began this chapter with some comments about Shakespeare written by students in the context of a final exam. I would like to close with some more comments on Shakespeare from yet another marginalized perspective, comments from another woman of the theater, the eighteenth-century actress, essayist, and novelist Eliza Haywood. Writing in *The Female Spectator* (1745), Haywood maintains that "some of Shakespeare's comedies, and all his tragedies, have beauties in them almost inimitable; but then it must be confessed, that he sometimes gave a loose to the luxuriancy of his fancy; so that his plays may be compared to fine gardens full of the most beautiful flowers, but choked up with weeds through the too great richness of the soil: those therefore which have had those weeds plucked up by the skillful hands of his successors, are much the most elegant entertainments" (Davis and Finke 1989, 360). Haywood's critical voice was effectively marginalized by Alexander Pope, who, in book 2 of his *Dunciad*, savagely depicts Haywood as the bovine, sluttish prize of a pissing contest among publishers he despised. But Haywood's metaphor of weeds in an untended garden reminds us of the cultural work that produces the literary text; she reminds us that weeds are not particular *kinds* of plants, but *any* plant that for some reason or another a gardener does not want around (Eagleton 1983, 9). In other words, value—whether in plants or in literary texts—is always value-for, for someone and for some purpose. Haywood's discussion of Shakespeare's faults and the correction of those faults by such playwrights as Thomas Otway calls attention to what the "Shakespeare idolatry" has covered over. She continues:

> I was a little surprized, when I heard that Mr. Cibber, junior, had revived the tragedy of *Romeo and Juliet*, as it was first acted; *Caius Marius* being the same play, only modernized, and cleared of some part of its rubbish, by Otway, appearing to so much more advantage, that it is not to be doubted, but that the admirable author, had he lived to see the alteration, would have been highly thankful and satisfied with it.
>
> It were indeed to be wished, that the same kind corrector had been somewhat more severe, and lopped off not only some superfluous scenes, but whole characters, which rather serve to diminish than add to the piece. (Davis and Finke 1989, 360)

What twentieth-century audiences have been taught to value about Shakespeare is very different from what the eighteenth, or the seventeenth, or the nineteenth, century valued. To be sure, Haywood is repeating here late seventeenth- and eighteenth-century truisms about Shakespeare which can be found in Dryden, Johnson, Shaftesbury, and elsewhere. Critical debates about Shakespeare's felicities and infelicities raged throughout the seventeenth and eighteenth centuries. Even Johnson, who claimed in *Preface to Shakespeare* that his dramas were "the mirrour of life," censured Shakespeare for sacrificing convenience to virtue, for being more careful to please than to instruct, and for indulging excessively in "quibbles." But perhaps because Haywood has been so thoroughly reviled and silenced, her preferences strikingly reveal the complex relationship between aesthetic judgment and the political values it articulates. Such value judgments about Shakespeare's language as the following may strike the modern reader as gratuitous, even funny on first reading:

> Mr. Otway . . . has improved and heightened every beauty that could receive addition, and been extremely tender in preserving all those intire which are above the reach of amendment. . . . Some poets, perhaps, to show their own abilities, would have put a long soliloquy into the mouth of young Marius, when he finds Lavinia at her window . . . ; whereas this judicious emendator

leaves his author here as he found him. . . . Nor is the tenderness
and innocence of Lavinia less conveyed to us, when in the fulness
of her heart, and unsuspecting she was overheard by any body,
she cries out,

> O Marius! Marius! wherefore art thou Marius!
> Renounce thy family, deny thy name,
> And in exchange take all Lavinia.

(Davis and Finke 1989, 361)

But we need to consider what kinds of values Otway's version of
Romeo and Juliet encodes and what appeal those values might have
had for Haywood not just as an eighteenth-century writer but as a
woman who deserted her husband to become a writer. Haywood
calls attention to the cultural work that has been required to create
and perpetuate the Shakespeare we idolize today. She reminds us
of the work done by nineteenth-century scholars to recover (or
recreate) the texts of plays that had been rewritten throughout the
seventeenth and eighteenth centuries. It is not obvious from Haywood's remarks or from this labor of recovery that Shakespeare's
plays exhibit some kind of fundamental and transhistorical aesthetic values. Rather, they demonstrate the hegemonic function of
"canons," which do not operate by fiat but which have to be continually renewed, recreated, defended, and modified, as well as
resisted, limited, and challenged. They demonstrate that value is a
site of dialogical contestation whether it is in *The Awakening* or
Romeo and Juliet.

Afterword:
From Text to Work

Roland Barthes's 1979 essay "From Work to Text" outlined a program for poststructuralist theory by proclaiming the end of the literary "work." The work, Barthes said, as an object that occupies library space, as a document with fixed and stable meaning that can be consumed by a passive reader, would be replaced by the text, conceived of as a "methodological field" (74). This text would be situated entirely in language and would remain in a continual state of production. Henceforth, the activity of the literary critic would take place solely within the realm of language production, of textuality. Critical flights of fancy would no longer be constrained by such conventional limitations as authors or their intentions or even, in some cases, the words on the page. As I have suggested, this movement from work to text was profoundly disturbing for many feminists. It seemed to dissolve the object of feminist investigations, the material woman who suffers oppression or the woman writer who triumphs in spite of it, into immaterial language—air—which seemed, to quote Falstaff, "a trim reckoning" indeed. Deconstruction seemed to offer to replace the newly discovered woman writer of feminist literary criticism with the tyranny of the (usually male) critic, who could appropriate for himself whatever creative power we used to attribute to the (usually male) author.

This book participates, along with several others—Mary Poovey's *Uneven Developments* and Nancy Armstrong's *Desire and Domestic Fiction* to name just two—in attempts to refine poststructuralist feminist inquiry by shifting the focus from text to work. This movement is not a return to the work considered as a static object, a noun, but to work as a verb, conceived of as the cultural, intellectual, and ideological activity that constitutes individuals and texts within specific social formations. In this sense, work includes practices that are material as well as discursive; analyses of this work must account for the free play of linguistic and literary production and for the specific power relations that constrain this free play as well as the resistances to that power.

In "From Work to Text," Barthes organizes his theory of the text around seven propositions. By way of summary, I would like to revise those seven propositions and suggest their implications for a feminist theory of complexity which explores the cultural work of gender.

(1) Unlike the text, which is experienced exclusively in the activity of language production, cultural and ideological work—and this includes the work of gender—is experienced not only in discursive practice but in countless material practices of everyday life as well. The method that explores the cultural work of gender must examine the interrelationships between the symbolic and material orders. Neither gender nor sex is an "eternal verity," a given; they are the work of specific cultural practices, which have histories. If there is any such thing as a "woman's sentence," it can only be the product of the interplay among material and discursive practices; it does not point to anything essentially female. In examining the historical practices of such apparently ahistorical concepts as love, kinship, and pain, I have tried to show how such practices participate in the production of gendered individuals. These historically situated practices, in turn, can be seen as both producers and products of linguistic and literary productions, including poetry, religious writing, political treatises, or even of something as amorphously abstract as "style" or literary "value."

(2) A theory of complexity, of cultural work, must examine the power relations that attempt to determine and fix the "limits and rules of rationality and readability" (75) as well as the practices of resistance that transgress them. It must negotiate the boundaries between the order that produces reason and meaning and the chaos that challenges and resists culturally hegemonic meanings.

Such negotiations are always tricky; the analysis must account for the apparent coherence and stability ideological order seems to promise and at the same time show the cracks and gaps in the façade which continually threaten its collapse. If I have occasionally seemed to lose track of that balance in my analyses, if I make larger claims for the resistance and subversion of the medieval trobairitz and mystics than may seem warranted, or if I seem to stress the failures of a Wollstonecraft or a Chopin to transcend the ideologies of gender, it is because I feel that feminists have generally seen medieval women almost solely in terms of their oppression, that they have located the emergence of organized feminist resistance in the eighteenth century with Wollstonecraft and others or the success of gynocriticism in figures such as Chopin. My aim has been to show that women have always been able to resist the ideological work of gender, just as they have always fallen prey to its ordering principles.

(3) While recognizing the persuasiveness of poststructuralist theories of the sign which hold that the signified is endlessly deferred through the disruptive free play of signifiers and that such disruption is potentially subversive of structures of order (including gender), theorists of cultural work also examine those hegemonic practices that create the illusion of a center that closes off this free play—practices that create the illusion of fixed meanings. If, at least since the eighteenth century, gender has been organizing individuals into two opposing and mutually exclusive sexes, then it is crucial to examine both how that organization has naturalized and fixed differences and how its control has been, in Poovey's words, "uneven" and unstable (Poovey 1988b, Laqueur 1990).

(4) In poststructuralist theory the text is a tissue of intertextual references, citations, echoes, and languages, which are ultimately "anonymous, irrecoverable, and yet *already read*" (Barthes 1979, 77). In theories of complexity, if intertextuality answers to dissemination rather than truth, it is also the occasion for dialogue and the transgression of the boundaries of the disciplines as they have been constituted to serve the administrative needs of such institutions as the university. Feminist theory did not require poststructuralism to intuit that its "work" must be truly interdisciplinary in Barthes's sense of that term. "Interdisciplinary ac-

194 Feminist Theory, Women's Writing

tivity," he writes, ". . . cannot be accomplished by simple confrontations between various specialized branches of knowledge. Interdisciplinary work is not a peaceful operation: it begins *effectively* when the solidarity of the old disciplines breaks down . . . to the benefit of a new object and a new language, neither of which is in the domain of those branches of knowledge that one calmly sought to confront" (1971, 73).

(5) If the author, in poststructuralist theory, is no longer paternal or privileged, neither can she be maternal and protected. I have, somewhat disingenuously, used the phrase "woman writer" throughout this book only to call into question its foundationalism as the organizing principle of feminist inquiry by constantly locating writing in a complex network of gender and other social relations that fracture the author's apparent solidity as the locus of meaning in her texts. I do this most explicitly in my analyses of *The Book of Margery Kempe* and *A Vindication of the Rights of Woman*, but this aim is implicit in my choice of texts throughout. In adopting this necessary but somewhat duplicitous practice, quite frankly, I attempt to have it both ways. If the woman writer visits her texts only as a guest, I do not want her to be *merely* "ludic." If she is not the origin or end of the text, its sole source of meaning, her political presence is nevertheless important, if only because authorship is still the ideological means—and perhaps the illusion—by which the institution of literature constitutes and organizes literary texts.[1] It is important for feminist theory to proceed strategically on two

[1]Of course Barthes himself was aware of the political fallout the death of the author would create. As Vincent Leitch suggests: "The job of deconstructing the authority of the *author* involves desedimentizing a historical formation, which long ago installed itself as a purposeful ideology. So long has this notion reigned that it seems 'natural' to us now. Yet this 'social natural' serves demonstrable political and economic purposes. Propounding the death of the author, Barthes uncovers the pernicious combined forces of empiricism, rationalism, individualism, positivism, and capitalism—as they influence and direct a theory of literature and criticism. Deconstruction, of the telquel variety produced during the late 1960s and early 1970s, springs forth with an ideological agenda and a political mission" (1983, 106). Yet as it proliferated in American universities in the 1980s, deconstruction seemed to lose the force of this ideological agenda and political mission. The death of the author served more to aggrandize the (male) critic than to expose the pernicious effects of patriarchal order as an ideological formation. That it did perhaps suggests why the Paul de Man scandal has proved so painful for American academics who have invested so heavily in deconstruction.

opposing fronts: recognizing that "woman" is a production of culture, feminists must simultaneously insist that women have always been producers of culture.

(6) If the text is produced by the reader, all readers—and all the texts produced by readers—are not equal. Once again, the material practices of social institutions—universities, English and literature departments, publishers, book reviews—and particular social relations, such as those of gender, make some productions more likely than others. This is the argument of the last chapter. If reading is an act of collaboration between an "author" and a "reader," it is also an act of consumption, bound up in the modes of production and reception which organize the activity of reading in a particular social formation.

(7) Finally, it is not enough simply to declare the utopian or sexual pleasure of the text without examining the political consequences of erotic pleasure, especially for women, whose sexuality has always been tied to the reproductive labor of society and controlled according to the reproductive needs of the dominant classes. If the sexual and linguistic promiscuity of the libertine pose is seen as liberating for the troubadour poets or for radicals like Shelley or Byron, its consequences for women—whether for Castelloza in the twelfth century, Aphra Behn in the seventeenth, Mary Wollstonecraft in the eighteenth, or even for a fictional character like Edna Pontellier—are often disastrous. Feminist theory has much work to do to articulate a feminist analysis of sexuality which reclaims eroticism for women as well as for men.

The texts examined in this book range widely over time and place—from twelfth-century France to nineteenth-century America —perhaps more than is usual or even comfortable given the specialization that has characterized literary studies in the last half of the twentieth century. But my theoretical argument is tied to particular and local histories and to the identification of disparate examples of "cultural noise," of information excluded from universalizing histories of order, so that my method has been to link chapters paratactically rather than hypotactically. My aim is to identify ruptures and gaps within a literary history that in this century has been resolutely linear and teleological. It has not been my intention to offer a new teleology to replace the old one, to show how feminist theory got here from there; nor am I interested in writing the "history of the woman writer." Rather my hope is to glimpse in the margins of several local histories the possibilities for a different genre of history altogether, one that challenges the ontological necessity of categories of gender at the same time as it recognizes the importance of the political struggles and local resistance of women everywhere.

Bibliography

Abel, Elizabeth, ed. 1982. *Writing and Sexual Difference*. Chicago: University of Chicago Press.

Abels, Richard, and Ellen Harrison. 1979. "The Participation of Women in Languedocian Catharism." *Mediaeval Studies* 41: 215–51.

Adams, Hazard, ed. 1971. *Critical Theory Since Plato*. New York: Harcourt, Brace, Jovanovich.

———. 1988. "Canons: Literary Criteria / Power Criteria." *Critical Inquiry* 14: 748–64.

Altieri, Charles. 1983. "An Idea and Ideal of a Literary Canon." *Critical Inquiry* 10: 37–60.

Armstrong, Nancy. 1987. *Desire and Domestic Fiction: A Political History of the Novel*. New York: Oxford University Press.

Armstrong, Paul B. 1983. "The Conflict of Interpretation and the Limits of Pluralism." *PMLA* 98: 341–52.

———. 1990. *Conflicting Readings: Variety and Validity in Interpretation*. Chapel Hill: University of North Carolina Press.

Bakhtin, M. M. 1981. *The Dialogic Imagination*. Trans. Michael Holquist and Caryl Emerson. Austin: University of Texas Press.

———. 1984. *Rabelais and His World*. Trans. Hélène Iswolsky. Bloomington: Indiana University Press.

———. 1986. *Speech Genres and Other Late Essays*. Ed. Michael Holquist and Caryl Emerson. Trans. Vern W. McGee. Austin: University of Texas Press.

Barthes, Roland. 1967. "Le Discours de l'histoire." *Social Science Information* 6: 65–75.

———. 1979. "From Work to Text." In *Textual Strategies: Perspectives in Post-Structuralist Criticism*. Ed. Josué V. Harari. Ithaca: Cornell University Press: 73–81.

Bauer, Dale M. 1988. *Feminist Dialogics: A Theory of Failed Community*. Albany, N.Y.: SUNY Press.

Baym, Nina. 1981. "Melodramas of Beset Manhood: How Theories of American Fiction Exclude Women Authors." *American Quarterly* 33: 123–39.

——. 1984. "The Madwoman and Her Languages: Why I Don't Do Feminist Literary Theory." *Tulsa Studies in Women's Literature* 3: 45–59.

Beauvoir, Simone de. 1974. *The Second Sex*. Trans. H. M. Parshley. 1952; rpt. New York: Vintage.

Behn, Aphra. 1984. *The Lucky Chance*. Ed. Fidelis Morgan. London: Methuen.

Belenky, Mary Field, Blythe McVicker Clinchy, Nancy Rule Goldberger, and Jill Mattuck Tarule. 1986. *Women's Ways of Knowing: The Development of Self, Voice, and Mind*. New York: Basic Books.

Bell, Rudolph. 1985. *Holy Anorexia*. Chicago: University of Chicago Press.

Belsey, Catherine. 1980. *Critical Practice*. London: Methuen.

Benhabib, Seyla, and Drucilla Cornell, eds. 1987. *Feminism as Critique*. Minneapolis: University of Minnesota Press.

Bennett, William. 1985. "To Claim a Legacy." *American Education* 21: 4–15.

Benstock, Shari, ed. 1988. *The Private Self: Theory and Practice of Women's Autobiographical Writings*. Chapel Hill: University of North Carolina Press.

Benveniste, Émile. 1971. *Problems in General Linguistics*. Trans. Mary Elizabeth Meek. Coral Gables, Fla.: University of Miami Press.

Berg, Elizabeth. 1982. "The Third Woman." *Diacritics* 12: 11–21.

Berger, John. 1972. *Ways of Seeing*. London: Penguin Books.

Bergin, Thomas C. and Raymond T. Hill, eds. 1973. *Anthology of the Provençal Troubadours*. New Haven: Yale University Press.

Bloch, Howard. 1983. *Etymologies and Genealogies: A Literary Anthropology of the French Middle Ages*. Chicago: University of Chicago Press.

——. 1987. "Medieval Misogyny." *Representations* 20: 1–24.

Bloch, Marc. 1961. *Feudal Society*. Trans. L. A. Manyon. Chicago: University of Chicago Press.

Blonsky, Marshall, ed. 1985. *On Signs*. Baltimore: Johns Hopkins University Press.

Bloom, Allan. 1987. *The Closing of the American Mind*. New York: Simon and Schuster.

Bogin, Meg. 1980. *The Women Troubadours*. New York: Norton.

Booth, Wayne. 1982. "Freedom of Interpretation: Bakhtin and the Challenge of Feminist Criticism." *Critical Inquiry* 9: 45–76.

Bordo, Susan. 1982. "The Cultural Overseer and the Tragic Hero: Comedic and Feminist Perspectives on the Hubris of Philosophy." *Soundings* 65: 181–205.

——. 1987. *The Flight to Objectivity: Essays on Cartesianism and Culture*. Albany, N. Y.: SUNY Press.

Bourdieu, Pierre. 1977. *Outline of a Theory of Practice*. Trans. Richard Nice. Cambridge: Cambridge University Press.

Bridenthal, Renate, and Claudia Koontz, eds. 1977. *Becoming Visible: Women in European History*. Boston: Houghton Mifflin.

Brown, Alice. 1987. *The Eighteenth-Century Feminist Mind*. Detroit: Wayne State University Press.

Bynum, Caroline W. 1982. *Jesus as Mother: Studies in the Spirituality of the High Middle Ages*. Berkeley: University of California Press.

——. 1987. *Holy Feast and Holy Fast: The Religious Significance of Food to Medieval Women*. Berkeley: University of California Press.

——. 1991. *Fragmentation and Redemption: Essays on Gender and the Human Body in Medieval Religion*. New York: Zone Books.

Cannon, John, ed. 1981. *The Whig Ascendancy: Colloquies on Hanoverian England*. New York: St. Martin's Press.

——. 1984. *The Aristocratic Century: The Peerage of Eighteenth-Century England*. Cambridge: Cambridge University Press.

Chodorow, Nancy. 1978. *The Reproduction of Mothering: Psychoanalysis and the Sociology of Gender*. Berkeley: University of California Press.

Chopin, Kate. 1976. *The Awakening*. Ed. Margaret Culley. New York: Norton.

Christian, Barbara. 1987. "The Race for Theory." *Cultural Critique* 6: 51–63.

Cixous, Hélène. 1976. "Laugh of the Medusa." Trans. Keith Cohen and Paula Cohen. *Signs* 1: 875–93.

——. 1981. "Castration or Decapitation?" Trans. Annette Kuhn. *Signs* 7: 41–55.

Clark, Katerina, and Michael Holquist. 1984. *Mikhail Bakhtin*. Cambridge: Belknap Press of Harvard University Press.

Culler, Jonathan. 1982. *On Deconstruction: Theory and Criticism after Structuralism*. Ithaca: Cornell University Press.

——. 1988. *Framing the Sign: Criticism and its Institutions*. Norman: University of Oklahoma Press.

Davies, P. C. W., and Julien Brown. 1988. *Superstrings: A Theory of Everything?* Cambridge: Cambridge University Press.

Davis, Robert Con, and Laurie Finke, eds.. 1989. *Literary Criticism and Theory: The Greeks to the Present*. New York: Longman.

Davis, Robert Con, and Ronald Schleifer, eds. 1989. *Contemporary Literary Criticism: Literary and Cultural Studies*. 2d edition. New York: Longman.

de Certeau, Michel. 1984. *The Practice of Everyday Life*. Trans. Steven F. Rendall. Berkeley. University of California Press

——. 1986. *Heterologies: Discourse on the Other*. Trans. Brian Massumi. Minneapolis: University of Minnesota Press.

——. 1988. *The Writing of History*. Trans. Tom Conley. New York: Columbia University Press.

Delany, Sheila. 1983. *Writing Woman: Women Writers and Women in Literature, Medieval to Modern*. New York: Schocken Press.

———. 1987. "Mothers to Think Back Through: Who Are They? The Ambiguous Case of Christine de Pizan." In *Medieval Texts and Contemporary Readers*. Ed. Laurie A. Finke and Martin B. Shichtman. Ithaca: Cornell University Press: 177–97.

de Lauretis, Teresa, ed. 1986. *Feminist Studies, Critical Studies*. Bloomington: Indiana University Press.

———. 1987. *Technologies of Gender: Essays on Theory, Film, and Fiction*. Bloomington: Indiana University Press.

Delmar, Rosalind. 1986. "What Is Feminism?" In *What is Feminism?* Ed. Juliet Mitchell and Ann Oakley. New York: Pantheon Books: 8–33.

Derrida, Jacques. 1970. "Structure, Sign, and Play in the Discourse of the Human Sciences." In *The Structuralist Controversy: The Languages of Criticism and the Sciences of Man*. Ed. Richard Macksey and Eugenio Donato. Baltimore: Johns Hopkins University Press: 247–72.

———. 1981. *Positions*. Trans. Alan Bass. Chicago: University of Chicago Press.

———. 1982. With Christie V. MacDonald. "Choreographies." *Diacritics* 12: 66–76.

Dreyfus, Hubert L., and Paul Rabinow. 1982. *Michel Foucault: Beyond Structuralism and Hermeneutics*. Chicago: University of Chicago Press.

Dronke, Peter. 1984. *Women Writers of the Middle Ages: A Critical Study of Texts from Perpetua (203) to Marguerite Porete (1310)*. Cambridge: Cambridge University Press.

Duby, Georges. 1974. *The Early Growth of the European Economy: Warriors and Peasants from the Seventh to the Twelfth Century*. Trans. Howard B. Clarke. Ithaca: Cornell University Press.

———. 1983. *The Knight, the Lady, and the Priest: The Making of Modern Marriage*. Trans. Barbara Bray. New York: Pantheon.

———. 1988. *A History of Private Life: Revelations of the Medieval World*. Trans. Arthur Goldhammer. Cambridge: Belknap Press of Harvard University Press.

Eagleton, Terry. 1983. *Literary Theory: An Introduction*. Minneapolis: University of Minnesota Press.

———. 1984. *The Function of Criticism: From "The Spectator" to Poststructuralism*. London: Verso.

———. 1986. *Against the Grain: Essays, 1975–1985*. London: Verso.

Eble, Kenneth. 1956. "A Forgotten Novel: Kate Chopin's *The Awakening*." *Western Humanities Review* 10: 261–69.

Egan, Margarita, trans. 1984. *The Vidas of the Troubadours*. New York: Garland.

Eisenstadt, S. N. and Luis Roniger. 1984. *Patrons, Clients, and Friends: Interpersonal Relations and the Structure of Trust in Society*. Cambridge: Cambridge University Press.

Eisenstein, Hester, and Alice Jardine, eds. 1980. *The Future of Difference*. Boston: G. K. Hall.

Eisenstein, Zillah. 1981. *The Radical Future of Liberal Feminism*. New York: Longman.

Elias, Norbert. 1978. *The Civilizing Process: The History of Manners*. Trans. Edmund Jephcott. New York: Urizen.

Eliot, T. S. 1950. *Selected Essays*. New York: Harcourt Brace Jovanovich.

Ellmann, Mary. 1968. *Thinking about Women*. New York: Harcourt.

Emerson, Caryl. 1983. "The Outer Word and Inner Speech: Bakhtin, Vygotsky, and the Internalization of Language." *Critical Inquiry* 10: 245–64.

Erlich, Bruce. 1986. "Amphibolies: On the Critical Self-Contradictions of Pluralism." *Critical Inquiry* 12: 521–49.

Finke, Laurie. 1984. "Painting Women: Images of Femininity in Jacobean Tragedy." *Theatre Journal* 36: 357–70.

———. 1986. "The Rhetoric of Marginality: Why I Do Feminist Theory." *Tulsa Studies in Women's Literature* 5: 251–72.

———. 1989. "Towards a Cultural Poetics of the Romance." *Genre* 22: 109–27.

Fish, Stanley. 1980. *Is There a Text in This Class? The Authority of Interpretive Communities*. Cambridge: Harvard University Press

———. 1985. "Consequences." *Critical Inquiry* 11: 433–58

Flexner, Eleanor. 1972. *Mary Wollstonecraft: A Biography*. New York: Coward, McCann, and Geoghegan.

Flynn, Elizabeth A., and Patrocinio P. Schweickart, eds. 1986. *Gender and Reading: Essays on Readers, Texts, and Contexts*. Baltimore: Johns Hopkins University Press.

Foucault, Michel. 1970. *The Order of Things: An Archaeology of the Human Sciences*. New York: Pantheon.

———. 1972. *The Archaeology of Knowledge*. Trans. A. M. Sheridan Smith. New York: Pantheon.

———. 1977a. *Discipline and Punish: The Birth of the Prison*. Trans. Alan Sheridan. New York: Random House.

———. 1977b. *Language, Counter-memory, Practice: Selected Essays and Interviews*. Ed. Donald Bouchard. Ithaca: Cornell University Press.

———. 1978. *History of Sexuality*. Vol. 1: *An Introduction*. Trans. Robert Hurley. New York: Pantheon.

———. 1979. "What Is an Author?" In *Textual Strategies: Perspectives in Poststructuralist Criticism*. Ed. Josué V. Harari. Ithaca: Cornell University Press: 141–60.

———. 1980. *Power / Knowledge: Selected Interviews and Other Writings by Michel Foucault, 1972–1977*. Ed. Colin Gordon. New York: Pantheon.

———. 1984. *The Foucault Reader*. Ed. Paul Rabinow. New York: Pantheon

Froula, Christine. 1983. "When Eve Reads Milton: Undoing the Canonical Economy." *Critical Inquiry* 10: 321–47.

Frye, Northrop. 1957. *Anatomy of Criticism: Four Essays*. Princeton: Princeton University Press.

Gallop, Jane. 1982. *The Daughter's Seduction: Feminism and Psychoanalysis*. Ithaca: Cornell University Press.

———. 1987. "The Problem of Definition." *Genre* 20: 111–32.

Gardiner, Judith Kegan, Elly Bulkin, Rena Grasso Patterson, and Annette Kolodny. 1982. "An Interchange on Feminist Criticism: On 'Dancing through the Minefield.'" *Feminist Studies* 8: 629–75.

Gellrich, Jesse. 1988. "Orality, Literacy, and Crisis in the Later Middle Ages" *Philological Quarterly* 67: 461–73.

Gilbert, Sandra, and Susan Gubar. 1979a. *Madwoman in the Attic: The Woman Writer and the Nineteenth-Century Literary Imagination*. New Haven: Yale University Press.

———, eds. 1979b. *Shakespeare's Sisters: Feminist Essays on Women Poets*. Bloomington: Indiana University Press.

———. 1985a. *The Norton Anthology of Literature by Women*. New York: Norton.

———. 1985b. "Sexual Linguistics: Gender, Language, Sexuality." *New Literary History* 16: 515–43.

———. 1988. *No Man's Land: The Place of the Woman Writer in the Twentieth Century*. Vol. 1. New Haven: Yale University Press.

Gilligan, Carol. 1982. *In a Different Voice: Psychological Theory and Women's Development*. Cambridge: Harvard University Press.

Godwin, William. 1974. *Memoirs of the Author of "A Vindication of the Rights of Woman."* 1798; rpt. New York: Garland.

Goldin, Frederick, ed. and trans. 1973. *Lyrics of the Troubadours and Trouvères*. New York: Anchor Books.

Gould, Stephen Jay. 1981. *The Mismeasure of Man*. New York: Norton.

Green, Judith A. 1986. *The Government of England under Henry I*. Cambridge: Cambridge University Press.

Greenblatt, Stephen. 1988. *Shakespearean Negotiations: The Circulation of Social Energy in Renaissance England*. Berkeley: University of California Press.

Greene, Gayle, and Coppélia Kahn. 1985. *Making a Difference: Feminist Literary Criticism*. London: Methuen.

Guralnick, Elissa S. 1979. "Radical Politics in Mary Wollstonecraft's *Vindication of the Rights of Woman*." *Studies in Burke and His Time* 18: 155–66.

Habermas, Jürgen. 1962. *Strukturwandel der Öffentlichkeit*. Berlin: Neuwied, Luchterhand.

Harari, Josué V., ed. 1979. *Textual Strategies: Perspectives in Post-structuralist Criticism*. Ithaca: Cornell University Press.

Haraway, Donna. 1985. "A Manifesto for Cyborgs: Science, Technology, and Socialist Feminism in the 1980s." *Socialist Review*, no. 80: 65–107.

———. 1988. "Situated Knowledges: The Science Question in Feminism and the Privilege of Partial Perspective." *Feminist Studies* 14: 575–99.

———. 1989. *Primate Visions: Gender, Race, and Nature in the World of Modern Science*. London: Routledge.

Harding, Sandra. 1986. *The Science Question in Feminism*. Ithaca: Cornell University Press.

Hawking, Stephen. 1989. "Is the End in Sight for Theoretical Physics?" In John Buslough, *Stephen Hawking's Universe: An Introduction to the Most Remarkable Scientists in Our Time*. 1985; rpt. New York: Avon Books.

Hawkins, Harriett. 1983. "The 'Example Theory' and the Providentialist Approach to Restoration Drama: Some Questions of Validity and Applicability." *Eighteenth Century: Theory and Interpretation* 24: 103–14.

Hayles, N. Katherine. 1989. "Chaos as Orderly Disorder: Shifting Ground in Contemporary Literature and Science." *New Literary History* 20: 305–22.

——. 1990. *Chaos Bound: Orderly Disorder in Contemporary Literature and Science*. Ithaca: Cornell University Press.

Herlihy, David. 1976. "Land, Family, and Women in Continental Europe, 701–1200," In *Women in Medieval Society*. Ed. Susan Mosher Stuard. Philadelphia: University of Pennsylvania Press: 13–46.

——. 1985. *Medieval Households*. Cambridge: Harvard University Press.

Hirsch, E. D. 1976a. *The Aims of Interpretation*. Chicago: University of Chicago Press.

——. 1976b. *Validity in Interpretation*. New Haven: Yale University Press.

——. 1987. *Cultural Literacy: What Every American Needs to Know*. Boston: Houghton Mifflin.

Hirschkopf, Ken. 1985. "A Response to the Forum on Mikhail Bakhtin." *Critical Inquiry* 11: 672–78.

Hodge, Robert, and Gunther Kress. 1988. *Social Semiotics*. Ithaca: Cornell University Press.

Hohendahl, Peter U. 1982. *The Institution of Criticism*. Ithaca: Cornell University Press.

Hollister, C. Warren. 1971. *The Making of England: 55 B.C. to 1399*. Lexington, Mass.: D. C. Heath.

Holquist, Michael. 1983. "Answering as Authoring: Mikhail Bakhtin's Trans-linguistics." *Critical Inquiry* 10: 307–20.

Irigaray, Luce. 1985a. *Speculum of the Other Woman*. Trans. Gillian Gill. Ithaca: Cornell University Press.

——. 1985b. *This Sex Which Is Not One*. Trans. Catherine Porter. Ithaca: Cornell University Press.

Jacobus, Mary, ed. 1979. *Women Writing and Writing about Women*. London: Croom Helm.

——. 1982. "Is There a Woman in This Text?" *New Literary History* 14: 117–41.

—— 1986. *Reading Woman: Essays in Feminist Criticism*. New York: Columbia University Press.

Jardine, Alice. 1985. *Gynesis: Configurations of Woman and Modernity*. Ithaca: Cornell University Press.

Jardine, Alice, and Paul Smith, eds. 1987. *Men in Feminism*. London: Methuen.

Jehlen, Myra. 1981. "Archimedes and the Paradox of Feminist Criticism." *Signs* 6: 575–601.

Johnson, Barbara. 1980. *The Critical Difference: Essays in the Contemporary Rhetoric of Reading*. Baltimore: Johns Hopkins University Press.

Julian of Norwich. 1978. *Showings* (Long Text). Ed. Edmund Colledge and James Walsh. New York: Paulist Press.

Kamuf, Peggy. 1982. "Replacing Feminist Criticism." *Diacritics* 12: 42–47.

Kauffman, Linda, ed. 1989. *Gender and Theory: Dialogues on Feminist Criticism*. Oxford: Basil Blackwell.

Kaufman-McCall, Dorothy. 1983. "Politics of Difference: The Women's Movement in France from May 1968 to Mitterrand." *Signs* 9: 282–93.

Kelly, Joan. 1984. *Women, History, and Theory: The Essays of Joan Kelly*. Chicago: University of Chicago Press.

Kempe, Margery. 1940. *The Book of Margery Kempe*. Ed. Sanford Brown Meech and Hope Emily Allen. London: Oxford, EETS.

———. 1985. *The Book of Margery Kempe*. Trans. B. A. Windeatt. New York: Penguin.

Kendrick, Laura. 1988. *The Game of Love: Troubadour Wordplay*. Berkeley: University of California Press.

Keohane, Nannerl O., Michelle Z. Rosaldo, and Barbara C. Gelpi, eds. 1982. *Feminist Theory: A Critique of Ideology*. Chicago: University of Chicago Press.

Kessler, Suzanne J., and Wendy McKenna. 1978. *Gender: An Ethnomethodological Approach*. Chicago: University of Chicago Press.

Kieckhefer, Richard. 1984. *Unquiet Souls: Fourteenth-Century Saints and Their Religious Milieu*. Chicago: University of Chicago Press.

Kofman, Sarah. 1985. *The Enigma of Woman: Women in Freud's Writing*. Trans. Catherine Porter. Ithaca: Cornell University Press.

Kohler, Erich. 1962. *Trobadorlyrik und höfischer Roman*. Berlin: Rutten and Loening.

———. 1964. "Observations historiques et sociologiques sur la poésie des troubadours." *Cahiers de Civilisation Médiévales*, 7: 27–51.

Kolodny, Annette. 1975. "Some Notes on Defining a Feminist Literary Criticism." *Critical Inquiry* 2: 75–92.

———. 1976. "Review Essay: Literary Criticism." *Signs* 2: 404–21.

———. 1980a. "Dancing through the Minefield: Some Observations on the Theory, Practice, and Politics of Feminist Literary Criticism." *Feminist Studies* 6: 1–25.

———. 1980b. "A Map for Re-reading: Gender and the Interpretation of Literary Texts." *New Literary History* 14: 451–67.

Kristeva, Julia. 1980. *Desire in Language: A Semiotic Approach to Literature and Art*. Trans. Thomas Gora, Alice Jardine, and Leon S. Roudiez. New York: Columbia University Press.

———. 1981. "Women's Time." Trans. Alice Jardine and Harry Blake. *Signs* 7: 13–35.

———. 1987. *Tales of Love*. Trans. Leon S. Roudiez. New York: Columbia University Press.

Lacan, Jacques. 1982. *Female Sexuality: Jacques Lacan and the Ecole Freudienne.* Ed. Juliet Mitchell and Jacqueline Rose. New York: Norton.

Laqueur, Thomas. 1990. *Making Sex: Body and Gender from the Greeks to Freud.* Cambridge: Harvard University Press.

Latour, Bruno. 1987. *Science in Action: How to Follow Scientists and Engineers through Society.* Cambridge: Harvard University Press.

———. 1988. *The Pasteurization of France.* Trans. Alan Sheridan and John Law. Cambridge: Harvard University Press.

Latour, Bruno, and Steven Woolgar. 1986. *Laboratory Life: The Construction of Scientific Facts.* 2d edition. Princeton: Princeton University Press.

Leitch, Vincent B. 1983. *Deconstructive Criticism: An Advanced Introduction.* New York: Columbia University Press.

Lévi-Strauss, Claude. 1966. *The Savage Mind.* London: Weidenfeld & Nicolson.

———. 1969. *Elementary Structures of Kinship.* Trans. James Harle Bell, John Richard von Sturmer, and Rodney Needham. Revised edition. Boston: Beacon Press.

Lipking, Lawrence. 1983. "Aristotle's Sister: A Poetics of Abandonment." *Critical Inquiry* 10: 61–81.

MacKinnon, Catherine A. 1982. "Feminism, Marxism, Method, and the State: An Agenda for Theory." *Signs* 7: 515–44.

Macpherson, C. B. 1962. *The Political Theory of Possessive Individualism.* Oxford: Oxford University Press.

Malson, Micheline R., Jean F. O'Barr, Sarah Westphal-Wihl, and Mary Wyer. 1989. *Feminist Theory in Practice and Process.* Chicago: University of Chicago Press.

Markley, Robert. 1987. "Style as Philosophic Structure: The Contexts of Shaftesbury's *Characteristicks.*" In *The Philosopher as Writer: The Eighteenth Century.* Ed. Robert Ginsberg. Selinsgrove, Pa.: Susquehanna University Press: 140–54.

———. 1988. *Two Edg'd Weapons: Style and Ideology in the Comedies of Etherege, Wycherley, and Congreve.* Oxford: Clarendon Press.

———. 1991. "Representing Order: Mathematics, Natural Philosophy, and Theology in the Newtonian Revolution." In *Chaos and Order: Complex Dynamics in Literature and Science.* Ed. N. Katherine Hayles. Chicago: University of Chicago Press: 125–48.

Marks, Elaine, and Isabelle de Courtivron, eds. 1981. *New French Feminisms.* New York: Shocken.

McDonnell, Ernest W. 1969. *The Beguines and Beghards in Medieval Culture.* New York: Octagon Books.

McLaughlin, Eleanor. 1973. "The Heresy of the Free Spirit and Late Medieval Mysticism." *Medievalia et Humanistica* 4: 37–54.

Medvedev, P. N. / M. M. Bakhtin. 1985. *The Formal Method in Literary Scholarship: A Critical Introduction to Sociological Poetics.* Trans. Albert J. Wehrle. Cambridge: Harvard University Press.

Meese, Elizabeth. 1986. *Crossing the Double-Cross: The Practice of Feminist Criticism*. Chapel Hill: University of North Carolina Press.

Miller, Nancy K. 1982. "The Text's Heroine: A Feminist Critic and Her Fictions." *Diacritics* 12: 48–53.

———, ed. 1986. *The Poetics of Gender*. New York: Columbia University Press.

Mitchell, W. J. T. 1985. *Against Theory: Literary Studies and the New Pragmatism*. Chicago: University of Chicago Press.

Moi, Toril. 1985. *Sexual/Textual Politics: Feminist Literary Theory*. London: Methuen.

———, ed. 1986. *The Kristeva Reader*. New York: Columbia University Press.

Moorman, John. 1968. *A History of the Franciscan Order from Its Origins to the Year 1517*. Oxford: Clarendon Press.

Morson, Gary Saul, and Caryl Emerson, eds. 1989. *Rethinking Bakhtin: Extensions and Challenges*. Evanston: Northwestern University Press.

Myers, Mitzi. 1988. "Pedagogy as Self-Expression in Mary Wollstonecraft: Exorcising the Past, Finding a Voice." In *The Private Self: Theory and Practice of Women's Autobiographical Writings*. Ed. Shari Benstock. Chapel Hill: University of North Carolina Press: 192–210.

Newman, Louise Michele, ed. 1985. *Men's Ideas / Women's Realities: "Popular Science," 1870–1915*. New York: Pergamon.

Newton, Judith. 1981. *Women, Power, and Subversion: Social Strategies in British Fiction 1778–1860*. London: Methuen.

———. 1984. "Making—and Remaking—History: Another Look at 'Patriarchy.'" *Tulsa Studies in Women's Literature* 3: 125–41.

Newton, Judith, and Deborah Rosenfelt, eds. 1985. *Feminist Criticism and Social Change: Sex, Class and Race in Literature and Culture*. London: Methuen.

Nicholson, Linda J. 1986. *Gender and History: The Limits of Social Theory in the Age of the Family*. New York: Columbia University Press.

Nussbaum, Felicity. 1988. "Eighteenth-Century Women's Autobiographical Commonplaces." In *The Private Self: Theory and Practice of Women's Autobiographical Writings*. Ed. Shari Benstock. Chapel Hill: University of North Carolina Press: 147–71.

Nussbaum, Felicity, and Laura Brown, eds. 1987. *The New Eighteenth Century: Theory, Politics, English Literature*. London: Methuen.

Ohmann, Richard. 1983. "The Shaping of a Canon: U. S. Fiction, 1960–1975." *Critical Inquiry* 10: 199–223.

Paden, William D., ed. 1989. *The Voice of the Trobairitz: Perspectives on the Women Troubadours*. Philadelphia: University of Pennsylvania Press.

Paden, William D., et al., eds. 1981. "The Poems of the *Trobairitz* Na Castelloza," *Romance Philology* 35: 158–82.

Pagels, Elaine. 1988. *Adam, Eve, and the Serpent*. New York: Random House.

Paulson, William R. 1988. *The Noise of Culture: Literary Texts in a World of Information*. Ithaca: Cornell University Press.

Peat, E. David. 1988. *Superstrings and the Search for the Theory of Everything*. Chicago: Contemporary Books.

Petroff, Elizabeth Alvilda. 1986. *Medieval Women's Visionary Literature*. New York: Oxford University Press.

Poovey, Mary. 1984. *The Proper Lady and the Woman Writer: Ideology as Style in the Works of Mary Wollstonecraft, Mary Shelley, and Jane Austen*. Chicago: University of Chicago Press.

——. 1988a. "Feminism and Deconstruction" *Feminist Studies* 14: 51–65.

——. 1988b. *Uneven Developments: The Ideological Work of Gender in Mid-Victorian England*. Chicago: Chicago University Press.

Rabine, Leslie Wahl. 1983. "Searching for the Connections: Marxist-Feminists and Women's Studies." *Humanities in Society* 6: 195–221.

——. 1988. "A Feminist Politics of Non-identity." *Feminist Studies* 14: 11–31.

Rabinow, Paul, ed. 1984. *The Foucault Reader*. New York: Pantheon.

Remley, Paul. 1989. "*Muscipula Diaboli* and Medieval English Antifeminism." *English Studies* 1: 1–14.

Rich, Adrienne. 1979. *On Lies, Secrets, and Silence: Selected Prose, 1966–1978* New York: Norton.

Richards, I. A. 1925. *Principles of Literary Criticism*. New York: Harcourt, Brace, Jovanovich.

Richetti, John. 1983. *Philosophic Writing: Locke, Berkeley, Hume*. Cambridge: Harvard University Press.

Robinson, Lillian. 1978. *Sex, Class, and Culture*. London: Methuen.

——. 1983. "Treason Our Text: Feminist Challenges to the Literary Canon." *Tulsa Studies in Women's Literature* 2: 83–98.

——. 1986. "Is There a Class in This Text?" *Tulsa Studies in Women's Literature* 5: 289–302.

Rooney, Ellen. 1986. "Who's Left Out? A Rose by Any Other Name Is Still Red; or, The Politics of Pluralism." *Critical Inquiry* 12: 550–63.

Rorty, Richard. 1979. *Philosophy and the Mirror of Nature*. Princeton: Princeton University Press.

Russ, Joanna. 1983. *How to Suppress Women's Writing*. Austin: University of Texas Press.

Sampson, Edward E. 1985. "The Decentralization of Identity: Toward a Revised Concept of Personal and Social Order." *American Psychologist* 40: 1203–11.

Saussure, Ferdinand de. 1966. *Course in General Linguistics*. Trans. Wade Baskin. New York: McGraw-Hill

Scarry, Elaine. 1985. *The Body in Pain: The Making and Unmaking of the World*. New York: Oxford University Press.

Schultz-Gora, Oscar, ed. 1888. *Die provenzalischen Dichterinnen: Biographien und Text nebst Anmerkungen und einer Einleitung*. Leipzig: Fock.

Schweickart, Patrocinio P. 1986. "Reading Ourselves: Toward a Feminist Theory of Reading." In *Gender and Reading*. Ed. Elizabeth A. Flynn and

Patrocinio P. Schweickart. Baltimore: Johns Hopkins University Press: 31–62.

Scott, James. 1985. *Weapons of the Weak: Everyday Forms of Peasant Resistance.* New Haven: Yale University Press.

Scott, Joan W. 1988a. "Deconstructing Equality-Versus-Difference; or, The Uses of Post-structuralist Theory for Feminism." *Feminist Studies* 14: 33–50.

——. 1988b. *Gender and the Politics of History.* New York: Columbia University Press.

Sedgwick, Eve Kosofsky. 1984. "Sexualism and the Citizen of the World: Wycherley, Sterne, and Male Homosocial Desire." *Critical Inquiry* 11: 226–45.

——. 1985. *Between Men: English Literature and Male Homosocial Desire.* New York: Columbia University Press.

Serres, Michel. 1982. *Hermes: Literature, Science, Philosophy.* Ed. Josué V. Harari and David F. Bell. Baltimore: Johns Hopkins University Press.

Shapiro, Marianne. 1978. "The Provençal *Trobairitz* and the Limits of Courtly Love" *Signs* 3: 560–71.

Showalter, Elaine. 1975. "Review Essay: Literary Criticism." *Signs* 1: 435–60.

——. 1981. "Feminist Criticism in the Wilderness." *Critical Inquiry* 8: 179–205.

——. 1983. "Critical Cross-Dressing: Male Feminists and the Woman of the Year." *Raritan* 3: 130–49.

——. 1984. "Women's Time, Women's Space: Writing the History of Feminist Criticism." *Tulsa Studies in Women's Literature* 3: 29–43.

Siebers, Tobin. 1989. *The Ethics of Criticism.* Ithaca: Cornell University Press.

Smith, Barbara Herrnstein. 1983. "Contingencies of Value." *Critical Inquiry* 10: 1–35.

Smith-Rosenberg, Carroll. 1985. *Disorderly Conduct: Visions of Gender in Victorian America.* New York: Alfred A. Knopf.

Spender, Dale. 1980. *Man-made Language.* London: Routledge and Kegan Paul.

——. 1983. *Feminist Theorists: Three Centuries of Key Women Thinkers.* New York: Pantheon Books.

Spivak, Gayatri Chakravorty. 1985. "Scattered Speculations on the Question of Value." *Diacritics* 15: 73–93.

Stallybrass, Peter, and Allon White. 1986. *The Politics and Poetics of Transgression.* Ithaca: Cornell University Press.

Steward, Susan. 1983. "Shouts on the Street: Bakhtin's Anti-Linguistics." *Critical Inquiry* 10: 265–82.

Straub, Kristina. 1989. "Women, Gender, and Criticism." In *Literary Criticism and Theory: The Greeks to the Present.* Ed. Robert Con Davis and Laurie Finke. New York: Longman: 855–76.

Suleiman, Susan Rubin, ed. 1986. *The Female Body in Western Culture: Contemporary Perspectives*. Cambridge: Harvard University Press.

Thompson, Michael. 1979. *Rubbish Theory: The Creation and Destruction of Value*. Oxford: Oxford University Press.

Todorov, Tzvetan. 1984. *Mikhail Bakhtin: The Dialogic Principle*. Trans. Wlad Godzich. Minneapolis: University of Minnesota Press.

Tompkins, Jane. 1985. *Sensational Designs: The Cultural Work of American Fiction, 1790–1860*. New York: Oxford University Press.

Topsfield, L. T. 1975. *Troubadours and Love*. Cambridge: Cambridge University Press.

Trask, Haunani-Kay. 1986. *Eros and Power: The Promise of Feminist Theory*. Philadelphia: University of Pennsylvania Press.

Treichler, Paula. 1984. "Escaping the Sentence: Diagnosis and Discourse in 'The Yellow Wallpaper.'" *Tulsa Studies in Women's Literature* 3: 61–77.

———. 1985. "The Wall behind the Yellow Wallpaper: Response to Carol Neely and Karen Ford." *Tulsa Studies in Women's Literature* 4: 323–30.

———. 1986. "Teaching Feminist Theory." *Theory in the Classroom*. Ed. Cary Nelson. Urbana: University of Illinois Press.

Vance, Eugene. 1975. "Love's Concordance: The Poetics of Desire and the Joy of the Text." *Diacritics* 5: 40–52.

Veeser, H. Aram, ed. 1989. *The New Historicism*. London: Routledge.

Vickers, Nancy. 1981. "Diana Described: Scattered Women and Scattered Rhyme." *Critical Inquiry* 8: 265–79.

Vlaspolos, Anca. 1980. "Mary Wollstonecraft's Mask of Reason in *Vindication of the Rights of Woman*." *Dalhousie Review* 60: 462–71.

Vološinov, V. N. / M. M. Bakhtin. 1976. "Discourse in Life and Discourse in Art (Concerning Sociological Poetics)." In *Freudianism: A Critical Sketch*. Ed. I. R. Titunik and Neal H. Bruss. Trans. I. R. Titunik. Bloomington: Indiana University Press: 93–116.

———. 1986. *Marxism and the Philosophy of Language*. Trans. Ladislav Matejka and I. R. Titunik. Cambridge, Mass.: Harvard University Press.

Wardle, Ralph. 1951. *Mary Wollstonecraft: A Critical Biography*. Lincoln: University of Nebraska Press.

White, Hayden. 1987. *The Content of the Form: Narrative Discourse and Historical Representation*. Baltimore: Johns Hopkins University Press.

Wiebe, Robert. 1967. *The Search for Order, 1877–1920*. New York: Hill and Wang.

Williams, Raymond. 1977. *Marxism and Literature*. Oxford: Oxford University Press.

Wilson, Katharina, ed. 1984. *Medieval Women Writers*. Athens: University of Georgia Press.

Wittgenstein, Ludwig. 1966. *Lectures and Conversations on Aesthetics, Psychology, and Religious Beliefs*. Ed. Cyril Barrett. Oxford: Blackwell.

Wittreich, Joseph. 1987. *Feminist Milton*. Ithaca: Cornell University Press.

Wollstonecraft, Mary. 1796. *An Historical and Moral View of the Origin and Progress of the French Revolution*. London.

———. 1975. *A Vindication of the Rights of Woman*. Ed. Carol H. Poston. New York: Norton.

———. 1976. *Letters Written during a Short Residence in Sweden, Norway, and Denmark*. Ed. Carol H. Poston. Lincoln: University of Nebraska Press.

Woolf, Virginia. 1932. *The Second Common Reader*. New York: Harcourt, Brace.

Yaeger, Patricia S. 1984. "'Because a Fire Was in My Head': Eudora Welty and the Dialogic Imagination." *PMLA* 99: 955–73.

Zagarell, Sandra A. 1986. "Conceptualizing Women's Literary History: Reflections on *The Norton Anthology of Literature by Women*." *Tulsa Studies in Women's Literature* 5: 273–87.

Zumthor, Paul. 1972. *Essai de poétique médiévale*. Paris: Seuil.

Index

Reading Women Writing

A SERIES EDITED BY SHARI BENSTOCK
AND CELESTE SCHENCK

Greatness Engendered: George Eliot and Virginia Woolf
by Alison Booth

Talking Back: Toward a Latin American Feminist Literary Criticism
by Debra A. Castillo

H.D.'s Freudian Poetics: Psychoanalysis in Translation
by Dianne Chisholm

From Mastery to Analysis: Theories of Gender in Psychoanalytic Feminism
by Patricia Elliot

Feminist Theory, Women's Writing
by Laurie A. Finke

Colette and the Fantom Subject of Autobiography
by Jerry Aline Flieger

Cartesian Women: Versions and Subversions of Rational Discourse in the Old Regime
by Erica Harth

Narrative Transvestism: Rhetoric and Gender in the Eighteenth-Century English Novel
by Madeleine Kahn

The Unspeakable Mother: Forbidden Discourse in Jean Rhys and H.D.
by Deborah Kelly Kloepfer

Women and Romance: The Consolations of Gender in the English Novel
by Laurie Langbauer

Autobiographical Voices: Race, Gender, Self-Portraiture
by Françoise Lionnet

Library of Congress Cataloging-in-Publication Data

Finke, Laurie.
    Feminist theory, women's writing / Laurie A. Finke.
        p.   cm. — (Reading women writing)
    Includes bibliographical references and index.
    ISBN 0-8014-2547-6 (alk. paper). —ISBN 0-8014-9784-1 (pbk. : alk. paper)
    1. Feminist theory.   2. Feminism and literature.   I. Title.   II. Series.
HQ1190.F56   1992
305.42'01—dc20   91-55566